William J Fay

FREEDOM TO BE FREE

Orbis Books • Maryknoll, New York 1973

Freedom to be Free

ARTURO PAOLI

Translated by
Charles Underhill Quinn

Second Printing

Originally published as *Dialogo della liberazione* © 1970,
Morcelliana, Brescia

Copyright © 1973, ORBIS Books, Maryknoll, New York 10545

Library of Congress Catalog Card Number: 72:93340

ISBN Number: 0-88344-143-8

Manufactured in the United States of America

Contents

Introduction vii

1. Freedom in Truth. 1

2. Freedom from the Law 15

3. Freedom from "Sin". 29

4. Freedom from Death 43

5. The Freedom of Love 57

6. Freedom in Friendship 71

7. Political Love 87

8. Virginal Love 105

9. Freedom through the Cross . . . 123

10. Poverty as Freedom 143

11. Dialogue of Freedom 161

12. The Sign of Freedom 179

13. Obedience as Freedom 197

14. The Center of Freedom 213

15. The Free Woman 231

16. The Spirit of Freedom. 249

17. The Outrage of Youth. 267

18. Freedom in Peace. 287

Conclusion 301

Introduction

"Don't you see you're destroying one another?"

"Yes. But doesn't the automatic smile of the nun who served you coffee seem like destruction to you? And what about the little priest who said mass for the nuns this morning and then went off happily with the Mother Superior's gift of a new sweater under his arm? Isn't that destruction? Isn't it destruction never to grow out of childhood, unreality, a walking sleep? Our destruction is at least involved with life. Theirs is outside of it. And I want to live. . . ."

Michael's logic left me speechless. We were sitting face to face. On our right a window looked out on a magnificent park in which the old converted villa was set. It was now a religious house. The look in Michael's eyes made everything seem ugly and mediocre to me, starting with myself and my own life. For a moment I wondered whether the look in the eyes of youth were not something like the look in God's eyes. There was a phrase in the old *Dies irae* that spoke of a meeting with God in which all things would be sifted. This would not be a trial, but rather a mere exchange of glances, an instant which dissolves all logic. A life destroyed or a life on fire? A life aborted or a life consummated? Destruction can't be avoided because you can't avoid death. All you can do is accept death or endure it. Go out to meet it or let it enter by force.

Michael's question gnaws at me and humiliates me deeply. There is no answer to it. Had my generation time to experience this look in the eyes of youth, and to sense that this look of challenge may be the eye of God, there would be a new creation. For this, we should have to accept the destruction of a history, of a person, and of the great wealth spoken of by Saint Luke. If I agree to be alone with God, who will be my defense attorney at that moment? No one, because I have no defense. We have to have the courage to say that a person is destroying himself with alcohol, with drugs, with prostitution, with nonlove, with nonhistory, with doing useless things, with suffering imaginary tortures.

The sign of a life destroyed is excommunication: "Go away from me, you accursed!"—you who are not reconciled with me or with one another. Yet, out of one kind of destruction can come communion, because out of the scorched earth can grow immense compassion: "Much was forgiven her since she loved much." But out of a second kind of destruction nothing can come because it is clandestine, like an undiagnosed leukemia, sunken in boredom. Despair is the opposite of hope. Boredom the opposite of well-being, civilization, and culture. Despair is only a step away from communion. Boredom is accepting the fact that freedom does not exist.

We are irritated by youths' impatience, by their nonacceptance of uncomfortable situations, of phony people, of the actors' masks we have become so used to wearing. But this irritation of ours turns us away from the truth, which makes us grow and gives us the courage to accept change. Were we able to bear this shattering look in the eyes of youth, which makes us feel so helplessly empty, we should have the courage to be poor, and the "kingdom of God" would already be with us.

What is the alternative to self-destruction? Michael and I spoke of it for a long time and we discovered in the Bible a recurrent theme, which we shall try to follow through: liberation.

It seems to us that the meaning of life may be this: to journey toward freedom, because freedom is the permanent part of history. It is the great human truth which we see as a certain value, a constant motive for revolutions, for man's personal as well as his communal quest.

1

FREEDOM IN TRUTH

"Jesus then said to the Jews who had believed in him, 'If you continue in my word, you are truly my disciples, and you will know the truth, and the truth will make you free' " (John 8:31-32).

Liberation is a "way toward the truth," and it is here perhaps that the misunderstanding begins. At twenty, you discover you are in an existential position that is false. Your environment has conditioned you to choose a career, a group of friends, a state in life, and then all of a sudden you realize you are not being true. The discovery of "not being true," and therefore of "not doing what is true," happens at that moment in your life when you discover a lack of harmony in yourself, a sensation of profound discontent, of doing everything wrong and of being lost in doubt about everything. Who am I? What am I doing? What is all this for? You discover that the truth is not merely the willing adherence of the intellect to a reality outside of yourself, but a combination of both intelligence and truth. And you discover it the moment your whole being, your person, is not in agreement with the truth you accept, or which people have gotten you to accept.

This discontent, this doubting of everything, this not knowing what to do, is all the same thing and has the same source: not having discovered a vocation, feeling absurd in the world. Often this state of insecurity affects persons who thought they had a vocation and discover that they no longer have. What has happened? They have sensed a vocation but at a level which is not the truest or the deepest. It is a state of neurosis to live one's life on a nonpersonal level, to embrace a truth or an ideal not at the root of your being but out of self-surrender, a real alienation resulting

1

from a passion that may be enthusiasm, fear, or desire. One moment you are caught up and you give yourself to something that seems to be the truth. Then, all of a sudden, reality dawns and you get the profound impression that the whole thing is a hoax, that you're acting out a comedy, that you're out of place. When life requires a serious commitment, when the wind shakes the tree to its roots, you realize that you have no roots.

"The truth will make you free." But what truth? And how are we to live it? Jesus had the courage to tell the world: "I am the truth," not in the sense that he was the sole truth, but in the sense that he was its unique basis, the ontological support of all truths. When somebody asks me why I believe in Christ, I do not know how to answer in a few words. At the basis of my faith there are certainly the proofs of the Gospels' historicity, of the historical person of the dead and risen Christ, attested to by generations of believers and by their martyrdom. But, little by little, I have felt these proofs dissolving in me, becoming a vague background into which all truths flow. The famous phrase of Saint Augustine, "Christ, the solution of all difficulties," seems to me to be the constant hypothesis of all my knowledge.

It seems to me that without Christ everything is absurd. Every step I take, deepening my knowledge, is like a verification of Christ's existence; it is like having the surprise of meeting him all over again. How can I explain why I am a Christian? I should have to give the history of all my experiences, of my whole life. And I feel that Christ is not the facile apologetic solution to the uncertainty and anguish of doubt. He is not next to or above the truth that opens out before me: He is within it. I shall try to explain with an example.

Recently I have been reading *Psychanalyse et anthropologie* by Géza Róheim (Paris, Gallimard). The author presents an hypothesis with regard to the formation of language. The first men had come together to eat, and while eating made mumbling sounds which later became articulated into words. Spontaneously I went to John 6 where word, food, and community are three intertwining and interrelated values. This theory is not definitive and to make of it a proof of the Gospel's truth or vice versa to prove this theory from the Gospel is absurd and would not even occur to me. But everything that man discovers as he gropes along on the way to knowledge projects rays of light that help him discover the depth of the Gospel. For this reason I say that everything is very profound.

For the truth to free us, we have first of all to admit that we are not free and that in itself truth is more of an alienation than a salvation. This is a situation which the Gospel continually denounces. The Jews answered Jesus: "We are descendants of Abraham and have never been in bondage to any one. How is it that you say, 'You will be made free'?" *(John 8:33).* Man has always tried to build himself a solid truth which is an alienation and which allows a person to hand in his resignation and to unload all responsibility onto it. They answered: "We were not born of fornication. We have one Father even God." And Jesus said: "If God were your Father, you would love me, for I proceeded and came forth from God; I came not of my own accord, but he sent me" *(John 8:41-42).*

In all the renascent forms of Pharisaism there is the alienation of truth, that is, truth accepted on a superficial level, which is not the true one. There is a wretched mix-up of the true and the false, of truth accepted with falsehood, of a complicity between truth and error, which creates a most dangerous situation for man. It is antilove because it is truth used as a weapon. One is faced with truth in a dualism of reciprocal alienation. Jesus did not say, "I possess the truth" or "I give the truth." He said: "I am the truth," which might seem to be a more proud and less human statement, but that is not so. I do not wield truth as a weapon which I have in my hands. The truth has become me. What ought to be, the ideal, coincides with being: The truth has become me. There is no other way for Christ to defend himself than to die because he cannot duel with this kind of weapon. The truth is in him, it has become him. The man who believes in him must reproduce his person. To a certain extent he must be Christ, and this profound likeness is the end of alienation, of dualism, and therefore the end of the anguish of nonbeing, the anguish of death. How deeply perceptive that phrase from Paul which I read so often now appears to me: "But as at that time he who was born according to the flesh persecuted him who was born according to the Spirit, so it is now" *(Galatians 4:29).* The greatest sign of insecurity is fanaticism, which is security won by aggressiveness. Because I have frozen the truth at the level of my present awareness and have made that awareness the measure of truth, I fight in the name of truth, that truth which has reached another level.

Pharisaism is basically a neurosis, a pathological state of the faith. And the neurotic defends himself by seeking to reverse roles, by making the other person look insane and setting him off against the truth that he possesses. To say that the faith can be an alienation, that moral truth can be an alienation and therefore an opiate, lets loose a furious protest, a fierce torrent from the whole Sanhedrin: "He has uttered blasphemy. Why do we still need witnesses?" *(Matthew 26:65).* Jesus had stated his equality with the Father, that he had reached that unreachable and unrepeatable fullness toward which man aspires with his whole being: the total coincidence between what is and what ought to be, between love and loving, the overcoming of inner tension, existential anguish, the fear of not being because there is no longer any nook or cranny that has not been reached by being.

Jesus cannot defend himself before the Sanhedrin because they are questioning him about an obedience to an external law which they have chosen as the measure of truth and as the arbitrary level of love. But this measure has disappeared in Christ. He himself has become the measure, the measure of the possibility of the divine penetrating man and assimilating him to itself. For this reason, they cannot tolerate Christ. He rightfully deserves to be put to death. The only people who understand him are those who have lost control, those who have no levels, either because they have entered spaceless infinity or because they have given up what ought to be: those who are on fire with the love of God, or the publicans and prostitutes. It is only those who are no longer concerned with what ought to be, either because the law has been provisionally destroyed by the horror of existence, or because it has been emptied by a renunciation of what ought to be in favor of an existence accepted in the obscurity of faith.

We are inevitably confronted by existential anguish, by the dualism between what we really are and what we should be: the ideal we have formed or which has been imposed on us by the conditioning of our existence or as the liberation from this conditioning. We liberate ourselves from it with a kind of fictitious, provisional transcendence, which is continually assaulted by the anguish that reappears under the form of boredom or that more heroic form of flight toward death. This is the solution of letting oneself live, of choosing nothing and choosing everything. It is a position that can give rise to heroic moments, a receptiveness to what comes, that can also proceed from God. But it is a pseudoliberation into which Pharisaism has easy entry: Making sin a law or a norm is as pharisaical as making Moses' norm one's absolute. Sin happens when we make the transgression of a norm the ideal. Violation and formal obedience become joined and intertwined in this absolutizing of a norm. I have found as many Pharisees among the law's observers as among atheists and sinners.

But the flight from what ought to be can become an emptiness, a poverty, a disposibility. For this reason Jesus came to "heal the sick, and to call sinners and the contrite of heart." The Pharisee cannot be helped because he has left insecurity behind by an absolutization that is beneath the level of truth. He is a person without courage. He does not have the courage to live, to go down into the roots of being, and he therefore fashions for himself a fictitious level of existence. One of the many caricatures left us by the Gospel is outlined in the following text: "And when you fast, do not look dismal like the hypocrites, for they disfigure their faces that their fasting may be seen by men. . . . But when you fast, anoint your head and wash your face, that your fasting may not be seen by men but by your Father who sees in secret" *(Matthew 6:16-17).*

If this Father were an Absolute to be confronted, we should avoid one alienation only to fall into another one. I can sin by vanity by seeing myself reflected in a law as much as in a Father who is hidden in mystery. But we must take the whole of the Gospel. The relationship with the Father matures in a unity in which it is no longer possible to see oneself. It is the disappearance of dualism. In the Trinity, the three are one, completely identified in the total equality of being. Vanity, judging others, persecuting others, defending a truth as an absolute, with aggressiveness, are all manifestations of the same cause: not going right down to the roots of being, not being liberated. The redemption Christ brought to the world always seems to me to be a return of man to being, saving him from all alienation in order that he might rediscover his original being. Man is repelled by this idea of being saved, of needing a Savior. In reality, salvation comes from us, but it could not come without this presence of being in us. The "fall forward," that desire to grow, to be, which is basically, in the state of our present existence, the incentive to reach out to the possibilities of being, is assured in depth by our being rooted in being, in which all things were created, the visible and the invisible *(Colossians 1:16).*

Three major foes are opposed to this liberation: sin, the law, and death. The law counters it insofar as it is the possibility of objectifying an absolute and setting it up as the norm for personal maturity. Sin is the reverse of law and the reification and absolutizing of a freedom cut off from laws and therefore neurotic. All three foes vanish when death is swallowed up in "victory," and nonbeing ceases to threaten from the shadows, when being and existing become identified in me. This is possible only in the supreme equation: "I have been crucified with Christ; it is no longer I who live, but Christ who lives in me; and the life I now live in the flesh I live by faith in the Son of God, who loved me and gave himself for me" *(Galatians 2:19-20).*

Truth has become liberation when from being "outside" it passes "within," from being transcendent in the space-time sense it has become immanent, so immanent that it is no longer possible to be measured by it. Apologetics is prior to contemplation. In contemplation apologetics becomes witness and transparency. If the apologist is progressing along the road of freedom, he must become a martyr, a witness. The term "martyr" means a witness as well as a person who dies violently, because the truth made flesh, made a liberation and personal freedom, cannot be defended as something other than oneself. The martyr is the antitype of the Pharisee. The Pharisee has need of the martyr in order to discover the truth. Only the incarnate truth can free him from the deception of written truth, from the tragic game of absolutizing the law.

John 19 tells us that Christ was pierced with a lance in order to make sure that he was dead. It is a curious context, in which the evangelist forcefully states that he is telling the truth: "He who saw it has borne witness—his testimony is true, and he knows he tells the truth—that you also may believe." And again another passage says, "They shall look on him whom they have pierced" *(John 19:35-37)*. The aggressiveness of the Pharisee pierces Christ's person with a lance and must come face to face with the Truth. The Truth has become Christ's heart, made visible by the lance's blow; it became love and is the highest point of assimilation. It is the sign that the Truth has come to liberate and to make itself the liberator. Truth becomes love when it reaches the root of existence; it becomes a communion with the person by transforming its defender into a martyr. A defense of truth which does not become a martyrdom is like a flower that has dried up and rotted without yielding fruit. The apostles, those who were sent out to preach, to proclaim and defend the truth, were all martyrs. And this was due not only to the historical circumstance that their truth was not accepted, but to a much more profound reason. Since they were assimilated to the truth with perfect proportion, they could proclaim and defend it only as witnesses. Paul could not illustrate this better than when he said, "I saw the risen Christ. I bear in me the signs of the Passion and the Resurrection." The truth becomes a person and to strike out at it there is nothing else to do than to strike out at the person.

For this reason, being persecuted for the truth, being a martyr, will always be a sign of identification with the truth, a sign that the truth has entered within, has become the person, and has achieved its liberating effect.

But how can we make the truth free us? We must have the courage and the desire to know ourselves in depth, in the light of God who is the truth. The in-depth knowledge of ourselves, however, can be narcissism, a neurotic state. Our generation has the courage and the curiosity for self-knowledge, sharpened by psychoanalytical techniques. On the scientific level, these techniques have undoubtedly contributed toward freeing us from many illusions and therefore toward dealing a hard blow at Pharisaism. But in these techniques it is impossible, according to Tillich, to distinguish clearly the line of demarcation between, on the one hand, man's universal existential situation based on finitude and, on the other, the psychosomatic sickness which is considered to be an attempt to escape this situation and its anxieties, by taking refuge in the stronghold of the mind (*Theology of Culture*, New York: Oxford, 1959).

The merit of psychoanalysis is that it discovered the dynamism of the person as a necessity of liberation, but its limitation is to have cut the person off from the root of being, and therefore it is necessarily descriptive and not philosophical. Since it lacks a metaphysics of the person, it itself becomes a metaphysics and can be nothing else but the metaphysics of anguish. There is an anguish of overcoming, an anguish which I would call "methodological," which is the law of limited and therefore necessarily alienated being. And there is a metaphysical anguish which is the consequence of a discovery of the roots of the person outside of being. This metaphysics necessarily leads to neurosis, that is, to alienating choices, and particularly in the area in which psychoanalysis would want to free the person. The only advantage is a change in level, a quantitative level in regard to the Pharisaical choice which is made without coming to terms with oneself and by overcoming alienation through a doctrinaire leap. Saint Catherine spoke in great depth of "never leaving the cell of the knowledge of God and the cell of the knowledge of self." Obviously, we cannot know God if we do not go down into the roots of being, allowing ourselves to be pushed by him toward the remote depths in which he dwells, in that deep part of the self beyond which the finite and the limited do not exist but only the origin and the beginning.

Psychoanalysis does not go astray when it endeavors to discover the roots of the human. Anguish is a sign of bad structural functioning, and it is necessary to go to the origins, to the roots of the human, in order to discover the cause of this anguish. But psychoanalysis merely defers the moment of alienation, the dualism that is the cause of the anguish, and does not resolve it. The root is dead because it is separated from the basis humus; it is alienated from its origins because its identification with being is impossible. It is in this identification that its peace is ultimately to be found. Psychoanalysis removes human illusions from us and obliges us to seek deeper. Everything reached before this level is suspect of alienation and therefore laden with anguish—the anguish of not being, of being without meaning.

Saint John of the Cross gives a way to reach these depths, which brings us to that dark nothingness in which the limited being loses itself through the existential leap into the divine being. Here is found an end to the duality and to the fear of death by passing through death, accepting this disappearance into nothingness, which is at the ultimate level of existence. It is the point where we reach a state of poverty accepted with steadfast courage: giving up the quest to overcome the limitation and alienation with a provisional ideal. Poverty of possession and poverty of dependence. This poverty can be sustained only through a profound search for God and through the rejection of idols. It can be sustained only through trust in finding the root of being at an unknown depth, and therefore in accepting that all other roots be cut off. Speaking of Abraham's faith as an exemplary faith, although monstrous from a human point of view because it was an affirmation of life beyond death, the Letter to the Hebrews says, "By faith, Abraham, when he was tested, offered up Isaac, and he who had received the promises was ready to offer up his only son, of whom it was said, 'Through Isaac shall your descendents be named.' He considered that God was able to raise men even from the dead; hence, figuratively speaking, he did receive him back" *(Hebrews 11:17-19)*.

Here there is no alienation because it was overcome by total poverty. The being dies in this total self-giving; it cuts its existential roots in order to be grafted onto the roots of Being: "Abide in me, and I in you. As the branch cannot bear fruit by itself, unless it abides in the vine, neither can you, unless you abide in me. I am the vine, you are the branches. He who abides in me, and I in him, he it is that bears much fruit, for apart from me you can do nothing" *(John 15:4-5)*. It is a rebirth, and therefore a descent deep into the roots of being. It reaches the roots because faith is a totality. It confronts man with the most profound choice, death, and therefore with the meaninglessness of life. Faith is salvaged through the renunciation of substitute certainties. The same faith must disappear as an intellectual virtue, as a force of the self, because the leap from dualism to identity, from alienation to unicity, is impossible without the difficult leap into nothingness. This sheds light on the acts of absurd faith of the mystics who state that they will continue to love even if beyond life there is nothing. It is an act of faith in being and at the same time a rejection of dualism, of the self as separated from being. It is the extremely difficult passage from faith to love: "Love never ends; as for prophecies, they will pass away; as for tongues, they will cease; as for knowledge, it will pass away" *(1 Corinthians 13:8)*. Here the allusion to a future life is clear, but it can apply to that anticipation of future life which is contemplation.

To arrive at this root of being and the union that transforms, we must accept the void, that is, the active renunciation of all things insofar as they are not God, and passively accept the work of grace, which completes in us its task of emptying us of all attachment. Every "aggressiveness" and "concupiscence," which are the two great creative forces of the person, the two moments of the rhythm of preservation and growth, which at a certain point give us the sense of existing and of existing as alienated people, are voided in this poverty. And yet, are we not witnessing here the end of the person? Is this not the end of anguish, of an anguish that makes the person exist and grow, constituting the force that perpetually refurbishes concupiscence and aggressiveness, the force of desire, the force of conquest and of the defense of the desired good? But being is life and not conflict. It is a totality in peace without rivalry, and therefore without aggression.

Love between man and woman, which is typical, begins in conflict. Its internal dynamic is made up of the burden of concupiscence and aggression, but it aspires to unity, friendship, and an encounter in peace. And this aspiration is called "being in love," "abiding in love." It will never be possible perfectly and definitively, but it is the aspiration of love. The aspiration of love is to fill the void of nonbeing, occupied by aggressive fear and desire, and to bring about the peace of unity. This is not the wall of death; it is the starting point for a relationship of assimilation and unification. Man passes from the aggression of the crowd to life in common, which is not merely a juxtaposition. It is the joy of being together, of being one, of being assimilated. The world is discovered as something beautiful and as order to the extent that we are poor, that is, to the extent that we have lost concupiscence and aggression and have become capable of a contemplative relationship. We allow ourselves to be penetrated by the beauty of things and we no longer look upon them with an eye to economy, with an eye to conquest. Work becomes poetry, *poiesis*, a "doing," a creation that is neither aggressive nor alienating. Marx had the intuition that work must disappear, although he certainly did not think that a metahistorical man would live in idleness. He was thinking of the end of alienating work, of a relationship with nature that would be freed from concupiscence and aggression, a creative and distributive relationship, freed from anguish. It would be the joy of communion with nature, identified with the community, the community discovered as another self as well as the coherence and the preservation of the self.

Liberation means touching the very depths of the poverty of limited and alienated being and accepting this insertion into the infinite being, which is the principle and foundation of every being. However, can this be reached only through contemplation? If this were the case, there would be very few people who could achieve this liberation. And if Christ is the universal liberator, if he is the truth made a person and made love, he must be accessible even to those who are unfamiliar with the techniques of contemplation. I am convinced that this is so, even if I think that contemplatives are like the guides along a road which every man and every historical period must take.

Existential poverty arises everywhere, and anguish continually follows us. If we listen to ourselves for a moment, we feel the need for a rebirth, a purification, a need for going down to the roots of being, a desire to begin again, to go back to the source. I believe every man feels this within himself. In politics this can be expressed by the wish to make over a new world in truth. The following is a comment by a Marxist writer: "The person speaking to you is among those struggling for society, for a society which on the level of civilization would offer the maximum possible integration among individuals and society. It also would offer the greatest possibility for the development of the individuality of every man, not in an illusory egotistical form like that offered by bourgeois society. I do not believe that communist society by itself will achieve such moral progress that the lie of the individual is eliminated. But we cannot exclude the possibility that the human adventure in the universe may achieve this through other ways, technically and scientifically, like the ways opened up today by sciences such as cybernetics" (L. Luporini, *Morale e Società*, Rome: Editori Riuniti, 1966).

This liberation is explained on the moral level as a search for consistency, a being identical with ourselves, not playing the role of the just man, not thinking we are just, but being so. On the religious level it is manifested as a desire to eliminate dualism—God and me—which looks on God as an idol responsible for all my failures and even my wickedness. The Gospel certainly speaks of "your Father and my Father," but it also says, "The Father and I are one," and Jesus prays that "they all may be one; even as thou, father, art in me, and I in thee, that they also may be one in us" *(John 17:21)*

Our eagerness to defend a truth on the metaphysical level has led us to accentuate the dualism between God and me. I believe in the transcendence of God, of the Being that is distinct from me, but the Gospel proclaims that this Being is a life-giving principle, the deep root of the person, who is continually renewed insofar as he knows and discovers what is deception and accepts with love what is truth in himself.

Thirst for truth is a thirst for God. It is a thirst for justice because the supreme justice is the truth in which all values are discovered in their true essence. This thirst for truth is distinguished from curiosity in that curiosity is an external attitude of the person. It does not involve commitment. It is the energy of a research activity which has the result of juxtaposing newly acquired knowledge to what is already known. The thirst for truth is motivated by the desire to commit myself. Let the truth be in me and change me. From being a spectator I become an actor. From an active subject I become a passive one, that is, I allow the truth to penetrate me, to make me its own, without alienations. Even more, it strips me of alienation.

The curious person is characterized by his static attitude, which is expressed through pride and aggression. One who seeks the truth has a constant underlying vulnerability because he has discovered the anguish of deception, of nonbeing. Saint Teresa spoke of descending into hell. Perhaps we do not understand this very well, but I think it is very true. It is a descent into the hell of death, of the absurd, of disappearance, feeling devoured by deception. On the level of social relations, this deception is injustice. On the level of interpersonal relationships, it is a love which does not descend to the roots of being, to that level in which the gift of self can be only exclusive and irreversible. On the level of a relationship with God, it is an almost mock acceptance of his law as a substitute for him.

What is important is a frontal attack on deception. There is an essential unity in the person which demands that the truth we seek in a particular direction should possess our whole person. In the Letter to the Galatians Paul speaks of the fruits of liberation, because no one can say he is freed by truth simply because he accepts a scientific theory. The fruits are "love, joy, peace, patience, kindness, goodness, faithfulness, gentleness, self-control" *(Galatians 5:22)*.

These are not rhetorical words falling from the mouth of an orator carried away by his own eloquence. They are a repetition in other terms of the Beatitudes. The meaning could be conveyed as follows: The fruit of liberation in the truth is a *profound interior consistency* (faithfulness, patience), in the direction of love, which is a hunger and thirst after justice to the point of absorbing my selfish desires, all my concupiscence (gentleness, self-control). And therefore, since there is no longer anything personal to defend, anything explicit or properly our own, it is manifested as goodness, kindness, and gentleness, and leads to peace and joy.

We have all known people in various fields who have had great internal consistency, the result of purification and profound poverty. It directs the whole person, his whole existence, toward fulfilling a vocation, which is the central and sole focus of this existence. We need the vision and the honesty to discover that this unity of existence, this deep human maturity, can take place outside of an explicit faith because being is the principle and the common basis for all men and all things. And this interior consistency is not stubbornness, and the joy is not some stereotyped external smile. Peace is not inertia or some passive acceptance of injustice. Within these external and Pharisaical imitations all too easily can be seen aggression and all the defense mechanisms, as well as concupiscence and the anguished preservation of an individualistic self—even if this self does not coincide with the self of carnal passion and seems more disposed to self-denial and less strong.

Saint Paul's synthesis is quite difficult: "Against such there is no law. And those who belong to Christ Jesus have crucified the flesh with its passions and desires" *(Galatians 5:23-24).* From this a contemplative such as John of the Cross was able to describe for us the stages of this reduction to nothingness, to death, through the leap in being which is unity, and therefore the supreme victory over alienation. Man can arrive at this point through a path that is not openly religious. God reveals himself as a self-binding and overwhelming ideal in the innermost depths of being, the true and unique meaning of life. He can have such a force of attraction and liberation as to bring a person to death and to the ultimate qualitative leap.

Only at this point does the truth become a liberating truth, one that is singular and therefore unifying. It is the only truth that can redeem a person from his alienations and his diffuseness: "The truth will make you free." Its characteristic therefore is harmony, the elimination of clamoring and contrasts, which are the sign of a plurality in opposition. In a person, this harmony is joy and peace. In relations with others it is kindness and gentleness. In relation to things it is self-control, that is to say, poverty.

At this point liberation appears to us as the integral reconstruction of the person. It is not one or another aspect: It is the whole New Man which is the sign of liberation. Obviously, there are waverings and retrogressions; man cannot hope to reach a definitive maturity, but these waverings do not reach the root of being, the depth of the person.

Saint Paul was thinking of this when he bid the Ephesians to be "rooted and grounded in love" *(Ephesians 3:17)*.

Only when brought to this level can a vocation be called eternal and lasting. This is so not because of juridical bond, which does not preserve us from essential revisions and therefore from rejecting and changing, but because of the qualitative change that has been brought about. On the consciousness level, the commitment of vocation has been taken freely and consciously and therefore seems binding. But if liberation of the preconscious and the subconscious has not been achieved, genuinely reaching the ultimate origin, Being, the ultimate and first principle and the root of all beings, the subsconscious will continually threaten this decision taken at a very small and very limited emerging point.

God is not at the top of this huge floating iceberg. He is its foundation, its base. Paul was thinking of Christ's cosmic universality when he wrote to the Ephesians "that you ... may have power to comprehend with all the saints what is the breadth and length and height and depth, and to know the love of Christ which surpasses knowledge, that you may be filled with all the fullness of God" *(Ephesians 3:18-19)*. But it seems to me that this can be attributed to the little world of the person.

Here we have posited the vast problem of the perpetual vow. Can a man bind himself forever? Is he free? To be free he must be liberated and to be liberated he has to have gone down to the roots of being where the mystery of life and death meet at their origin. A time of testing is required before the definitive choice. But it would be necessary to be certain that within this time of testing there is the discovery and the liberation of the whole surface of the person down to the last detail. And this is not the result of a long apprenticeship in the knowledge of the law and of a gradual training of the will. It is an interior rebirth. In his conversation with Nicodemus, Jesus said, "Truly, truly I say to you, unless one is born anew, he cannot see the kingdom of God." Nicodemus asked him: "How can a man be born when he is old? Can he enter a second time into his mother's womb and be born?" And Nicodemus was not so far off the track, since he saw rebirth as a return to one's beginnings, going back beyond infancy. Jesus answered: "Truly, truly I say to you, unless one is born of water and the Spirit, he cannot enter the kingdom of God. That which is

born of the flesh is flesh, and that which is born of the Spirit is spirit"
(John 3:4-6).

Here we are touching upon the root of the mystery: "How and when
does this happen?" It is the great human mystery: For it is an ideal which
makes the holy and the wicked, giants and buffoons, slaves and freemen,
symphonies and cacophonies, architectural structures and piles of rock.

2

FREEDOM FROM THE LAW

Freedom faces three dangers, which objectify man and make him a "thing": *the law, sin, and death.*

These are the three adversaries that continually appear in the thought of Paul. Law, especially: Paul has the complex of a man who had a strict upbringing in his adolescence with very rigid educators, and—although he is now free from this—he is incapable of remembering this time of his life without a certain anger. The law is interposed between God and man, and can therefore produce the *religious man* who is not properly speaking the Christian ideal. It can be interposed between man and man and therefore stand in the way of dynamic personalization. It can stand between man and the world and thereby mediate between man and history, cutting off his temporal roots and emptying both time and the person of their significance. It can come between man and himself and become an obstacle to identification.

In the Gospel, the victim of the law is pictured either sarcastically or tragically in all the varieties of his ruination. The prayer of the Pharisee in the temple: a man-God, man-Being relationship. The priest and the Levite on the road to Jericho: an interpersonal relationship. The Pharisee who lives outside of time: you know how to interpret the earth and the sky; how is it that you cannot understand the signs of the times? *(Matthew 16:1-3, Luke 12:56)*—disconnectedness with history.

Another example is the rich man of Luke 12 who pats his stomach with great satisfaction: "Soul, you have ample goods laid up for many years; take your ease, eat, drink and be merry." This is one more result of a society structured on the law.

15

The Pharisee in the temple measures faithfulness to God not by identification with him, but by his identification with the law: "I fast twice a week, I give tithes of all that I get" *(Luke 18:12)*. He hypostatized the law and made it a god in order to save himself from personalization and from giving himself to others. This is the eternal temptation of the person and is the price one pays for fleeing from the liberation of one's own self. In order to live on a level of individualistic liberty, one pays this tribute to the idol: One objectifies and worships oneself, thereby avoiding a true encounter with God throughout one's whole life. It is a kind of atheism hidden beneath the veil of a hysterical and tense obedience, which has the inevitable consequence of judging others and persecuting them. A person who has truly encountered God is so lost in the limitless ocean that he no longer has any objective terms of comparison for judging others. To make a judgment about a greater or lesser love or a greater or lesser manner of being is practically impossible. To judge how many ounces I must eat for two days in a week and then to judge how many others should eat is easy and reducible to a quantitative formula. Therefore, "I am not like the rest of men" is the logical continuation of "I fast and tithe." God is not present there. It is I who decide my relationship with God and not he who decides.

And what prevents the priest and the Levite from seeing their neighbor in the injured man of Jericho is fidelity to the law. The man—who is unknown to them—does not enter into their formula. He is not included in the list of persons to be helped and assisted as one's neighbor, and therefore they are able to continue on their way. For them, love does not mean total availability, pure attention, or, I would say, an available emptiness. It is the "thingification" of a certain ideal of love, which is solidified in a determined historical moment of the community. And the whole community has collaborated in this "thingification," which protects the community itself, giving it the value of something absolute and permanent. It has thus become bogged down in a tradition that is closed off from history and contrary to it.

We have all been contaminated by this morality crystallized in time and solemnified by the unanimous consensus of the community. "These people do not talk to each other. Those don't visit each other." "That is not done." "That is not right." Many of these taboos are disappearing. But are we not also falling into the temptation of "thingifying" transgression, that is, the obverse side of the law? There is no escape hatch. We can save ourselves from the law by taking only one direction.

This "thingification" of the law stands in the way of receptivity to history, to the "sign of the times." The law is something fixed. History is continuous creation, the dynamism of constant renewal, and as such it is a constant break with norms that are made according to some moral schematization. Relativism is the great fear of Pharisees of every age. They killed and will always kill prophets because prophecy begins with the destruction of a fixed and permanent law, steadfast in all its parts and even in its interpretations.

"Of how much more value is a man than a sheep! So it is lawful to do good on the sabbath" *(Matthew 12:12)*. Beneath this "thingification" is hidden the fear of death as something final, and therefore the denial of the spirit of the Resurrection. This is the case because there is no presence in history without the aceptance of time, and thus none without faith. Time cannot be accepted without faith in the Resurrection, either the ultimate Resurrection in Christ in whom all things will be "recapitulated," or a resurrection this same historical time. And is this second resurrection not implied in the first? To defend a schema of salvation that would survive time is to deny the resurrection and to fear death. For this reason there will always exist in man the temptation to build an archeological city, a necropolis outside of historical time with its god and its immutable law. Against this, Christ's great prophecy is raised in vain: "And as for the dead being raised, have you not read in the book of Moses, in the passage about the bush, how God said to him, 'I am the God of Abraham, and the God of Isaac, and the God of Jacob'? He is not the God of the dead, but of the living; you are quite wrong" *(Mark 12:26-27)*.

They were incapable of distinguishing between a relativism of diminishment and one of interpretation, between legalistic, formalistic relativism, and the prophetic relativism which is a surpassing in the spirit. Jesus defined this kind of relativism with the words "I have not come to destroy but to build up." Lovers of legalism become entrenched in the city of the dead with their law, and their idols, and they hand out grades and honors.

Jesus repudiated this city and "suffered outside the gate. . . . Therefore let us go forth to him outside the camp, bearing abuse for him" *(Hebrews 13:12-13)*.

The man of the law gives authorization to the man of economics since economics is a law. The economists shape a language that without much change can be transposed to the moral sphere. Providence becomes foresight, obedience and fidelity become perseverance in work, poverty and avarice become thrift, prudence the defense of the sacrosanct nature of ownership. They are two distinct but not separate worlds in that the transition from one to the other is almost unnoticeable. Without realizing it the economist uses moral terms, and the moralist economic ones. The economist is an obedient man like the man of the law: Both claim dependence on an objective law, which oppresses them with its rigidity at the same time that it sustains them. Jesus was perfectly familiar with the psychology of the man of economics, and he hit upon the key point: "Take heed, and beware of all covetousness; for a man's life does not consist in the abundance of his possessions" *(Luke 12:13)*. And in Matthew: "No one can serve two masters; for either he will hate the one and love the other, or he will be devoted to the one and despise the other" *(6:24)*.

The abdication of the person in favor of the economic or moral law achieves the same result: the incapacity to grasp the true value of things and of persons as values in themselves. This can be done only when the liberated person is the subject of the act of knowing and doing.

The person has interiorized a motivation that prevents him from grasping values in themselves: The capitalist wonders, "What is the purpose of this?" And in the economic sphere there is a ready answer that cuts short and bars the way for arriving at the discovery of value *in se*, of the ultimate meaning of the thing.

A while ago I spoke with a plant manager about a person who was part of a team within his group. He took out a pencil, made an exact calculation of the work hours, the quantity of work produced, the relationship between profit and cost, and the person disappeared beneath this faultless geometric structure.

With the man of the law there is an analogous situation because the action, the "thingified" behavior within the law, prevents him from getting to the roots of consciousness and thereby discovering the person as a true, contemplating, and responsible subject. Consequently he cannot have that total availability which leads to the objective values of reality. The lack of profound peace, anguish in other words, is the sign of a permanent inadequacy because the mediation of the law prevents the person's total correspondence with objective reality.

To me this seems to be the profound sense of Jesus' rebuke to Martha. The key lies in this passage: "A woman named Martha received him into her house" *(Luke 10:38)*. Between her and Christ stands economic utility: Hospitality is a law. The guest must be properly received.

Some people say, "We can't invite anyone to come and see us because we are ashamed." There are certain rites, certain preparations, certain acts of hospitality that must be performed in order to avoid being embarrassed. Mary overcame all of this in order to concentrate on the person who had come into her house. She grasps the whole value of the event without recourse to any kind of intermediary. She is absorbed in the contemplation of the truth because she is liberated.

Of course the law has a function because the form of things and relationships and even of revolt and nonconformity is always a law. Paul says that "the law was a kind of tutor to conduct us to Christ" *(Galatians 3:24)*. In the Christian view the law must lead us to Christ, to the person with whom my own person identifies. This is the making over of the person in his original purity, regenerated by grace. This is the person who has achieved reflective ability: "Blessed are the pure of heart for they shall see God"; the person who has become completely available: "Blessed are the poor in spirit because theirs is the kingdom of God"; the person who has become patient and longsuffering: "Blessed are the merciful for they shall obtain mercy."

In a work of the Marxist writer Karel Kosik we read the following: "One who knows the truth and sees reality as it is cannot be happy [Blessed are those who weep]. One who is happy in the modern world does not know truth and looks at reality through the prism of convention and deception. This is the antinomy that revolutionary praxis must resolve" *(Morale e società*, Rome: Editori Riuniti, 1966). Blessed are those who hunger and thirst after justice. Blessed are the merciful.

For us Christians the root of the profound identification of the person with himself, and therefore the end of dualism between the law and the person, is a profound identification with Christ, who is the truth and the principle of action motivated solely by love. The law is the tutor to lead us to Christ insofar as in itself the law reveals the contradiction of the person—between what he ought to be and what he really is—and his powerlessness to overcome this contradiction. At this point, a new principle of action is presented to me, a permanent engrafting in truth and love. Although it leaves intact my being in the world and my being with others, it communicates to me a new principle of vision that is freed from all deception in poverty, a principle of operation freed from selfishness in love. It is not a liberation from one master in order to serve another. It is a self-liberation in freedom purely and simply because it returns the person to his original simplicity: "For in Christ Jesus neither circumcision nor uncircumcision is of any avail, but faith working through love" *(Galatians 5:6).*

We cannot boast here of a sign, of an objective value, of measurable and ponderable benefits. Faith and love are only total readiness to see and grasp the value of things in all their dimensions and a receptivity produced through the sole motivation of love. Therefore heteronomy is resolved in a true autonomy: Heteronomy is only a stage in a person's life. To use a current expression, it is its dialectical moment that must function as an impetus to a search for freedom from deception (faith) and from individual concupiscence (love). It is a moment that will never be overcome definitively because total and definitive freedom is impossible for the person. There will always be temptations to "turn back," to turn from integrity to plurality, from profound unity to atomization: "O foolish Galatians! . . . Who has bewitched you, before whose eyes Jesus Christ was publicly portrayed as crucified? Let me ask you only this: Did you receive the Spirit by works of the law, or by hearing with faith? Are you so foolish? Having begun with the Spirit, are you now ending with the flesh?" *(Galatians 3:1-3).*

Liberation from the law can come about only in one direction, in the spirit. And it can happen only through constant searching: in the line of poverty as simplification and renunciation; in the line of humility as solidarity with other beings; in the line of justice as a constant desire for objective truth; and in the line of truth as a constant search for liberation from deception in all its forms. Few people aspire to be spiritual men because Pharisaism is a temptation that runs through and with history. Every society makes its own choices and constructs its own models and therefore constructs a theory of the role player which it defines as a theory of the person.

I am writing these lines in a rather primitive village, inhabited by a race halfway between the Indians and Western man. Here the ideal of the group is *machismo* (maleness), which means seducing one girl and then going on to another one. Depth psychology has uncovered the roots of this aggressive sexuality in the fear of incest. Here, to be a person means to be a conquistador, according to the cruel and violent law of all conquests. For the most part love is blocked and inhibited by this image, which would be destroyed by genuine love. In this context the ideal of evangelical chastity is alienating because it cannot be seen as a regeneration of man through fontal grace, which is essentially love, and therefore the total giving of oneself to another. On this level it cannot be looked upon in any other way except as the opposite of virility, experience, strength, and cunning: It is the antiperson. It is only to be hoped that the presence of this value in a mystical person may give a few rays of light—to which Bergson alludes—which would be capable of capturing the attention and the desire of a person living the morality of his group. The ideal of the spiritual man can be grasped only in the person who lives it, because it cannot be reduced to a formula. As I said above, it is a witness or a martyrdom.

We cannot attain this "life of the spirit" without a poverty of simplification, without reducing our desires to the sole ideal of establishing a new order of truth in the world. To the rich man Jesus said, "You lack one thing; go, sell what you have, and give to the poor, and you will have treasure in heaven; and come, follow me" *(Mark 10:21)*.

Not all renunciation is liberating, because it can be done calculatedly, imposed by a superman spying upon us. This results in the most dangerous kind of alienation since it is incarnate in our own person. "Come, take up your cross and follow me." In his own way the Pharisee is a man of renunciation: "I fast—I pay the tithe," but his purpose is to be united with that superman in whom man is alienated by fleeing from himself and his real responsibility. Chastity is one of the most dangerous virtues in this regard because it has at its disposal a unique energy potential, and it can easily construct a superego. Jesus felt this and spoke of three categories of eunuchs. The choice of poverty can be dangerous if it is framed within a juridical structure that defines its limits and function as in a dowry system, because it is from this that the "poor man" role originates.

A juridical structure, a law, necessarily creates a role player, and thereby produces alienation, the opposite of liberation. Jesus did not make poverty an ideal. He shunned the schema of the poor-man role and behaved like a normal man in times of plenty: "And they said to him, 'The disciples of John fast often and offer prayers, and so do the disciples of the Pharisees, but yours eat and drink.' And Jesus said to them, 'Can you make wedding guests fast while the bridegroom is with them?' " *(Luke 5:33-34)*. "For John came neither eating nor drinking, and they say, 'He has a demon'; the Son of Man came eating and drinking, and they say, 'Behold a glutton and a drunkard, a friend of tax collectors and sinners' " *(Matthew 11:18-19)*.

For this reason the juridical structures of poverty do not succeed in making real poor people. These poor are the product of real situations, and poverty becomes a value of liberation when it is presented as an obstacle to the realization of the person and is confronted in struggle. It is a voluntary poverty when it is sought and discovered dynamically in that anxious and constant search for justice.

With Don Bosco poverty was an authentic force for liberation because all of his individualistic desires were absorbed, and overwhelmed, by the ideal of saving youth from depersonalization, from the perdition to which the society in which they lived condemned them. But the moment his successor becomes a special type with a particular method, the alienation is almost fatal.

Consequently, do we conclude that it is impossible to institutionalize a movement and therefore equally impossible to establish a rule? Paul gives the answer: The law is acceptable if it is considered as "a tutor to conduct us to Christ." It is a way to the liberation of the person, which is an unrepeatable personal history and can never be reduced to a schema.

The grave danger for each of us is that in arriving at the level of the role player, we stop there, without ever reaching the level of the person. We attain the superego, but never reach the true self.

We can never arrive at this level without a deep humility. This does not mean sinking down into the depths of despair and tormenting ourselves with remorse for often imaginary sins, with the precise—even if half-conscious—objective of creating a victim or penitent type. It means agreeing to live on the level of other beings, and not only of persons, but of all beings. The truly spiritual person is one who, after wavering in the land of dreams, open to exaltations of angelical abstractions and destructive self-denigration, has arrived at the peaceful acceptance of his own self, a common poverty, a common destiny, a modest history, which has its splendor in itself insofar as it is in the light of truth.

Progress in the spirit is not measured by an increase along the line of excess, but by that progressive return to being a man, by that reentry into normalcy, which is the acceptance of the self and of the life of all men. To be a Christian is basically to be a man, and if the renunciations appearing outside of the norm are accepted, they must be assimilated positively into a synthesis and must mature into the formation of a real person.

The truth of these renunciations is discovered through the capacity to understand all human situations. No one is true from the first moment: Life would no longer be a liberation if it were not a journey from alienation to liberation. And when someone accuses a religion or a law of being alienating, he is not wrong. He is placing this religion or law in the line of other alienations, but this has the illusion that it contains a hope and a value that other alienations do not have.

The spirit is a spirit of truth, and it cannot be received when we are complacent in the midst of lies. In order to combat this deception in us where it is least visible and hardest to reach, we must fight it outside of ourselves, not so much in man as in his projections. Man is both responsible for them and at the same time their victim. Fighting error, the struggle against the power of darkness, is an eternal attitude of the man who aspires to enter into the light of truth.

For this reason the spiritual man "judges all and is not judged by anyone." This is a phrase which, when taken literally as it sounds, may seem to contradict the "do not judge" concept of the Gospel. But it has a very profound meaning. Spiritual man cannot be judged because he does not correspond to any schema, he does not reproduce any "working model," and has achieved that freedom and that interior maturity which gives him the faculty of being able to judge the concrete situations in which he lives. And he discovers the truth in this state of tension against deception, in that coherent and untiring struggle which is defined as "hungering and thirsting after justice."

The objective is to free man from the successive slaveries to the laws which he himself has built and which continually postpone the creation of the free man. This struggle, however, constitutes the immanent dynamic of history, either of the history of an individual man or of the great history of mankind itself.

Since there is an interaction between man and society, there is a complicity between the two to construct a kind of comfort in alienation. For this reason the Gospel is a program of personal liberation: "Go, sell what you have and give to the poor, then come and follow me." But at the same time it is an open judgment on society: "You have heard what was said to the ancients: thou shalt not kill . . . But I say to you; whoever rages against his brother will be condemned in the judgment. . . . You know that it is said: thou shalt not commit adultery, but I say to you that whoever looks at a woman with desire has already committed adultery with her in his heart" *(cf. the entire fifth chapter of Matthew)*.

Jesus did not come to destroy the law, but to subvert at its roots a society that had become crystallized around a certain vision of the law. Jesus did not demolish either the Sanhedrin or the Israel of his time which had produced the hypocrite, the spiritual role player who prevented the person himself from being spiritual, true, and authentic. He presented himself as a sign of contradiction. We see the truth of the liberation he proposed to man insofar as we see its historical and real contradiction. This proposal is unthinkable without the open denunciation of the contradiction represented by the society to which Christ makes his proposal of liberation and genuine spiritualization. In Jesus' time the law was one. The Torah governed civil and religious society and they were identified with one another. Christ's death, decided by a religious and civil tribunal, can be considered the result of a political and religious condemnation. The separation that later came about and is becoming increasingly more evident, never succeeded in dissolving the reciprocal implications based on the unity of the person. The tragedy of alienation becomes complicated because we are made to serve two masters, secular and religious. The tyranny of both is aggravated by the jealous absolutism of each. Recent centuries are characterized by the aggressive defense of an autonomy that has permitted both powers to consummate in secret, on their own account, the alienation of the person—in the ideal empyrean of the superego or the fetid subcellar of slavery.

For this reason we cannot speak seriously of the liberation of the person without entering into the problematic of politics. Truth requires this because the political structure conditions a person's form of loving others. To accept this structure naively and dissociate the moral imperative from the real political structure is to be an accomplice of deception. To love a man does not mean to love abstract mankind, but man in the concrete—the man who fell and was injured at Jericho, on a definite road, on a given day, hurt by people who have names, addresses, and definite motives. And the injured man needs this particular help required by his real condition. How can I say I love a person, if I am partly responsible for an economic system that prevents him from being free and from realizing himself as a person? And I am responsible for my own time, not for others. The conviction that to liberate man from these alienations is not to liberate him definitively because other alienations will arise does not free me from my responsibility, which is bound up with a particular time and a concrete stage of history.

Only by entering into the problematic of politics and by doing so as a sign of contestation, with a demand for liberation, can I discover the deception that concretely alienates man and prevents him from being a person.

Someone told me once that in the world today it is impossible to be a Christian because the Gospel postulates an equality and a fraternity that cannot exist, once society has transformed the person into an economic relationship. However, this was even more true in the historical time of Christ in which this equality was denied on the juridical plane as well as on that of political praxis. In order for my preaching of brotherhood and equality to be authentic, I must reject any economic type of relationship that gives the lie in deeds to what I am saying in words. And I must combat it not only on the level of the individual but on the political level as well. I cannot change, as if by magic, political structures, but I can contribute to changing them. I can fight against these structures just as Christ fought with all the strength of his person against the Pharisaical society of his time.

What is said of the economic structure could also be said of the authority structure, which creates a relationship in which fear and desire play their part, along with concupiscence, adulation, deception, and simulation. In the Gospel, in fact, there is a whole criticism of authoritarian structure: "And Jesus called them [the twelve] to him and said to them, 'You know that those who are supposed to rule over the Gentiles lord it over them, and their great men exercise authority over them. But it shall not be so among you; but whoever would be great among you must be your servant, and whoever would be the first among you would be the slave of all' " *(Mark 10:42-44)*.

The Church has not always avoided the danger of crystallizing authority in a given person. It thus reflects other societies, but with the disadvantage of a more fundamental and perduring crystallization because it is less exposed to revolutions and to all the challenges of history. Truth is not a correspondence between the thing and the intelligence on a level that is apparent. It is this only on a deeper level, which is the only genuine one which I must seek. This is a penetration process that is not without its pains and its risks. This approach also condemns a certain kind of obedience, sought as a mere relationship of dependence and therefore of humiliation of the person, solely as an ascetical means of combatting one's own pride and individualism. Obedience that is not in truth is not liberating and is therefore in fact a slavery to the law.

Authority is "in truth" when it defends a person's right to "do what is true" and makes use of the wisdom given it by its position of coordination, and of the light it receives from God, to be of assistance in our progress along a road that becomes increasingly freer of alienations.

Therefore authority must be represented by a sign of service and not of comfort, of humiliation and not of pride.

To the mother of two of his most important followers, who asked for some authoritative place for her sons, Jesus stated clearly: "You do not know what you are asking. Are you able to drink the cup that I am to drink?" *(Matthew 20-22)*. Only on this condition can one neutralize the risk of power becoming the object of concupiscence.

Desire for authority is very strong, and more than other desires, it is able to make us deviate from the search for truth. Blind obedience is the obedience of a corpse. It is demanded on the presumption that the authority has such profound wisdom and such certain knowledge of the truth that it could make us trust in it with our eyes closed. But we forget that every man is responsible before the truth and that he discovers it to the extent that he commits himself personally to seeking it, to fighting for it, and to defending it. In this case authority is no longer a substitute for the person who is searching, but a stimulus and a guarantee of freedom and the right of the person.

If the law fulfills its function as a tutor to lead us to Christ, there is no reason for the distinction between autonomy and heteronomy, because the law has become absorbed in the person. It has become an instrument of liberation; it serves solely as a denunciation of all possible alienations, of everything that stands in the way of my reaching the truth. The law liberates only in a negative sense: "If it has not been for the law, I should not have known sin [i.e., alienation]," said Paul *(Romans 7:7)*. The sign of his identification with the truth is the interpretative and prophetic capacity to grasp truth in time and history. Because justice is the truth of existent beings, the truth which is justice and love is the contemplation of beings liberated from the deceptive appearances which sinful man has given them.

A passage from Paul's Letter to the Romans comes to mind: "For creation was subject to futility, not of its own will. . . . We know that the whole creation has been groaning in travail together until now" *(Romans 8:20-22)*. And the law is love insofar as the person is spurred on by a thirst for truth and seeks to restore men to justice. "Do what is true," which is a dominant motif of the Gospel, seems to me to have this meaning. Even if it is holy in itself, even if it is the law of God, the law always offers us the possibility of hypocrisies and of playing a character role.

Of itself, sanctifying the day of the Lord demands content. This inevitably creates the "good Christian" type who is at peace because he has fulfilled his obligation of being in a certain place at a time when a priest celebrated a rite 15 feet away from him. The only thing that would place him in communication with God and thereby in dialogue with him, a dialogue without the limits of time or space, would be a search for truth in this direction: It would have to be the occasion for him to lose himself and to renounce for good the possibility of measuring himself against someone else, which for man is equivalent to death. "He who finds his life will lose it, and he who loses his life for my sake will find it" *(Matthew 10:39)*.

Nobody can speak of autonomy in the absolute sense, because this would suppose an eternal and solitary person, but only in the sense that the law is so rooted in a person that it reaches the point of disappearing. By giving up its own content it becomes the pure capacity of judging and understanding. "Honor your father and your mother" is now no longer a precept, but a type of relationship guided by justice and love. In this light we may look at the whole of the law. For this reason, Christ's synthesis is a simplification, not in the sense of a dispensation but in that of a surpassing: " 'Teacher, which is the great commandment in the law?' And he said to him, 'You shall love the Lord your God with all your heart, and with all your soul, and with all your mind. This is the great and first commandment. And a second is like it, You shall love your neighbor as yourself. On these two commandments depend all the law and the prophets' " *(Matthew 22:36-38)*. By being a tutor to lead us to Christ who is the truth, the law has fulfilled its task. It has emptied itself and has permitted the person to exist in love. There is no other alternative for the law: either to make itself an idol or a tutor, a guide. Love is defined by a relationship with the Other and with others.

3

FREEDOM FROM "SIN"

The second foe to be conquered is "sin." There is no more dynamic or more human description of sin than that celebrated one of Paul in the seventh chapter of the Letter to the Romans: "We know that the law is spiritual; but I am carnal, sold under sin. I do not understand my own actions. For I do not do what I want, but I do the very thing I hate. Now if I do what I do not want, I agree that the law is good. So then it is no longer I that do it, but sin which dwells within me. For I know that nothing good dwells within me, that is, in my flesh. I can will what is right, but I cannot do it. For I do not do the good I want, but the evil I do not want is what I do. Now if I do what I do not want, it is no longer I that do it, but sin which dwells within me. So I find it to be a law that when I want to do right, evil lies close at hand. For I delight in the law of God, in my inmost self, but I see in my members another law at war with the law of my mind and making me captive to the law of sin which dwells in my members. Wretched man that I am! Who will deliver me from this body of death?" *(Romans 7:14-25)*.

Sin is a law of death, of falling backward, of the denial of the growth of a person. Only by separating it from the law and reducing it to being can we have a clearer notion of sin. Today more than in the past there is much discussion as to the nature of sin. Just what is sin? The discussion is caused by three factors. The first is always present: Man is always tempted to go beyond himself as a finite, contingent being, denying the possibility of limitation, whereas sin is the acknowledgment of limitation. There is no sin when there is no limitation, when there is total correspondence between being and existing, when my present existence in reality consumes my whole power to be. I cannot think of myself as anything other than what I in reality am at this moment of existence.

The second cause of this rejection of sin is the legal and juridical extrinsicism with which sin has been presented in our Christian morality, that is, as a quantitative entity expressed in a law. And therefore, its opposite, nonsinning, inevitably gives rise to the figure of the hypocritical Pharisee. Sin is not seen as a negative law inscribed in being. Rather it is defined by an extrinsic law. On this root man's Satanism prospers, that is, his desire to contrast a Promethean morality of affirmation with one that is basically only a denial of being.

The third cause is the dreadful ambiguity of a certain kind of morality which, precisely because it has no reference to personal being, gets lost in an interminable casuistry which completely distorts values. Everyone agrees in admitting the ambiguity of man and of history, the possibility that we may relapse, the unceasing inadequacy between what I am and what I ought to be. The difference is in the conclusion: Should I accept the human situation of ambiguity, this sinful being, or should I fight against it?

The Christian answer is obvious once we see that in the biblical perspective of all history is the history of salvation, of liberation from sin. Sin is a conscious rejection of being more and therefore of loving more. Before I see sin outside myself, objectified as a concrete notion, a projection of myself, I discover it within me as the "law of my members," which opposes my quest to be more. Seen as a negation of an external proposal, as a willful opposition to a tentative offer, sin requires savage energy which is discharged solely in the creation of a superego. Fleeing from one sin makes me fall into a worse one.

In reality a kind of athlete's view of morality has created satisfied heroes, combatants taking a deserved vacation on the beach, the champions of the sports magazines. Sin is a power of diminishment which I carry within myself, in my members. It is verified in diminishment in the sphere of faith and love, in the lessening of love toward what is invisible and cannot be appreciated with material categories—an ideal, a vocation, the search for a true value in the precariousness of the world and of history.

Sin means falling into plurality, a plurality fraught with desires, and therefore fraught with fears, which are the aggressive defenses of desires. *Good* is unity. It is the permanent within the provisional. It is the value I seek in a certain form and toward which flow my deepest vocation, my notion of the divine and of truth, my life ideal, and the unitive and creative center of my person.

This good I seek, as the unique good within the ambiguity of things, is both outside of and within me—as a vocation, as an element of unification, as the creative force of the person. The sign of fidelity will be precisely the progressive concentration of the person on the One, victory over plurality, diffuseness, and distractions. Sin is a proposal external to my true self. It is the projection of my plurality and my own ambiguity and at the same time an invitation to new pluralities and ambiguities. It is a new provocation to come out of myself, and dissipate into plurality. In his members each of us bears the law of sin, because as I grow there grows within me a seed of violence and ambiguity. The depth psychologists see it hidden in sex, insofar as sex is man's vital principle and the fire of his life. Perhaps this monistic emphasis helps us to discover truths that have been ignored. The truth is that our essence is love—if it is true that we are made in the image of God who is love—and that our existence is love. But it is especially here that our finiteness plays its role: Our loving is not love. Love is only in God. And therefore aggression in loving, violence in loving, which create man's terrible ambiguities, are also part of this search for proportion, this search for a form of loving which consumes and fulfills all my possibilities and my demands for love. Man's ambiguities are the monstrous objectifications of sin. Man's enslavement and exploitation are made into history with hunger, destitution, social rebellion, and explosions of anger which extend from a street fight with knives to a nuclear explosion. These are the signs of this violent search for love.

Even the desire for possessions is love. The Gospel offers a sure remedy to heal man's roots and as a consequence a peaceful attitude of retreat from things. The nonviolence of the Gospel is not—it seems to me—antithetical to the struggle for justice, which in certain cases may also be violent. It seems rather a standing at a distance from the violence of man in order to win a position of freedom, and therefore of knowledge in truth and of love in justice, meekness, and peace. Blessed are the pure of heart, blessed are the meek, blessed are the peacemakers.

The objectification of law and therefore of sin as a consequence seems necessary from the fact that none of us knows the forces of a person's diminishment or growth. The prodigal son of chapter 15 of Luke's Gospel thought he was going off to seek happiness and growth. Everything within him longed for it. But instead he experienced the forces of deterioration. This tale, which is basically the story of man, focuses on

God's forgiving and reconstructive love, of course. But this love does not excuse us from the duty of fighting sin and searching within our own personal history for the way toward being more and loving more. The law enters the history of liberation only when it is subjectified through faith and becomes the law of my personal being more and loving more. Calling the limit of a person and his ambiguity "sin" and recognizing it as such implies faith in a Person-God, that is, a God understood as the Being with whom I can have a relationship, which coincides with the fullness of my being and is the acknowledgment on my part of the possibility of rejection. The discovery of God as Being is made through sin, that is, through a direct experience of oneself, of one's own being as a creature, of the possibility of sharing in God's fullness, which is man's original and ultimate beatitude, and of the possibility of losing it.

I do not mean that it is necessary to sin in order to have an experience of God. But it is necessary to have an existential, personal experience of sin as something negative, an experience of the nonbeing in me and of its permanent threat. This experience can be brought about from the outside, through social pressure or with educational methods, and it can end up by creating a weak and anxious person, constantly tempted to escape into victimization or into the fabrication of a provisional superego which frees him from anguish. Or else it can arise from within as a revelation of a concrete and radical proposal of being, with the characteristic of a total and definitive surrender, an enslavement which coincides with the greatest liberation.

Charles de Foucauld had the "good fortune" not to know sin before his conversion or to have so forgotten what it was that he could say he did not know it. Unexpectedly, being was revealed to him as the point of confrontation with his own nonbeing—with his wasting of himself in the gutter of uselessness, ennui, and despair. He was truly one of life's prodigal sons, because he felt that beneath the positive surface he was deteriorating day by day. And at this point God presented himself to him as a unique and unconditional gift: "At the moment that I believed that God existed I understood that I could do nothing else but live for him." "Today salvation has come to this house, since he also is a son of Abraham" *(Luke 19:9).* " 'Woman, where are they? Has no one condemned you?' She said, 'No one, Lord.' And Jesus said, 'Neither do I condemn you; go, and do not sin again' " *(John 8:10-11).* It is the total acceptance of being out of the anguish of nonbeing and the despair of having rejected it. For this reason it is said that contrition must be total and directed toward God, rather than merely toward "what one has lost."

Recognizing that one is a sinner seems to be an alienation because it is to acknowledge that one is not autonomous; it furthermore casts one into a state of abjection, which diminishes his courage and causes in him morbid reactions and unhealthy renunciations. However, if we think about it, man's autonomy can never extend beyond the metaphysics of his own orbit and it can never get out of the circle of his own thought. Che Guevara, an idol of today's youth, has said: "To build socialism, we have to create along with its material basis the 'new man.' For this reason it is most important to make a proper choice of one's instrument for mobilizing the masses. This instrument must be basically of a moral nature, although we must not neglect the correct use of the material stimulus, especially one that is social."

Marxism has counted a great deal on changing structures for man's liberation, for saving him from "sin," which is identified with capitalism. At the height of his political activity, Che Guevara moved further and further away from the hope that new structures could automatically transform the person. In a speech given at Algiers in February 1965 he said: "Socialism cannot exist if a change is not brought about in people's consciousness that can effect a new brotherly attitude toward mankind, an individual attitude within the society in which socialism is being built or has already been formed [he refers here to the Soviet Union against which he was directing his criticism], a socialism of a worldwide vision in relation to all the peoples suffering capitalist oppression." These are words which have a ring similar to that of *Populorum progressio,* which was published two years later. Socialism does not resolve the moral ambiguity in which every religious morality seems to be floundering: either the typical hypocrite, the Pharisee, emerges, or else the roots of the person are reached with an unconditional liberation which may not coincide with the projects foreseen by bureaucratic planning.

A friend of mine from Buenos Aires, a most sincere woman and a winner of the Lenin peace prize, said that in her stay in Cuba she had attended a meeting of organizational women and her reaction was, "Who are these bigots?" She had the feeling she was at a Catholic Action meeting; she found the same atmosphere in both places. If we accept a liberation at the roots and discover autonomy on that level which is deepest in man, we necessarily touch on being and love. The speech of Che Guevara which I quoted goes on: "Let me say, at the cost of seeming ridiculous, that the true revolutionary is guided by great sentiments of love. It is impossible to think of an authentic revolutionary without this quality. . . . Under these circumstances it is necessary to have a large dose of a sense of justice and truth in order to avoid falling into dogmatic extremism and cold scholasticism and thereby into isolation from the masses. Every day it is necessary to struggle so that this love for living mankind might be transformed into concrete facts and deeds, into acts which will serve as an example for mobilization."

It is not possible to achieve this love without giving up a partial vision, a "party-caste morality." Only in this way can we discover morality as a vision and task of the liberation and growth of the person.

In this context, capitalism, that is, money as a center of interests and the motive for living, appears as the sin of man. The autonomy of the person as asserted by Marxism becomes the creation of a person without eschatology, a person who is totally fulfilled in the completion of his earthly vocation. In the strict sense of the term, however, this morality cannot be called autonomous because it is in search of a model that is beyond alienations. To find a motive for what must be done, this morality is obliged to establish a metaphysics of the phenomenon toward which the whole historical process tends, seen as a process of liberation. All of this is to be found in nature and in man. No residue of transcendence remains. It is curious how, when speaking of morality, the Marxists at every moment abjure the metaphysical dimension of the person which is at the basis of political liberation. This dimension attracts them as a hope and frightens them like a specter. Perhaps Christian moralists could learn something from this fear and avoid falling into too facile a transcendence, which can become an alienation. And in the face of this severity, more than one Marxist could be exorcized from the fear of transcendence by discovering it in its dynamic of personal liberation and creation. Indeed, with a few variations, this constitutes the hypothesis of a dialogue between the two groups.

To remain open to events, not to choose, not to accept moral categories and therefore not to accept sin as a negative category—these in the last analysis, are a product of metaphysics. This is the person as a conditioned being, a category internal to time and space and therefore incapable of true freedom. It is a tragic position into which the sense of sin can easily be inserted, and thereby the revelation of the Absolute. As the fullness of being, God is the necessary hypothesis of the moral act.

Today, in an age of moral anarchy in which the alternative is all or nothing, success or catastrophe, we see this much more clearly than in the age of moral rigorism, the age of Kant and the positivists. Perhaps our generation has a lesser perception of sin as enunciated in precepts because it cannot isolate sin from a certain kind of societal structure. But it has a clearer grasp of cosmic ruin, the possibility of collective destruction, and man's destructive power. Our generation repudiates the words of the Pharisee, "I tithe and fast twice a week," and consequently it is insensitive to the contrary. Tithes are of no importance to me. Fasts are ridiculous. However, we cannot be unmoved by Christ's lament over the Jerusalem that killed the prophets: "Behold, your house is forsaken and desolate." "There will not be left one stone upon another" *(Matthew 23:38 and 24:2)*.

If I could dialogue with the likeable Che, I should like to draw the conclusion that there therefore exist a revolution without love and one with love. This is not a problem of time. It is a qualitative problem. The man of love will not be a spontaneous product of socialist society. Man is responsible for love and he is so responsible that in accordance with revolutionary logic it may be possible to kill him, indeed it would be a duty to eliminate him, when love is lacking. This is the case because the lack of love on the part of some affects many through hunger, war, and underdevelopment. Therefore these few have to be eliminated. In whose name? In the name of a genuine, authentic, and profound love for man, revolutionary logic will answer. Therefore, admit "the sin of man," the lack of love. Do not admit hell or transcendence.

You think that this lack of love is imprinted in social deformations in these monstrous structures of society which are no less horrible than the gargoyles of Notre-Dame de Paris or the dances of death in Orcagna's frescos. Along with Che, however, feel the urgency of a "new" man, a man renewed in knowledge and in the possibility of loving. In order that the love of another may overcome the terrible weight of self-love, it is necessary that the other have a specific weight that is at least as great as the specific weight of the self. This supposes a clear knowledge of his essence. This knowledge must be nurtured on the hope of being able to love and with a love that is not sterile or pure idealism. Despair gives free vent to destructive aggression. Only hope can constitute a positive force of opposition to individualistic selfishness. And for the man who sins against love, who lives constantly in the sin of not loving, the capitalist, to give him a historical name, is there no hope of his conversion to love? No other way than elimination by violence? And are those who are doing the eliminating "out of love" sure that they are not acting out of destructive aggression, that they are acting truly out of love? Once the sinners are eliminated by violence, will there automatically rise up a generation of "saints" who know how to love? It does not seem so because we are back at the starting point, the hypothesis that motivates Che's moving criticism of a revolution that has already shown its "fruits." Once again then this "new man," this man capable of loving, would be the result of an internal conversion, a change, a *metanoia*. And this change cannot be effected without the discovery of error: "I have done wrong, I am doing wrong," and then, "I am able not to do wrong," "I can be something other than what I am, I can be a man who loves." And this process will be all the more true and radical the more there arises within me a disgust for what I do and how I do it, the vision of the seriousness of the consequences of my wrongdoing. This is what we Christians call "a sense of sin." The transcendence of "I have sinned against you alone," in the case of this secular sense of sin, is replaced by the image of what "I ought to be," by a model of myself. And this image is either superficial, bookish, a product of intellectual knowledge, and then my reaching for it will be an imitation of style and gesture, in a word it will be the eternal return of the Pharisee; or else this image will be vital, and will then attack the roots of my being.

It is the profound and vital person who attacks the role player, the alienated person. I cannot help but think of Paul's words, "rooted and grounded." The suffering occasioned by the situation can be neurotic, the expression of a generic nonacceptance of the self, which can be the nonacceptance of reality. This is pathological and not a sense of sin in our sense. We see this by its fruits because a person afflicted with this evil makes a great deal of movement, but always in the same place. He does not progress. When the sense of sin is genuine, it is accompanied by a realistic view: "I am able to be not this but something else." Therefore I decide to be something else. Luke's prodigal playboy did not succumb to the desperate tedium of a person who accepts to be less with the awareness that it is possible to be more. He sees clearly what ought not to be: "Here I am starving"; what could be: "Many day workers in my father's house are better off than I"; and he decides to be what he can be: "I shall set out and go to my father." In this perspective, the sense of sin and abjection does not seem destructive of the person, but rather creative and liberating. I do not see any other kind of dynamic that is capable of developing the creative forces of the person.

The sense of sin must be rediscovered outside of its sacramental and liturgical framework, which necessarily limits it to a specific group and to a characteristic precept that can be used by man's vanity and Pharisaism. It must certainly be rethought within a universal framework and shaped within man's historical responsibility. Today many Christians aspire to finding a broader liturgical framework, one that is more fitting than that of auricular confession, which easily becomes a psychological kind of consultation in which there are no obstacles to man's mythical tendency. For this reason they propose the discovery of sin and the act of conversion in a communitarian and historical context, which can be helpful in revealing sin as the integral rejection of the person and therefore as an attack against his integrity and a retrogression of both the community and history.

But this earthly transposition, this demythologization, cannot take away sin's innermost and most profound malice as a rejection of God as Being. Man's refusal to strive to be more is something of which I can accuse him when looking from the outside. But this indictment, together with what he feels rise up inside him from his conscience, has meaning only if it is true that he is not the inevitable product of a determined historical structure. He will be responsible only if his own fullness calls him deeply from within to tear himself away from all alienation in order to discover in himself his own truth as a conscious creature.

I cannot feel responsible on the basis of some precept which might be merely a quite debatable detail of the total world project, in which substantial discrepancies as well as doubts of every kind are possible. But I can feel myself responsible for the denial of Being, this Being which calls me to a painful liberation in order to reach down to my true self. All of this makes sense if God as the creative fullness exists. My asking for forgiveness is now directed to a Being who is outside of me, but, at the same time, it is also directed to the community and to history. To both of these my rejection has caused mortal wounds, voids of death, which become concentrated in the suffering of the person. It is difficult to see sin as an "evil to God," as an "offense to God." But it is possible and tragically transparent to see it as man's evil, as a lack of love. In this regard, the capitalist and socialist democracies are both playing chess—as Guevara saw—with the underdeveloped peoples who need their collaboration. But this is a rejection of Being only if Being is possible to man and therefore, I would say, if this Being exists. Sin is basically a rejection of that acceptance of the one, the more-man, the more essential, the truer and the more profound, by becoming easily lost in the alienations which can be reduced to my own use of creatures for myself.

For me there are many ways of calling God and of acknowledging him as the profound truth of our being as creatures. One of the most beautiful songs of repentance, Psalm 51, says, "Against thee, thee only, have I sinned," and then adds later, "Deliver me from bloodguiltiness." I have rejected you, true essence of my being, profound gravity of my life, my essential focus, the root and summit of my person, and thus I have shed blood in the world. I do not ask for freedom in order to construct the model of a just man, but rather for a freedom that is available, a freedom in justice and in will, which are the basic constants for any realization of truth in love. "Create in me a clean heart, O God, and put a new and right spirit within me. . . . Then I will teach transgressors thy ways, and sinners will return to thee." Once I have become a pure witness of a profound regeneration, of a freedom in love, of being a new man, I can teach your ways to those who want to live a consistent life of love.

For us Christians the vision of sin and our liberation from it are personified in Christ covered with wounds, rejected, crucified, dead, and risen. For us this is not a myth, but the essence of our faith. That this liberating action goes much beyond and outside of the sacramental sign which symbolizes the salvation process is true. It is also true that this liberation goes beyond the religious part of man's history and blurs the boundaries between sacred and profane history. This to me seems to be the meaning of demythologizing the history of salvation: It brings me to discover the signs of salvation outside the sacramental liturgical framework and makes me entertain the possibility that the sacramental sign may not be true. It may be an empty symbol, a sign without substance, if it is used to keep the Pharisaism of the believer alive.

From every quarter I am urged to speak of confession, which represents a general stumbling block of the Christian life. The stumbling block is no longer shame for sin, which our generation does not know, but the doubt that this "sacralization" of sin and repentance almost inevitably authorizes the Christian to isolate himself from others, from the whole history of the world. His insignificant humiliation before the priest would be the toll fee for maintaining the existence of the ghetto, that tiny company of the righteous awaiting heaven, authorized to swear upon the basis of an absolute and unmovable code.

Man today is essentially afraid of one thing, of not being a man. In the name of being an accepted part of a simple and normal community along with other men, he rejects the sacred as a category of the superego. This must always be kept present because it is the common basis of all the objections to the faith. For man to acquire trust in the sign of forgiveness, it is necessary that he see it as a deep part of his everyday history and as the suspension of a judgment that does not come to him from himself but from others, from the community. The sacrament of forgiveness may be framed in a community act without resolving its ambiguity. Basically, it is I who judge myself, I who double as judge and accused, and I who entrust the acts of this judgment to the authorized priest. He thus partly satisfies the judge by exalting my capacity to judge and partly the offender, increasing my sadistic complacency in remorse. The judgment must come to me from the community. Zacchaeus discovered his sin in the judgment of the people.

The Zacchaeus episode is a charming one. It has all the color of the life of a village where everybody knows everybody else. Everybody judges and criticizes everybody else mercilessly. Jesus' visit is obscured by this rural backbiting: "And when they saw it they all [not only the Pharisees, but everybody] murmured, 'He has gone in to be the guest of a man who is a sinner' " *(Luke 19:7)*. I can imagine the snickering that accompanied Zacchaeus' walk with his guest from the sycamore grove to his house: The wolf turned into a sheep—Zacchaeus caught on in a hurry. His sin, his lack of love, his cruelty to others are not measured by Zacchaeus himself on the basis of some code of his own. They are discovered by society and objectified in the injustices that "everybody" in Jericho knows. His repentance comes from this: "Behold, Lord, the half of my gifts I give to the poor; and if I have defrauded anyone of anything, I restore it fourfold." Jesus does not say a word to all the murmurers, who evidently are correct.

The attitude of the adulteress in John's Gospel *(Chapter 8)* is quite different. Here too the woman discovers her sin in the accusation of the community. But in this case it is not "everybody," but only the scribes and Pharisees who condemn her in the name of the law of Moses. The implication is obvious: "We are not like her," because they have never been caught in adultery. Jesus does not deny the sin of the adulteress: "Go and sin no more." He goes to the root of the evil: "Whoever among you is without sin, let him cast the first stone." Transferring the judgment from the person to the community does not heal the injustice. "Judge not" is just as valid for the individual as it is for the social group, which can be just as unjust and hypocritical as the individual.

However, the judgment of myself can be objective only if it comes from a public and communitarian context, and my private reflection must assume all this in my personal history. All historical reflection, whether Marxist, Christian, or some other, has discovered the great crimes of people who speak in the confessional only of telling "harmless white lies," the disturbing injustices of those who confess merely having "looked too long" at a miniskirt, the abysmal omissions of those who confess only that they missed one mass—in order not to feel out of place in front of the metal grill of a confessional. But some will have the dreadful doubt that they are reciting a farce of bad taste. It is to be hoped that the change in language that is inexorably taking place within the Church and the demand for greater clarity will influence the sacrament of reconciliation so that it will be the sign of a true desire for reconciliation.

Christ saves us in that the fullness of Being is united with the finiteness of man, not in the Olympian peace of arrival, of accomplishment, but in contradiction, in the painful effort to "become": "Therefore he had to be made like his brethren in every respect, so that he might become a merciful and faithful high priest in the service of God, to make expiation for the sins of the people. For because he himself has suffered and been tempted, he is able to help those who are tempted" *(Hebrews 2:17-18)*.

To say that in his person Christ is the soldering point between the infinite Being and the finite creature—brought by its own finiteness to seek a completeness in its actions, a completeness that is then discovered to be a healing in love—is not to eliminate the mystery. Liberation requires a leap of faith, faith in one who liberates us, a contingent person who lives in history but who is limited by time and space and who therefore can be said to be historical although not coextensive with history. For history in its totality to become salvation history, it is necessary that I who am living through a stage of history, a tiny part of this history, be able to save myself. And the community manifests this salvation which is coming about in history, coextensive with it and therefore fully visible only at the end of time: "For as often as you eat this bread and drink the cup, you proclaim the Lord's death until he comes" *(1 Corinthians 11:26)*. And this leap of faith is not an alienation, because it is a reality when I discover that the history of salvation is changed by me and on account of me into a history of perdition because I do not love. I discover that I am alienated in my sin and I seek liberation.

That liberation is projected in my acting in the world as freedom. Liberation in truth and in love is the only sign that repentance has not been pathological and that my calling out to the Savior has not been motivated by an egotistical fear and a desire to capitulate. The interior peace and joy which Paul defines as the fruit of the spirit are also suspect when they are isolated from the history of the person. There are many who sleep peacefully in mansions that were erected with violence and defended by the sword of injustice. But when a sign of freedom is present, such as the courage to look squarely at injustice and to fight it with an attitude of love in freedom—that is, free from economic conditioning or special interests of any type—then reconciliation is at hand. And a liberation is achieved and at the same time continues to be effected. It is in a state of becoming and as such brooks no complacency, no looking at ourselves in the mirror and murmuring the nauseating expression "I am not like the rest."

"Now when Jesus saw great crowds around him, he gave orders to go over to the other side. And a scribe came up and said to him, 'Teacher, I will follow you wherever you go.' And Jesus said to him, 'Foxes have holes, and birds of the air have nests; but the Son of man has nowhere to lay his head.' Another of the disciples said to him, 'Lord let me first go and bury my father.' But Jesus said to him, 'Follow me, and leave the dead to bury their own dead" *(Matthew 8:18-22).*

The encounter with Christ is not an encounter with the law. It is a liberation, a total receptivity. When this liberation arrives, the starting point for a long and indefinite journey, every kind of dependence is a return to death.

4

FREEDOM FROM DEATH

"The last enemy to be destroyed is death" *(1 Corinthians 15:26).* Freedom from sin implies a choice: I do not love, but I can love and I choose to love, and this decision is nurtured on concrete choices and definite programs.

These same choices free me from my alienation, but they do not free me from the anguish of the finite. To choose something means shutting off the possibility of choosing something else at the same time. The moral law seems to be an alienation precisely because in his choosing man is shut off from his "infinite," and his choosing is his way of being free. The creature, however, cannot eliminate his finiteness, and therefore he cannot eliminate anguish except in the peace of faith which is continually lost and regained. Faith as a virtue rooted in the person is not lost, but the profound peace in faith is continually lost because new factors present themselves, factors that have to be assimilated. Consequently the Christian is not exempt from the existential anguish of the person by the fact that he has a deep and permanent root, a certainty that underlies all the successive choices that are presented to him. In my opinion this is the crucial point where the alienation of the believer or his identity is decided. Since he has faith, a believer would seem liberated from the fatigue of the normal man's search in life itself for values, which present themselves indistinctly in the confused and contradictory flow of history. The believer already possesses a real set of fixed values, preserved from the tide and corrosion of history. Therefore it is impossible for the believer to share fully in the destiny of the common man, which is to acquire a way of behaving within the reality in which he is submerged.

Man has nothing or no one to save him. He alone must win his own salvation through concrete choices which will save or damn him. The believer and the Christian—for we are speaking of him here—already possesses a metahistorical content of faith. It is eschatological and permits him to enter into history as a pastime, in the expectation of the final manifestation of those values in which he believes and which he has chosen through faith. But is it true that faith has its own content in which values are hierarchized and therefore already selected by men other than myself? Is it true that only the determination of will is required of the believer, a capacity for implementing plans that have already been decided and values that have already been classified and possess the majesty of the divine seal and the awfulness of an ultraterrestrial sanction?

No. Faith gives only an ontological vitality, an essential holiness that guarantees the right and possibility to choose. Without faith we cannot choose, and without faith a moral life, founded on the capacity to establish values and choose among them, is impossible. It is obvious that I am not speaking only of explicitly religious faith. Rather, I speak of situating the human as a basic category of moral living, the search for what is fitting for man, for what fulfills him as a man bound to the earth, bound to space and history and therefore to time. Is not this healthy attitude which guides me in my search for values and concrete choices similar to faith? Is it not similar to faith in the fact that man exists, that the state in which I find him historically is a phenomenon of deformation and not the inevitable product of existence? Faith, then, gives me this and this alone: a certainty, which is obscure—because it is contradicted by reality—that this man, this person liberated in love, is possible, exists, and is in a state of becoming. In what way? In time, in history, and mysteriously since I cannot foresee the future. Faith does not shed any more light than the common man already has. Jesus' entry into Jerusalem could have given the illusion of triumph: We have arrived, at last we have won. And yet we find ourselves on the brink of humiliation, obscurity, and total defeat in every sphere.

In the Bolivian campaign, Che Guevara came to Samaipata on July 10, 1967, and harangued the crowd, urging the people to join the revolution that was in progress. On October 8, he was struck down, and with him died the hope of liberation for the poor of Bolivia. To see the triumph of the ideal, the righteous rewarded and the wicked punished, the affirmation of truth and justice, it is necessary to reconstruct a religious world apart from the Gospel, in which no guarantee is given. Jesus blocked the way for those who—like the friends of Job—want to fashion a two-penny theology and penetrate beneath the arid and colorless exterior of events in order to read the mystery that lies within. The Gospel tells us that the righteous man, the man of love and peace, will exist. We have the right to seek him. It is worth giving our lives in the pursuit of this ideal which lies beyond death. This kind of faith embraces a part of mankind that is much greater than that which is enclosed within the confines of the "people of God."

And faith in man is identified with faith in God. This to me seems to be the real meaning of "seeing Christ in one's brother" and "serving Christ in one's neighbor." But it is a truth, when taken as statically as it sounds, that can give rise to quite negative consequences. I shall never forget something which once happened to me in a religious school. A friend of mine, who was not a practicing Catholic and was openly at odds with the Church, asked me whether he could attend a mass I was going to celebrate. After the mass, we went to a copious breakfast, served in a setting which I found repulsive but which nevertheless showed the attention and meticulous care of the good nuns. After it was over, my friend, who had been very well impressed, thanked the sister who had served him. "No, don't thank me," said the sister. "We are serving Christ in our guests." This gave rise to an interminable discussion between us. If I had asked Che Guevara, "Who is this New Man you are looking for in your campaigns in the Sierra Maestra, the Congo, and the Bolivian altiplano? Who is the man you are serving and for whom you are giving your life?" Che would have answered that it was the man of justice and love, integrated in a community that has finally been liberated from its contradictions. A man who doesn't exist, but who will. And why will he? "Because I have faith that he will!" For a believer, this Man who ought to be, who is the final point of history, who has appeared as an anticipation and who is far from being known and understood in his full dimensions, has a name and that name is Christ—the whole Christ spoken of in the Pauline letters.

Therefore it is clear that the Christian is one who sees Christ in his brother just as Che saw the new man in the *peones* of Bolivia.

Faith must be enriched. It must be constantly redeemed and regained in the concrete choices presented to me day after day. For this reason the Gospel sets forth an urgent appeal for vigilance: "Be watchful and keep your eyes open." The foolish virgins are full of good intentions. They greet the guest with the same enthusiasm as their companions. But they lack initiative, are distracted, and put nothing of themselves into this obedience. They thoughtlessly run to meet the bridegroom. The servant who received the talent jealously defends his patrimony as a secure and inalienable possession. But this possession he so jealously and staunchly saved was taken away from him and given to the man who had much because he had made what he had increase.

Faith alone gives us a strong constitution and a profound strength, so that we may go in the direction of an attainable good. The goal is to produce in the person a likeness of Christ, the man free in love, toward whom the person tends. We have the root and the hope of this within us, but the likeness is constantly compromised by the force of death within and outside of ourselves. "Do not lie to one another, seeing that you have put off the old man with its practices and have put on the new man, which is being renewed in knowledge after the image of its creator" *(Colossians 3:9-10).* And a letter of Peter warns against "your adversary the devil [who] prowls around like a roaring lion, seeking someone to devour" *(1 Peter 5:8).* This vigilance is not a purely intellectual operation, but rather an active involvement which is clarified and grows in the dynamic construction of the "new man." The vital thrust which impels us to seek this "new man" is in contrast to a law of death which is so subtle and hidden that it is impossible to state it in written and well-defined form.

Death is not only the transgression of the written law. It is also a flight into the unreal, into nothingness and the void. Death is the negation of existence, and the "demon" constantly threatens us, the demon of the superego. Jesus' temptations constitute an exemplary episode that is most instructive. In the last analysis, the temptor is offering him a way out in the direction of a more convincing messianic character, more effective than a man defeated and worn out from fasting. In himself, in his person, and in his personal history, the Messiah begins the struggle against this role playing before waging war against the Pharisaical world. In the temptations of Christ can be seen the classical moral forms of man's sin, but what is important is that they all converge into one: the acceptance of a messianic person who comes from on high, who has everything to do and nothing to receive, who does not have to deal with events or reality because he is able to situate himself outside of and above reality. This chapter would be enough to uphold the Gospel as an eminently realistic and human doctrine.

The temptation of death, which Paul calls the "sting of death," tempts us strongly and is nurtured by the anguish of time and space. "Having to wait" is most difficult for the man who is capable of making supertemporal and superspatial syntheses. And having to achieve fulfillment here, in this space, with the awareness of a universal vocation, is another of the difficulties of the person. The temptation of time was foreseen in the Gospel: "As the bridegroom was delayed, they all slumbered and slept" *(Matthew 25:5)*. The temptation of time, which lasts between the invitation to and promise of the wedding and the moment of the wedding itself, produces the effect of impatience and discouragement, "letting oneself die." At other times it produces the effect of *hybris*, of arrogance, the flight toward a solution that may appear more human because it is more activist, but it is also fatal: "But if that servant says to himself, 'My master is delayed in coming,' and begins to beat the menservants and the maidservants, and to eat and drink and get drunk, the master of that servant will come on a day when he does not expect him and at an hour he does not know, and will punish him, and put him with the unfaithful" *(Luke 12:45-46)*. The temptation of space was also foreseen in the Gospel: "And [Jesus] came to Nazareth, where he had been brought up; and he went to the synagogue, as his custom was, on the sabbath day. And he stood up to read. . . . And all spoke well of him, and wondered at the gracious words which proceeded out of his mouth; and they said, 'Is this not Joseph's son?' And he said to them, 'Doubtless you will quote to me this proverb, "Physician, heal yourself; what we have heard you did at Capernaum, do here also in your own country." ' And he said, 'Truly I say to you, no prophet is acceptable in his own country' " *(Luke 4:14-30)*.

Time and space spur man to search for a way out, which can be either in the direction of liberation or of dependence, enslavement, and death. Freedom is expressed as a calling, as the meaning of my existence at this time, in this space, and in this community. In other words, it is the real acceptance of oneself in particular circumstances. Or on the other hand, it is possible to get out of time and space and move toward a superspatial and supertemporal role playing. In this choice, which is constantly being renewed, the person's psychic state plays a major function. At times an intervention in the psychic equilibrium can help him to return to reality and thus to life. However, there are people who live out their lives in a state of delirium. At times what may seem to us to be a descent toward death is actually a step toward life. A well-balanced spiritual life must show itself in a progressive liberation from the artificial role playing and in the increasingly more heartfelt adherence to an unrespectable personal vocation.

Often it is life itself, with its disillusionments, that helps a man leave the role player behind and accept his own self. It is rather sad for a person to discover that he has begun to live only in old age and to realize that for many years he has not been living in truth. The more serious thing is that a person who lives in death, in the nonexistent, projects himself into external structures as much as he can out of a need to calm his internal anguish. Indeed, since he cannot adjust to reality, he seeks to create a reality similar to his own self. The social structures of delirium—armaments, violent occupations of countries, the dramatic arrogance of monopolies, are all the projection of delirious people who have escaped into an abstract superego which always demands to be made historical.

Religious education is particularly in danger of creating these types of people because it lays great stress on the "model" rather than on the vocation, on dependence rather than on autonomy, and on obedience to the law rather than on obedience to the spirit.

The anguish of death pursues us because we feel its presence within us and in our choices. The atomic bomb is the almost mythical projection of this fear. In order to overcome it, we must hunt it in all its hidden lairs. The secret is to fill nonbeing with real being. It is well known that the fear of death even in its neurotic forms is to be found in certain social classes where there is a great disparity between the awareness of oneself and the awareness of one's vocation to something concrete, to something that needs to be done in the world. If being coincides with vocation, if I look upon time as a *kairos* which I must and can fulfill, as my own time, and if I look upon space as that piece of ground adapted to my being rooted in the universe and in history, death will utterly disappear. It will be conquered when my existence perfectly coincides with my vocation.

The Gospel expresses this truth for us in an apparently absurd antithesis: "He who finds his life will lose it, and he who loses his life *for my sake* will find it" *(Matthew 10:39)*. The words "for my sake" are of utmost importance, even though their meaning may be obscure. They cannot mean merely losing one's life with an extrinsic, added intention of making an offering to Christ. Their significance is something deeper, something ontological: losing one's life for the kingdom of God which is man's freedom, the total and integral construction of the person. Christ conquered death by passing through it. In his total acceptance of the time and space of the "Jerusalem which kills the prophets" and the Pharisaical community, his messianic vocation was concretized. The sign of the perfect coincidence of his existence as man and his vocation as Messiah is precisely death as the definitive and total gift of self: "Greater love has no man than this, that a man lay down his life for his friends" *(John 15:13)*.

In the Gospel there continually appears the contrast between the apostles, still under the influence of death and therefore tempted by nonbeing, and the Messiah, who discovers time and space as the signs of his vocation. When Jesus announced his passion, Peter "took him and began to rebuke him. But turning and seeing his disciples, he rebuked Peter and said, 'Get behind me, Satan! For you are not on the side of God but of men' " *(Mark 8:32-33)*. And they continually urged him to leave time and space, but "Jesus said to them, 'My time has not yet come, but your time is always here,' " *(John 7:6)*. A vocation can be charged with passion, but if it does not have roots in space and time, if it is not concrete obedience to a time and a space, it is laden with nonbeing and with death.

Only vocation as obedience has the strength to make me come out of myself and thereby storm death's citadel within me, within my self considered as an absolute, as something apart, as something deserving of every right. To the extent that I make myself obedient to my concrete existence, "though our outer nature is wasting away, our inner nature is being renewed every day" *(2 Corinthians 4:16)*. Without time or space, without history, there is no death, but neither is there life. In reality, the person cannot live outside of time and space, but he must conquer anguish, which is death. And he can do this only by ransoming time and space as a vocation, by transforming what occurs into history.

Therefore the anguish of death—which is the product of time and space because time continually pushes me out of space by hunting me out from a position that I believe to be inalienable—is conquered only with the victory over time and space. I accept death's work of dissolution, but at the same time I give myself over to it and fill it with myself in this very struggle. It is something like the bee who dies leaving its sting in the flesh of the other. We must leave our life in the flesh of the time and space which are ours, if we coincide with them through our vocation. Jesus entrusted himself to time and space and arrested them for eternity, because "heaven and earth will pass away, but my words will not pass away." My "not existing any more" terrifies me only when nothingness, nonexistence, has reached me interiorly, deeply penetrating my being, filling it with superficial actions and movements which have lost their essential truth.

These are the actions or the facial gymnastics of an actor, the shadowboxing of a prize fighter, the jests of a mime. This is not the unique, unrepeatable obedience, that completely new obedience to something or someone which has grasped you at the roots of your being, obliging you to an obedience that does not come to you from the outside, but with a force that is identified with the force of life itself. "But when he who had set me apart before I was born, and had called me through his grace, was pleased to reveal his Son to me, in order that I might preach him among the Gentiles, *I did not confer with flesh and blood" (Galatians 1:15-16).* This mysterious sense of life's seriousness is unexplainable in logical terms, but it can give a person the courage to accept dependence and it creates that mixture of security and fear, a sense of the necessity and at the same time of the contingency of one's own existence.

"How can a being" asks Tillich, "who is dependent on the causal nexus and its contingencies accept this dependence and, at the same time, attribute to himself a necessity and a self-reliance which contradict this dependence?" (*Systematic Theology*, Chicago: University of Chicago, 1951, I, 197). Through personal experience I am convinced that death, and therefore the threat of death, its sting, is to be found in the area of independence within me, in that space in which my self asserts itself by undertaking projects independently of time and space, that is, outside of its vocation as a definite person with a name and his own history.

The anguish of death is hidden deep inside me: " 'And I will say to my soul, Soul, you have ample goods laid up for many years; take your ease, eat, drink, be merry.' But God said to him, 'Fool! This night your soul is required of you' "*(Luke 12:19-20).* The anguish of death is hinted at in this extrapolation of the person, this flight from time and space, from nature and the community. The possessions this rich man has today are bound up with their function in community. And the Gospel emphasizes this: "And the things you have prepared, whose will they be?" *(Luke 12:20).* They are looked upon as an absolute possession of a person bound to space and time: "You have ample goods laid up for many years." If I eliminate this space of false autonomy, which I am able to create by separating myself from the concrete conditions of my existence, I eliminate the place of "nonbeing," the breeding ground of death.

I have often thought that this anguish of death—as a consequence of being uprooted from reality, as a consequence of the nonacceptance of the real, and therefore as a consequence of a disobedience which is ontological, even if it is not intentional—is an unreal suffering, which is strongly felt but which is nevertheless the expression of a nonexisting person. "Afterwards the other maidens came also, saying, 'Lord, lord, open to us'. But he replied, 'Truly, I say to you, I do not know you' " *(Matthew 25:11-12).* "For many, I tell you, will seek to enter and will not be able. When once the householder has risen up and shut the door, you will begin to stand outside and to knock at the door saying, 'Lord, open to us.' He will answer you, 'I do not know where you come from' " *(Luke 13:24-27)*. It would seem that two people were speaking a completely different language: I do not know you. Fear of death has nothing to do with fear of God. In this case it is the sign of a void that we have carried with us and have lacked the courage to fill with our personal choices. Sin and death have this in common: They are phantasms of reality. In both I abandon my vocation in order to do what I please; I decide to go outside of obedience to my existence as determined by the Creator.

The anguish of death can be conquered only by accepting the destruction of a false self which is projected and substantiated in desires, in false projects, in relationships which are ephemeral even though they may be grandiose and impressive. Today, from the perspective of history, we see clearly how the delirium of a false Hitler, Hitler's double, built the extermination camps, destroyed entire families, and filled the earth with mourning. These are the monstrous caricatures, the amplifications, of something that more or less happens to us all when we escape from history into myth, from an obedience which defines our vocation to the delirious pursuit of an imaginary project: "Therefore as sin came into the world through one man and death through sin, and so death spread to all men because all men sinned, . . . so by one man's obedience many will be made righteous" *(Romans 5:12 and 19)*.

Conversion, then, will be like a reawakening from a dream. The return to reality will be the discovery of the true proportions of one's self and of a compatibility with the real and simple life: "How was I able to do this? How could I have taken so long to understand this? It is the impression of passing from death to life. This would not happen if it were not a question of a reference to truth and if this truth were not incarnate in a history of man; for if it were outside of this history, instead of showing me the road to acceptance, it would fix me in evasion. The more the opportunity of adhering to the truth is manifested to me, the further away I get from my own being as a man on earth and in a community. I discover the truth—my vocation insofar as it is in me—inscribed in my being, even if it can be ultimately attributed to the will of the Creator. The truth made flesh, the truth made human existence, is Christ.

Christ is the Savior from death insofar as he is true human existence and has not rejected any of the limitations of man, anything real and concrete. He rejected only sin, which is an emptiness, man's nonbeing. Life is fidelity to him who projected his obedience into the world. In the world he placed a gravitational force, thus removing it from the emptiness to which man continually subjects it by making it a projection of his disobedience and therefore of his nonbeing.

Death and life confront each other in man as a law of existing in the world, now, in this particular history and community, and as an antilaw of rejection, escape, rejection of one's own time, space, and community. And they confront each other in the world as images of the ambiguity of the person, in which we discover in a disconcerting continuity the density of history and the subtle vanity of dreams. And man now senses the serious-ness of the commitment to live, nurtured by a love which is as strong as death. At times he notes that he is not serious and, looking at himself in the mirror, he feels that he lacks the courage to wait for another sunrise. Following in Christ's footsteps means that we must place ourselves in that cone of light where things are real and where the person is a real subject who adheres to himself, to the concrete law of his existence. And the signs of this are poverty, love, and humility, salvation from the alienation of space, the community, and time. "I mean, brethren, the appointed time has grown very short; from now on, let those who have wives live as though they had none, and those who mourn as though they were not mourning. . . . For the form of this world is passing away" *(1 Corinthians 7:29-31)*. That is, we must live in accepting our own true proportions, our limitations. And we do this not by creating for ourselves a phantasm of man, some lord of time and creatures, but by finding ourselves in the acceptance of the limits that define us and give the true dimensions to our history and our powers.

Christ's victory over time and space, brought about in obedience to his being as man, in the perfect acceptance of his messianic vocation, is the basis for the courage through which the believer "accepts the threat of losing individual substance and the substance of being generally" *(Systematic Theology*, I, 198).

For a man, to give up his self-image is really to lose his substance, because the sensation of living, being, having a substance, is more related to the role player than to the person. To be identical with one's self, to live one's own mission consistently, to accept fully and without reserva-tion one's own space and time, one's own history as a vocation, all mean to renounce the idea of seeing, touching, defining one's self. The dark night of the senses, of the spirit, of the intellect means this: giving up being something other than one's self and therefore accepting the fact that this other has to die.

I remember a conversation with a friend who confided in me his sadness at seeing his mother grow old. What impressed him more than physical deterioration was her spiritual degeneration. She had been quite generous and now had become mean. Where before she had been patient and tolerant, she now had become irritable and peevish. He thus watched develop in her a humanness that was new, but at the same time antipathetical and disagreeable. He had expected a progressive spiritual maturation. But perhaps it was the role player in his mother than was going to ruin, and what appeared was she herself, her true, infantile, and immature self. Perhaps she had not worked with what had been given to her and she had wasted time making a pillar of salt which was now crumbling. Perhaps this is the real "moment," the encounter with truth. Only truth will make us free, and in order to discover this truth we ourselves must be true. We cannot be true on our own; we need the assistance of life and time. Time which is not accepted, which is continually wasted, must involve us in its own mechanism and make us die in order that we might make the transition to resurrection.

All this is true if Christ has risen. Paul says that everything hinges on this event: "If Christ has not been raised, then our preaching is in vain and your faith is in vain. . . . Then also those who have fallen asleep in Christ have perished. If for this life only we have hoped in Christ, we are of all men most to be pitied" *(1 Corinthians 15:14, 18-19)*. Christ truly conquered time and space by fully accepting them. Accepting them means accepting destruction and estrangement, and therefore nonexistence, because the real dimensions of my existence have left me. But it also means accepting my identification, saving my self from total destruction. And this profound and resistant nucleus, which has succeeded in emerging in the arduous becoming of the elements, enters by means of obedience into time and space, into life that is more than life. All that dissolves is what is subject to time and space, and not that which finds the fullness of its existence in obedience to time and space. By the same law whereby we die we live. The same concrete, historical obedience is the law of my existence and my death. Of Christ it has been said that "by dying he destroyed death," and this can be also said of every Christian following in Christ's footsteps.

The resurrection is not a prize that comes from the outside to someone who has been well-behaved, the trophy given to an athlete who has won the race. It is the result of concrete choices which are repeated over the course of our life. Obviously it comes to me through grace, because without Christ's victory immortality would be a hope of the species and not of the person. But it is a category that is internal to me, a seed that flourishes within me—"seed of grace and seed of glory." Life and death are contained in me and are proposed to me in the choices I make, in my relationships with things and with people. Death is equivalent to deception, to darkness. Life is equivalent to truth.

"The coming of the lawless one by the activity of Satan will be with all power and with pretended signs and wonders, and with all wicked deception for those who are to perish, because they refused to love the truth and so be saved. Therefore God sent upon them a strong delusion, to make them believe what is false, so that all may be condemned who did not believe the truth but had pleasure in unrighteousness" *(2 Thessalonians 2:9-12)*. Deception is already death because it means leaving one's own truth to live in the vanity that is death.

The resurrection of Christ is the resurrection of the flesh, of our flesh. It is God's power applied to the sphere of space and time, the opening out of the finite into the infinite, beyond the victory over space and time. Without the resurrection, the Gospel is not the Good News, because instead of liberating us it would abandon us to time and death. Its plan of personalization would be reduced to the formation of a vanity that is worse than that of carnal man. Truly we would be the "most wretched of men."

The Gospel is either a proposal of permanent Being which gives us fullness, or else it makes us slaves of the law and places us outside of history by cutting us off from all hope. We cannot look upon Christ as a moral teacher, and much less as a guide to our insertion in history. Either he is the cornerstone upon which our life and history are built, or else we are shattered into pieces, losing our consistency as men. Hence faith in the resurrection makes us wager all our existence and all our hopes. Like Abraham, each of us is called at a certain moment to lift the sword against the son, against ourselves, to "lose our life." True faith, that profound faith that saves, which reaches the roots of the person, is an almost total act of courage. It is such an absolute loss of self that it is possible only through the certainty that Christ has risen and that we shall rise with him.

The choice of life is made by passing through death, and each person must live this death as a personal experience. The old woman about whom

I spoke above can enter into the life of faith only by discovering herself naked, poor, bereft of false dignity, made up of bits and pieces, by accepting herself as she is and accepting this "loss of substance" which is worse than death.

This self-emptying is true and has value only if Christ is risen and if this road of humility and death is his road. Only in this way, by accepting true death, can we escape the anguish of death. Our faith and our life, the life of the world and its hope, the hope of being done with a world of deception and bringing man back to his truth, the hope of leading him away from the alienations that prevent his self-identity, from the state of a puppet to that of a person, all of this depends on Christ's resurrection, on his victory over death.

The world's consistency and truth, the seriousness of history as the history of liberation and salvation, and thus laden with the values of regeneration, all depend upon the resurrection of Christ. The personal courage to live this faith by accepting the death and resurrection of Christ in us, not as a historical event outside of us but as a fact of our personal life, is the only original message which the Christian can give to the world: "Whenever you eat this bread and drink the cup, you celebrate the death of the Lord until he comes."

Looking at the world, that immense theater in which the wonderful action of the thinking and conscious being unfolds, we can have either, the sense of enormous vanity, of a gigantic and fearful apparition, or of an absolute and consistent reality preserved forever from vanity. It depends on whether we look at it with the eye of faith in the resurrection, that is, of faith in the fact that the world and history have been forever saved from the phantasm of nonbeing because our history, in time, is the history of the death and resurrection of Christ.

5

THE FREEDOM OF LOVE

The great force of the liberation of the person is love. On all levels we find the law of love as the law which constructs the person, as the concrete decision whereby the person knows and identifies himself, or is lost, that is, does not know himself because he has lost the points of contact with the true self and constructs a phantasm which is outside of the true essence of concrete man. The first level in which liberation must take place is the interpersonal encounter between man and woman. The man-woman encounter is decisive for the liberation of the superego from aggression and instability. For the man, the woman is the symbol of creation which attracts him as a value to be admired, possessed, and guarded; this must be done through a constant endeavor of enrichment because no value is sustained statically. In the formation of the couple, we find all the elements we have discovered above. It is the human opportunity par excellence.

Genesis, the great fresco of mankind, describes for us the woman's being created from the man who is immersed in a deep sleep: "So the Lord God caused a deep sleep to fall upon the man" *(Genesis 2:21)*. Adam awakened to find a "thou": "This at last is bone of my bones and flesh of my flesh" *(2:23)*. Here we have prefigured what was to become the awakening from dreams, from the fantasies of childhood, from the whole period of the formation of instincts and affectivity which gave rise to an interplay of offenses and defenses, of projections in images, while the physical maturity of the person was being formed within the family circle. Finally, the whole richness of the person is concentrated on a thou of flesh, with a face, a name, and a history.

For this thou man "leaves his father and his mother and cleaves to his wife, and they become one flesh" *(Genesis 2:24)*. In this discovery of the thou the separation from the family complex is completed and man accepts his destiny in the world. If the love is true in its origins, it is presented as an invitation by the other to abandon ourselves, our world of dreams, fantasies, and fears, the intrauterine world from which the person emerges in his state of consciousness in order to discover that he himself is a being in enslavement. For this reason the call of the other is heeded in the beginning as an invitation that is both intriguing and uncomfortable, as something easy and at the same time a commitment. It shares the nature of a game and of a serious commitment. It has the complexion of an adventure that is dreamed of and lived on the level of childhood and of an adventure that drives the person toward the unknown. The call of the other elicits a response of joy and of protest.

Forces are at play which can subsequently prove to be destructive, although in love's awakening they seem necessary in order to conquer rejection, fear, and self-preservation: They are pride, vanity, and concupiscence. I am a person who is interesting to you. I desire you because you please me. "I am she who would give you so much war," said Laura to her lover on his visit to the third heaven. And this is a sentence filled with feminine vanity. I cannot go out of myself by decree. It is only the other who can help me toward this liberation. My existence needs the other. This call is an invitation to enter into reality, in time and space. The other obliges me to make a definite choice, which closes off the road to the indefiniteness of dreams, for my existence, my future, is this other person.

Obviously my habit of dreaming does not cease in a moment, but my dreams are limited by an emerging reality: this particular person with this name and this face. In the Bible man's history is always represented as an exodus, a going out of self. And in this invitation to go out, to be transformed, man receives a name; he finds his true identity. Man has a name which signifies his vocation, what he will do in life, what he must be in life. Thus man finds himself; that self is man in the profound adherence to his vocation. "Now the Lord said to Abram, 'Go from your country and your kindred and your father's house to the land that I will show you'" *(Genesis 12:1)*. This search for oneself, which is the discovery of one's vocation, is not a magical and unforeseen happening. I do not discover my vocation as if it were a pair of shoes made to fit. It is the result of an arduous search, tormented by doubt, two steps forward and one back. The biblical story of Abraham is enlightening in this regard because the invitation to go out is given to him in his youth. But then things happen which seem to complicate matters and to go contrary to his hope for departure. Finally, at the age of ninety-nine—that is in his maturity, in proportion to the long life span which the Bible attributes to him—he receives definite clarification: "Behold, my covenant is with you, and you shall be the father of a multitude of nations. . . . As for Sarai your wife, you shall not call her name Sarai, but Sarah shall be her name" *(Genesis 17:4 and 15)*.

In this going out of oneself, in making one's own history, a person discovers his vocation and consequently who he is. He comes to this through what he is, that is, what he has come to do and what his place is in history. And the concrete invitation to come out of oneself, out of the dream of role playing, in order to discover and touch his subjective nature, comes through love. Love, then, contains within itself a deep demand for sincerity. It is defined as a dream stage, but instead it is the stage of awakening to reality. In fact, love does not bring peace until there is an intersubjective encounter, that is, until there is an encounter in truth of the two persons as they are, beyond the functions they have assumed, beyond the role they have. What is necessary is the encounter of "what they are" and not of "what they wish to be." Instinctively, the person who loves asks with anguish for "the truth," often without knowing what the truth is. He believes it is the word's conformity to a fact, an inevitable relationship of a happening. In reality it is something much deeper. It is a renunciation, a deep humility, and I think few people realize this.

While writing these notes, I met with a group of teachers from a secondary school in Venezuela, and we spoke for an entire afternoon about problems of education. Naturally, the basic problem was the erotic one. They remarked, although without being critical or citing false taboos, how eroticized the scholastic milieu had become. Almost never—and this they said with irritation—does a girl fall in love with one of the more studious boys, someone who has much promise for the future. And so almost never does the boy choose his partner with this criterion. This seems quite normal to me, because this special interest in study can be felt as an obstacle to the encounter in truth between two persons. Instinctively, these students feel that those who are not "first in their class" are available and are not yet committed to a role. This law of love may be and in fact many times is betrayed because of impatience, because of a bad upbringing—especially among upper middle-class families for whom the importance of the role cancels out the importance of "being a person"—

because of the habit of escaping into the realm of sex, and because of the lack of an education capable of awakening and deepening the taste and the appetite of the person.

Love remains on the level of deception, on the level of appearances, and does not reach the level of what one is. At times, when I meet men who are obviously playing a role, I wonder whether they have the courage to act the same way with their wives. And I see that they do, that even she plays this comedy and supports the role player, at times even to the point of using objective lies and distortion of facts. It seems to me that this is the clearest proof that here there is no love, for there is no true encounter between persons. Thus love demands poverty as a complement. Fables often speak of a prince or a potentate disguising himself as a pauper in order to be loved, because there is no love if a man is not loved for what he is. And beneath all of man's inventiveness, like nudism and free love, do we not see this demand for truth, for stripping away the conventions, the taboos, the "wealth" of a culture and a tradition which prevents an encounter on the level of the person, which is the true level?

The youth rebellion against the culture of adults has this origin. They are discovering that in fact culture prevents this stripping of the person, which is the condition of his "being true." Before accepting his role, before resigning himself to being what his milieu wishes him to be, the young person has a moment of protest, of rebellion. And this rebellion coincides with the discovery of the "thou," which demands a truth for which he is ill-prepared. Youth ends at the moment in which rebellion is quieted and man accepts being what his father and his grandfather were, resigning himself to frustration as the normal and common destiny of man.

For this reason, Tillich proposes that the word and notion "education" be replaced by the term "initiation," because education indicates the *terminus a quo*, the "whence," while initiation indicates the *terminus ad quem*, the "whither." It is therefore of utmost importance to arrive at this level of being and truth as such—before the fracture between subject and object—which has the nature of a mystery.

We have all assimilated the concept of education as an acquisition of values and ideas rather than as a liberation, a simplification. Real education ought to be a formation in truth by means of poverty, humility, and receptivity, while the whole of bourgeois education is exactly the opposite. It is an education in economic power, in the power of commanding, in the ability to know how to use others. The person thus comes to discover the other already deformed in this way and his whole affective capacity is often powerless to free him from nontruth and nonbeing.

When I look at our history from this point of view, I feel the need for redemption, for man cannot be a man solely on his own. The road to liberation is a very long and hard one because it is insecure. It is somewhat like the path of faith, which is not guaranteed by external, objective certitudes that can be weighed and measured. Its outcome is entrusted to an initial intuition, which can be likened to the initial act of faith, to each man's good will and courage. The temptation to look for supports and guarantees continually crops up. The feeling of being in a boat in the midst of a storm without any assurance that we shall reach the shore makes us so often cry out, "Master, save us, we perish."

So often have I heard this kind of disillusionment in love: "I have discovered that her interest in me is selfish. This girl is too self-centered." This is not completely true. They are words that describe something quite real, which is not exactly self-interest. It is rather fear. This bond that is so uncertain and irresolute, so compelling, is continually threatened by a break. For this reason the beloved thou is exposed to the ever-present temptation to become rooted, to be secure. Often this pseudoconcern compromises love. Love is aimed at liberating man from fear. It is a liberation from the motherland, from the mother's womb, in order to plant roots in a new earth: "Leave your own country . . . and go to other lands." And the impatience for the land can take the upper hand. But there is no other way: Liberation always passes through insecurity, which is death. In the liberation of love there are always moments of loneliness and doubt. We are powerless to fill up these voids, which are essential for our choice, for the total detachment of love.

Love is a person-to-person encounter and is truly intersubjective when the two begin to feel the dark night of insecurity, the test of faith. It is accepted by rejecting any other kind of security. Love demands an absolute exclusiveness and one can doubt if he loves one person more than another. On the level of feelings, an examination is never precise. Who can say whom he loves more, his mother or his fiancée, his friend or his fiancée? However, she is the only person upon whom my whole security depends. The doubt that I am not loved, the fear of being deserted, polarizes my whole life. It is all or nothing, existence or nonexistence. Other separations are painful for me, but this separation brings me death. Exclusiveness is not forged by an external choice or with juridical *apartheid*. It is an existential decision that lies within the flesh of the person.

Until one has gambled everything, he cannot say he has discovered love. Until he has agreed to lose himself through insecurity—if I lose you nothing can make me happy—he cannot say he has discovered the liberating love of the person.

A medieval poem, "The Accomplished Maiden," describes in one short verse this situation of the spirit: "Nothing cheers me, neither flower nor branch." If he misses this opportunity, the person will never be able to denude himself, to give himself fully, to get to the roots of his being and to be profoundly true. All forms of insincerity, dilettantism, not taking one's life seriously, not knowing oneself profoundly, and therefore falling into aggression, envy, and all the forms of substituting for seeming values the true value lost—all are connected with having missed this opportunity. One has missed the great moment of faith, the moment of exclusiveness which is never unilateral but always reciprocal. I cannot choose exclusively if I do not fully commit myself. This is not easy for a male to understand. He has so assimilated the harem-exclusiveness model—the right to exclusiveness which works in only one direction and which is comfortable and costs nothing because it has rained down from the sky of tradition—that he does not commit himself to achieving it. He discovers the woman's fear and her insecurities, and often he misunderstands her and does not know how to help her.

Exclusiveness can be carnal and then you have aggressive and frightened jealousy. And there is no other way of freeing exclusiveness from fear than by nourishing it with the renunciation of the other as a preconceived ideal created by my own imagination, by respecting the other's history, vocation, mode of existence, and being. True love is liberating insofar as it is an oblation, although not in the sense that I must give myself madly to the other. That could become an unbearable burden and a form of pressure that would limit freedom. I must desire with all my heart that the other be what he is, what is written in his vocation. True love is always a limitation, but one that is aimed at freedom. It is painful because it obliges me to concentrate my attention on the other. It is a limitation because it limits an anarchical freedom. But at the same time it is liberating because one must sense that the other obliges me to be faithful to myself, to faithfulness to my own manner of being, rather than to a manner of being that is thought up or dreamed of by the other, which would of necessity be false.

True love is creative, not of the role player, but of the person. For this reason true love is essentially religious, because it is limited by the

respect for a vocation that is basically a respect for God, by the acknowledgment that there is One before me and above me who has already
shaped the design of this person and already possesses him. For what is a
vocation if not a plan of existence with which this person's manner of
being should coincide? In love one discovers God as a limit but also as a
liberation. He is a limit to a full possession that would be tyrannical, a
limit to the arbitrary creation of the person which would end up by
destroying the being that attracted me and who appeared to me to be an
intuitively desirable thou.

The outline in Paul's Letter to the Ephesians is very clear in this
regard: "Even so husbands should love their wives as their own bodies. He
who loves his wife, loves himself. For no man ever hates his own flesh, but
nourishes and cherishes it, as Christ does the Church, because we are
members of his body" *(Ephesians 5:28-30)*. Each person is a member of a
body with its function and its history. To love it means to help it to be
what it is in its destiny, in this choice which is prior to the encounter
between the two. And this encounter must help to clarify, to achieve, to
give consistency, seriousness, and faithfulness. There is a jealousy of
suspicion and fear and a jealousy of respect. The first is carnal and selfish:
I want you to be for me. It is nourished by selfishness and fears. The
second is unselfish: I want you to be what you must be and I can help you
to be what you must be. To the extent that we discover that love liberates,
we sense that love is a force, a necessity. We discover within ourselves a
creative, vital force which makes us grow. This is the result of a slow
process, which does not come about without mistakes and some turning
back, without the humility of going back to the beginning and starting all
over again. Paul said that love does not "insist on its own way; it is not
irritable or resentful; it does not rejoice at wrong, but rejoices in the right"
(1 Corinthians 13:5-6). It does not wish to dominate and transform
according to its own plan but rejoices in truth. And this search for the
truth of the other is the practical means of shedding our role, of getting rid
of all the deceptions we have carried with us from adolescence, our
upbringing, and our environment.

Many people justify everything with love. Love is felt to authorize
going above law and tradition, and everything is classified as a taboo that
has to be swept away. Yet, love can never be dissociated from the truth.
To love means essentially to love in truth. A mother's love is strong,
passionate, and exclusive for her son. But often this love, which seems
sacred, which justifies itself because it is nurtured on sacrifice and suffer-

ing, is not in the truth and is destructive. The mother's love is not always directed toward the son's being what he should be, and maternity becomes maternalism. Losing its sacred character, its religious essence, it becomes intrinsically atheistic. I should call any kind of love of this type profane.

We are losing our sexual taboos. Little by little we are acquiring an awareness of the body and its role, an awareness that differs from that of past generations. We are almost completely freed of fear of the body. Undoubtedly this is progress, but anarchical love can pervert this creative and liberating value of love. The Circe of Homeric legend changed men into pigs by her love, and, without seeing in this legend an allusion to sex and the flesh, we can conclude that the force of love often causes the thou not to be what it should be because the love is not a love in truth.

The importance and ambiguity of love shed light on the educational attitude of the Church toward sex education concerning premarital chastity. It is obvious that centralizing the sexual problem and making it obsessive turns it into a taboo. And today we see the excess resulting from a correct intuition. Chastity is not everything, nor is it the principal virtue of the Christian. But if the person misses this center of liberation, he runs the risk of searching in vain for himself throughout his whole life. Initiation to chastity is not made through fears and threats, which easily give rise to inhibitions, provoke distorted responses, and create an aggressive and defensive position in a person in regard to the thou. Nor is it made with rhetorical and inhuman glorifications of virginity, which easily create a proud apartness and a self-sufficiency, permanently blocking the possibility of giving oneself to someone else. Catharism and Manicheanism are episodes in Church history which have left a much deeper impression on its teaching habits than we might suspect. This deformed kind of education has been responsible for producing educators who, though well intentioned, are too often overly empirical, completely in the dark about the problem of sex, without experience in love, and unfulfilled as persons. This explains the adverse reaction of many graduates of religious high schools and colleges or of people who have lived through the experience of a religious education.

Yet sexual discipline, the control over one's own body, the renunciation of pleasure for pleasure's sake, patience in bearing up under sexual pressure, which at times threatens like a river in flood, is still of universal validity in education. It must always, and from the very first moment, be aimed at the thou and emphasize the liberating function of love. The tragic aspect of sex is not that I can perform a forbidden act, but that I am able to distort its cognitive function. In the Bible, the act of sex is expressed by the word "know": Adam "knew his wife," which is not a prudish substitution for a questionable word, since for the ancients there was nothing questionable about it. The deep meaning of love is this profound knowledge of one another, this unique self-revelation of one person to another without any disguise, casting off the masks and poses we so often assume toward others. For love to be a liberating function we must have the will to know and to be known, a relish for the person and for being.

I may seem abstract and utopian, but I remember, when I was eighteen or twenty, that I did indeed feel this relish for being, that passion for self-preservation which I identified with my religiousness. A thought that impressed me then, and which I have never forgotten, was an expression of Saint Irenaeus, which, by the way, I found in a nonreligious book: *Gloria Dei vivens homo*, the glory of God is a man who lives, who lives as a person.

Education is difficult because man lives in time and lacks the category of the eternal, which means seeing, simultaneously and with a single vision, what is and what will be. For this reason, saying no to immediate pleasure and blocking one's instincts in order to achieve knowledge and liberation will always seem to be a moralism that is narrow-minded, inhuman, and inhibiting. And I think that this endeavor to join education with love can be accepted only within a comprehensive view, in a culture in which religion and philosophy, politics, science, art, and popular customs all converge to emphasize the person.

The consumer society certainly does not help us discover this sense of being. It is not only love for life. It is something much deeper and impossible to express in words. It is love of being as history, as charged with mission, as something which has a creative responsibility in time. Love of being can go hand in hand with a nonlove for one's own life: "Who loves his own life, loses it." Here the word "life" is equivalent to "being." And this love for being cannot emerge from a society where the ideal is to preserve. For there to be preservation, a part must be played by destruction and consumption—a consumption of goods which easily and inevitably turns into a destruction of persons. Initiation to love is initiation to being, to the sense of person, and this is not only in the religious sphere. It must be political, historical, in a word, cosmic. With love man finds his place in the world and in history as a creator of fuller being. Rather than the moralistic test which can be something negative, the test of authentic love will always be this: Does it give rise to the appetite for being more, that hope of not being lost, the relish for existence because I have something to do in the world, something which I and no one else can do?

Society is consuming itself, say the "drug culture" advocates in the United States. We wonder whether love will be the first act of liberation of the person which transforms society by revolutionizing it, or will renewed society itself convey this zest for being and stimulate this quest for being through love. I am unable to give a conclusive answer. Both camps must be involved and must struggle together for personal love and for political love. The will to be and the will to exist are like the love for freedom. It is something mysterious and profound which cannot be inculcated. Is it assimilated from the environment or does it originate and grow within us? This mysterious sense saves us from our ruination and prevents us from exchanging real love for what merely seems to be love. Love's great paradox is that it is both a bond and a liberation, a limitation and a freedom.

The bond comes from the fact that a person's being free is dependent on his relationship with the other. A person discovers his own freedom, his own true being, in encounter and involvement with the other. He senses that he is achieving his freedom to the extent that he seeks the other's freedom. The more he wants the other to be himself, in his own world, the more he frees himself from fears and aggression. The characteristic of love is freedom and unselfishness.

The other paradox of true love is wanting for oneself and at the same time, wanting for the other that he be as he is and therefore obedient to his own true world and his own true history. Both endeavor to harmonize the two worlds and the two histories without there being a perfect coincidence or an absorption of one in the other. Love is music, a concord of discordant sounds. In the film *La Strada*, Gelsomina was the center of a story of true love. When she met a man who loved her, she discovered the values of life which, in her own wretched existence of being battered about, used, and constantly deserted like a dog, had become submerged. She too had her part in the world, her own history; it is not the history of Zampanò, that is, as his appendix or tool. It is she, Gelsomina, a free being, a person created by herself and for herself. Therefore, her world is suddenly beautiful: The pebbles in the road reflect the stars. Life is beautiful when you are part of the cosmos, of order, when you are not absurd. And as a sign of this discovery, a song rises up inside her, her message of liberation. Because she is liberated, she too can liberate. It is no longer she, her body, her face, that liberates Zampanò. It is her memory, her song, her liberation, her freedom.

Love here is taken on a simple, primitive level, but it is love in truth and therefore has all the elements of liberation. God is in the wings. He is not seen, but he is there. He is there in outline and appears everywhere because he who finds his own true being finds God. The two poverty-stricken people give freedom to one another, because their common poverty unites them in a bond that is a bond of love and therefore liberating. However, the psychology of being born, of feeling loved, is more evident with Gelsomina. I do not know whether I can guess all of Fellini's intuitions because the artist intuits all at once what is discovered philosophically through analysis. But Gelsomina is ultimately liberated from being a thing, an appendage, a work horse, a body that receives blows and insults. She is discovered as a subject, freed from any role, made pure subjectivity, pure truth. It is a moment of unique coincidence, and for this reason she dies because her function coincides with her being. And as such, as a subject, something which Zampanò never discovered because he always looked upon her as a tool, as something to use, she is able to liberate him. She could not have been the force of his liberation without the mediation of death. I have often reflected on the themes of love and death, which are almost always united. Perhaps love tends toward death because it tends toward the supreme liberation, to that ultimate truth which is attained completely only through death.

Sex certainly helps this process of knowledge, the ultimate revelation of the beloved thou and his true essence, but it can also foster a "thingification" of the person. Sex in itself does not foster the appetite for being. It can become a drug or an instrument for easily mastering the other. For this reason I believe that the result of the simplification of sex reached by the present generation is beneficial. Not relying too much on it, not considering it too much in the history of the person, not making it an absolute—these seem important to me. Perhaps we have to break the magic of sex by bringing persons face to face and discovering what love is. But the stage of disillusionment, ennui, and anguish through which we are living is also inevitable.

In itself sex is a provisional function, as the Gospel says. It is not essential for being, even if it has a decisive importance in the formation and behavior of the person. Sex and its function pass away, but love does not pass away. At the moment we are emerging from a culture which has centralized sex, either by singing it moonlight serenades or by indicting it as the instigator of crimes. Through an increase in awareness, it has been put back in its place as a provisional function, and as such, a symbol used by the person in time. As a symbol it can signify gift, discovery, knowledge, and liberation, or domination, "thingification," and separation. It can be a symbol that represents reality and can also be an empty and deluding symbol. Sex certainly can enrich and liberate, but it also can empty, humiliate, depress, and separate.

I read with interest about the experiments taking place in the United States at Esalen in the "movement for human potential" and in Palm Springs, both on the California coast, which have something quite mad about them. It is interesting to note, however, the appearance in these anarchical experiments of the discovery of the true values and eternal laws of the person. Above all, there is the theme of liberation. The person can no longer live by that part of his reason which emerges like a mountain peak out of the clouds. He wants to live with the whole fullness of his being, with his emotivity and affectivity, with all that has been considered instinctive and irrational, and therefore inferior and unimportant to him. All of this richness of the person which has been kept in exile is precisely what threatens his equilibrium and seeks to be received and given value.

They are discovering the liberating value of religion, which, when rationalized, has perhaps satisfied the intellectual concern of man, but has not constituted his force of liberation. "We want to get religion out of the hands of the priests," is their slogan. It is the demand that religion become human, become a factor of liberation for the person. Why is the Gospel called the Good News if not because it is an announcement of the liberation of man, who, basically, asks only for this? They are searching with questionable means, but they are searching for the profound truth of interpersonal relationship. The psychologist Paul Brindim says: "I do all I can to raise the level of love in each of the groups. Tenderness and affection are not necessarily related to the sexual drive."

This is but one of the many lines of research in the world today. And we are wrong to dwell on the extravagant or shocking aspects of the experiments without looking more deeply into them. In their own way, they are prophetic experiments and we must know how to read them. Within them there is a profound desire for truth. Society has clothed man with lies and conventions and has alienated him in a role that does not truly belong to him; it has left aside the true, unrepeatable history which is his alone. He has to be stripped of these clothes. The first, easiest, and most obvious thing is to strip him of his clothes of cloth or nylon. The eternal temptation which Jesus and Paul discovered in the Hebrew people—to classify the sons of Abraham as those who had the sign in the flesh—is always in vogue and will always be so. In this search, however, there is a search for truth which is reached through love and for a tenderness freed from the impatience of sex. Is this the contemporary translation of the phrase: "Do the truth in love"? I do not think I am saying anything blasphemous. All the searching done with regard to the truth of the person, even if it is and will always be ambiguous, must be a verification of the Gospel, if it is true that Christ is the center of the universe and history and that his word is liberating for the person. We are sad when we see how slow these movements are and how much it costs man to find the truth. But we find peace in reflecting that perhaps man can find truth only in the shadows, in figures and symbols.

In the wandering through the desert, Christ is the rock and God the pillar of cloud by day and the pillar of fire by night. It seems man's destiny never to see God with his face uncovered. If he would see God, he would die. This is the conviction of all the generations of the Old Testament. And in the groping search of our day another aspect of the Gospel seems evident to me: its antimythical characteristic, which is precisely the opposite of the search for the superman. In order to find himself, the person is oriented toward an impoverishment, a reduction, a leaving behind. The Gospel does not invite him to stand on his toes, to flex his muscles. It invites him rather to relax, to be poor, to leave his possessions behind, to be a child, in order to discover a simplicity which comes prior to the complications of culture and traditions. The "movement for human potential" in one point in its program says this: "To release our innermost feelings, it is important that we feel like children and that we behave like children in front of ourselves and in front of others."

The whole spirit of the Gospel is an invitation to descend, to lower ourselves, to be humble: to be ourselves. It is true that Jesus offered himself as a model, but so that we would imitate him in meekness and humility of heart, in poverty and simplicity of the person, in order that we might be more true and more ourselves. Perhaps this is the meaning of the famous passage: "And as he was setting out on his journey, a man ran up and knelt before him, and asked him, 'Good Teacher, what must I do to inherit eternal life?' And Jesus said to him, 'Why do you call me good? No one is good but God alone' " *(Mark 10:17-19)*. He does not offer himself as an accomplished and finished model, but rather as an ideal to seek: "If any man would come after me, let him deny himself and take up his cross and follow me" *(Mark 8:34)*. Jesus invites us to a journey, to a movement, to a leaving behind of ourselves, a leaving behind of our egos which we have thought through, fondled, and sketched out with such passion. He invites us to follow him in the acceptance of our true task, which is the cross. Perhaps Christ is the secret of this way to truth, to our truth, which this generation so passionately seeks.

6

FREEDOM IN FRIENDSHIP

Without great effort, the Gospel could be seen as the story of a great friendship. The Messiah did not work alone. At the very beginning he chose collaborators for himself: "As he walked by the Sea of Galilee, he saw two brothers, Simon who is called Peter and Andrew his brother, casting a net into the sea; for they were fishermen. And he said to them, 'Follow me, and I will make you fishers of men.' Immediately they left their nets and followed him. And going on from there he saw two other brothers, James the son of Zebedee and John his brother, in the boat with Zebedee their father, mending their nets, and he called them. Immediately they left the boat and their father and followed him" *(Matthew 4:18-22)*. Here we see the creative lines of a friendship, an affinity at the starting point. All four were country people and fishermen who were waiting for the kingdom of God. It was an encounter which led toward a habitual life in common: "Follow me." It was a dynamic ideal to seek and create together: "I shall make you fishers of men." What did this mean? It was very vague and imprecise, but it was alluring enough for them to be induced to leave their nets and their father. We shall see it and we shall seek it together. They had no idea that the plan of the Leader who was inviting them would be much more vast and more true than the political liberation they were dreaming of. Little by little they would discover this, as they became aware of the history of their people and of what God intended to bring about in that history.

During the time that he lived with these four and the eight others who eventually joined them, Jesus sought to gather them around himself through love and the acceptance of a common idea. They discovered this

71

idea insofar as they achieved it by renouncing through this common vision their own particular ideas. The wealth of this friendship consisted in this: The "kingdom of God" corresponded to the real need, to the expectation of the whole people of Israel.

Jesus' lack of earthly success is due to the fact that this real need had not emerged in the level of consciousness of the majority and that prejudices stemming from a legalistic tradition, created interests, and all of man's alienating pressures prevented most people from seeing it. But his immediate success is due to the fact that freedom, that kind of spiritual freedom, released from the law and time, was historically necessary on the eve of the end of the political power of the kingdom and the eve of the diaspora. The time was ripe for Israel's mission to become truly universal: "The hour is coming when neither on this mountain nor in Jerusalem will you worship the Father. . . . But the hour is coming, and now is, when the true worshippers will worship the Father in spirit and truth, for such the Father seeks to worship him" *(John 4:21 and 23)*. A group of friends formed around one who had made the flesh of his flesh a vocation which the others also obscurely felt. And as their leader, he helped them to discover it, to clarify it, and to deepen it by putting it into operation.

But this vocation could not be sustained by one side only. It had to be rooted in history and therefore continually nurtured and kept alive in history. Nurturing and keeping alive does not mean the absence of a struggle, a kind of comfortableness. The society to whom the apostolic group announced liberation rejected them. It did not want to know about it, but at the same time it received it because it needed it: It interpreted the society's true historical exigency. This explains the paradox of the Gospel, that alternation between rejection and acceptance. In every way the presence of this group, what it said and did, provoked ferment and reaction because it was a living movement.

The work that Jesus proposed was preeminently religious, because Israel's political mission was to announce the true and living God to the world and to extend his mission of salvation to the very ends of the earth. In the political societies of that day there was a profound and unimaginable coincidence between the political and religious missions. Jesus was never able to clear up the ambiguity, not only with the priests and with Pilate, his enemies, but even with the twelve who lived so closely with him.

When a friendship is assured only by one side, that of the bond with the leader, it inevitably falls into ennui, staleness, or despotism. One, however, that has its roots in history remains fresh and creative and prevents the inflexibleness of authority. A religious community cannot think of being a friendship if it relies solely on the psychological ability or the ability to love, in the sense of friendship, on the part of the person in authority, or if it relies solely on the good will of its members. It must be opened to history; this common vocation which this group incarnates must be continually renewed by a symbiosis with history. Like an individual, a community is absurd without a vocation. And a vocation is not only a mission from on high. It must be animated, nourished, and enriched by the acceptance of history: "Go into all the world and preach the gospel to the whole creation" *(Mark 16:15).* Two heads, two soldering points which make a vocation alive are evident: the call from the one who has the message, the proposal of salvation; and creation, the whole of reality in permanent and continual creation, in the passage from nonbeing to being.

Being is ambiguous, contradictory, and in continual need of liberation. To freeze a vocation by cutting off its dependence upon creation, upon history, means to wither it. And the consequences are doubt, frustration, boredom within the group, and the despotism of authority. No force can save the authority from becoming dried up, arid, and juridical, even if it tries to remedy this betrayal with an emotional love. This vital insertion into history which continually recreates a vocation obliges the group always to rethink it. And this insertion is not easily discovered because it is not always presented as universally acceptable: "And wherever they do not receive you, when you leave that town shake off the dust from your feet as a testimony against them" *(Luke 9:5).*

On the political, scientific, or artistic level, the same thing happens. The historicity of the message cannot be measured by its acceptance or its immediate triumph. The nonacceptance in time, which is the drama of man, is augmented in society and becomes a threat that runs through the masses who kill the prophet and crucify him "outside the gate." Many times the only verification that remains is a hope, a dream, a vigorous human force, which is the opposite of frustration: "Whatever house you enter, first say, 'Peace be to this house!' And if a son of peace is there, your peace shall rest upon him; but if not, it shall return to you" *(Luke 10:5-6).* This is a valuable point: "Your peace shall return to you!" You may be received or you may be rejected, but you will not go away destroyed but rather enriched and strengthened in peace.

Can we have verifications that are more objective and sure? I think not. But for one who has acquired the capacity to sense being and to seek it in all its realizations, this verification is sufficient. For some this is so little that in history there will always be the restless masses, ready to kill the prophets; and there will always be prophets who are ready to die. To save ourselves as persons there is no other rhythm than this: to be open to the community. And to open up the community to history. Perhaps this explains why a friendship among a group of workers is easier than among a group of sisters, despite the fact that the latter have a deep religious sense. A friendship is not determined only within a group. It is also, and I would say especially, determined in its truest and deepest fecundity by its function in creation. It would seem that a religious community is preserved from this frailty by the fact that it is supposed to transmit values which are outside of time, values which man at all times needs ontologically: God, his salvation, eternity, faith, the internal security that faith generates. All of this is included in the sacramental symbol which synthesizes in itself all the benefits God wishes to give man and which man truly needs, even if he is not aware of it or rejects it.

But what is the salvation of man if not the fulfillment of the person, the passage from nonbeing to being, the rejection of the nonbeing which is in us and which continually threatens us? And these forces are in history, in the social and political structure. The Good News cannot be announced to man without helping him to discover and combat all the historical forces of deformation which prevent him from being a man. Piux XII said it was necessary for a man to become human in order to become a Christian. The Church intuits prophetically that liberation comes about in the world and in history, but in fact many structures of evangelization propose a nontemporal and therefore abstract liberation.

And all of this necessarily influences the composition and the state of the community which has been formed to carry forward the mission of the Church. To make friendship only an emotional, psychological, or spiritual problem is to see it only from one angle. And a one-sided decision to reform a religious structure is simply a waste of time. A contemplative community may seem to avoid these demands of communication with history. It cannot be said that there is no friendship between contemplatives, who seem open only to eternity and to the timeless. But they are not true contemplatives if they do not achieve liberation from all the historical alienations—wealth, fear, death—through the courage to exist in faith. Otherwise, contemplation would be a flight and an escape, and could be motivated out of fear and laziness. The authenticity of the motivation does not take long to make itself visible, to make itself a sign, because contemplation matures in a free and prophetic look at creation and history.

Saint Catherine saw tragically and clearly how the Church of her time should have been. Her remark, "to be what we should be," is a very contemporary idea. Saint Francis showed a warm relationship with creation and a brotherly relationship among men, which had its impact on political structures far beyond his intentions and resolved the Manicheanism of the Middle Ages. Father de Foucauld showed essentially a form of being and of serving which could guide and enlighten the technicians of human advancement, the organizers and leaders of new political structures which are rising from the dissolution of colonial structures. This solitary hermit bore witness to the gratuitousness of the adoration of the Absolute, adored and loved in itself; he is at the vanguard of the age of human cooperation and the advancement of the person, in the service of which all of man's technology and discoveries must be put.

A community can be a community of friends only if its structure is democratic and inserted in history. At Vatican II the need for friendship appeared constantly—that the bishop should be a friend to his priests and that they be friends among themselves. And this can happen only if the priest-bishop relationship is creative and not merely executive and functional. The basic vice of many ecclesiastical structures is that they are essentially organizational and executive structures. They have nothing to think out or to create because they originated with the conviction that the message had already been thought out, discovered, and defined. All that remains is to discover the organs of transmission and to perfect them. Until we discover the Gospel as a message of freedom for a time, a generation, a culture, a stage of history, the ecclesiastical structures will remain negative, and the relationship between the members will not be able to be one of friendship.

The ecclesial institutions are set apart from the groups that forge history and compose the avant-garde: the poor, the young, the workers, the researchers. These are the prophetic groups who, either through an explorative capacity for research or through militant political commitment, understand the times and cause progress. The ecclesiastical institutions are friendly with the groups in power. And these power groups infect them with their own leprosy, which is the reliance on money, on political protection, on the capacity to organize, all those seemingly effective ploys beneath which a profound frustration lies hidden. A historically frustrated structure cannot come up with a genuine reason for living for its members. And a group of frustrated people is the opposite of a group of friends. The endeavor made by religious communities to update themselves—economically, organizationally, intellectually—is practically useless. It is the origin of new frustrations. This updating process is seen as the key to effective proselytism rather than as a renewal of content. Here is the story of the Pharisees all over again: "You traverse sea and land to make a single proselyte, and when he becomes a proselyte, you make him twice as much a child of hell as yourselves" *(Matthew 23:15)*.

We must not consider the *aggiornamento* of Church institutions from within the institutions, but from the perspective of those who are growing with history. Even those who are in power are growing and are so agitated and "progressive" that they give the impression of being alive, of being the most dynamic members of society. But their progress is individual, and their levels of growth and progress presuppose the stability of the institutions. But the progress of the young, the poor, the proletariat presupposes change and the overthrow of institutions, and the growth of the researcher conditions the whole of social progress. Every kind of progress that is disengaged from these exponents of history is merely apparent and necessarily individualistic. The tragedy of the Church is this: The evangelists are not evangelizing in history, and therefore a dissociation harmful for the Church and for the world takes place.

Members of ecclesiastical institutions decide upon either a revolutionary action without God or else a worship of God dissociated from history. Entering into the process of the liberation of the world does not seem to be fidelity to the Gospel but a rebellion or a corruption of the Gospel. Within an ecclesiastical structure of religious or laity you can be a revolutionary, a modernist, as daring as you want, as long as you do not leave the organization and executive sphere. In this context you can say anything and positions can be radicalized. However, if someone should humbly and most modestly make a transition to another wave-length and touch upon the substance of the message, he is immediately put to death.

Perhaps to understand this it will be necessary for the crisis of Church institutions to become still more dramatic. I believe, however, that the most effective pressure for this change can be brought by the laity if they think through evangelization without prejudice, within the perspective of the poor and the seekers of the truth. Friendship cannot be thought of statically today, nor in the humanistic terms of Cicero or Seneca. Friendship is conditioned by its vital insertion in history and its growth is in strict dependence on the growth of history.

On my desk I have a thick dossier sent to me by a congregation of religious women. It contains the customary projects for reform. I found the first pages fascinating and the argument truly interesting. It is the

historical study of the political, economic, and cultural situation in seven-
teenth-century France, when this congregation was founded. Why did
these good sisters think it worthwhile to fill fifty sheets, single-spaced,
with this historical synthesis? Surely not for entertainment nor even for
the sake of erudition, but because they had the intuition that there must
be an intimate correlation between the origin of their congregation, its
spirit, and the historical period in which it was born.

For them to be consistent, this same work ought to have been done
for Latin America in 1968, where the same congregation was to be
established, to discover its goal and spirit. Either the congregation has
nothing to do with history—and then why this historical study of seven-
teenth-century France? Or else this study does have a place, and then this
methodology has to be used. But this study would have come about
spontaneously if the Church structure had a prophetic function in itself
and if its law had an agility which would permit a permanent state of
aggiornamento.

Many think that this historicization of the Gospel risks making it
into an ideology. Rather, the Gospel should inspire the formation of
ideologies and fit them continually to man's needs. For this reason it
promotes ideologies, but does not exhaust itself in any one. Even more,
this is precisely what it wishes to avoid in the prophetic relationship of
Church structures with history. In prophecy, in an eminently spiritual
synthesis, we have the unification of *interpretation, challenge, and a new
vision*. And is not this and this alone what the world and youth need? Men
who consider themselves wise often bring out outdated ideologies in
opposition to the new ones, without challenge and without vision. Prophets are profoundly of their own time and yet not of it. They accept it,
challenge it, find in it the signs of the kingdom, and at the same time see a
further stage.

A static ideology makes static men; therefore they are not friends
because they are not creators. Jesus opened no schools and never clearly
defined the kingdom: The perfect disciple is one who is poor, who hungers
and thirsts for justice, who is disposed to suffering everything, even death,
in order to carry forward the ideal of love. In the Gospel there is no trace
of any ideology. And this explains the challenge to the ideologies of the
Pharisees and the Sadducees. The kingdom of God appears as a continual
discovery of the concrete situations of men, a permanent creation. Events
become occasions for grace, of love on God's part, and are filled with this
content of grace. The episode of the centurion in Matthew 8 illustrates this

idea quite well. When Jesus offered to go to his house, the centurion saw this in the context of military discipline—a superior never visits the house of a subject: " 'For I am a man under authority, with soldiers under me; and I say to one, "Go," and he goes, and to another, "Come," and he comes, and to my slave, "Do this," and he does it.' When Jesus heard him he marveled, and said to those who followed him, 'Truly I say to you, not even in Israel have I found such faith' " *(Matthew 8:9-10)*.

The synthesis of the whole Gospel which Matthew makes in chapter 25 sheds light for us on the concept of a disciple as a seeker and a creator: "Come, O blessed of my Father, inherit the kingdom prepared for you from the foundation of the world; for I was hungry and you gave me food, I was thirsty and you gave me drink, I was a stranger and you welcomed me, I was naked and you clothed me, I was sick and you visited me, I was in prison and you came to me" *(Matthew 25:34-35)*.

The eschatological kingdom is built up during the earthly stage through creating human relationships. The kingdom of God must be sought and built in the concrete opportunities offered by history as the history of man's liberation. "I was hungry and you gave me food" is a powerful imperative for the man of faith who seeks God. It causes him to be watchful and not only to seek the hungry Christ who is very easy to find on all the streets of the world, but also to seek a way to feed all the hungry of the earth. It also causes him to seek a way to feed them in truth and love because the whole life of the Christian is accompanied by this musical background: "Do the truth in love."

Man is never just a stomach or a mouth. The identification of Christ with man and with the least of men, with the man in tatters, the filthy man, the man stripped of his dignity by the violence or indifference of his brothers, is deeply disturbing. This man has the specific weight of Christ, the Son of God. He has his dignity. He is a person like the Person who is the Model for all the reproductions of the person. And therefore, "You gave me food," not in an offhand manner as you might to force-fed chickens or to a watchdog!

It is clear that the program of feeding the hungry must be expressed concretely in a political ideology, which can never exhaust all the demands of the Gospel. And the Christian cannot wait too much nor dawdle around, because his time is short, very short. Moreover, he will have to collaborate with a political program if he does not wish to limit himself to individual almsgiving, which would be the more depersonalizing decision. John XXIII faced the problem of collaboration, which for many years had been taboo, and resolved it affirmatively (*Mater et Magistra* and *Pacem in terris*). The Christian must choose the program that is most evangelical, that is the most humanistic and personalistic. However, he cannot rely on a system to such an extent that he would lose sight of the fact that a Christian—through all his political, professional, family, and recreational activity—must be a *creator of friendship*, a creator of that *encounter among equals which liberates*, which helps us to discover and live our dignity as persons, as sons of God.

If it is not discovered in an interpersonal encounter among equals, dignity is merely rhetorical, a written right. For a Christian, friendship must be the perspective within which one's decisions are made. One evening, after a conference at the Catholic University of Medellín in Colombia, a young man asked my opinion about nonviolence. I answered that I felt when it was discovered and decided upon by the poor and oppressed as a means of liberation, it was Christian. When it is discovered by the oppressors and those in high places it seems to me to be a mousetrap. A girl asked me what I thought of "Blessed are the poor in spirit." I answered her that if it were a real discovery, by the truly poor, it seemed like a song to me, a psalm of praise to God, but on the lips of a rich man it would be a blasphemy and an insult. Jesus said it while among the poor and he himself was poor. A person who is not poor has no right to utter it because he cannot help but deeply corrupt it. Is it not true that the name of God can be uttered in a worshipful tone or in one that is blasphemous?

A key choice in friendship can have a liberating effect. However, when made outside of friendship it may be destructive. Friendship is the center of the humanization and personalization of history and of creation; it is like the condensation point of things within human love. Commitment in history is the bone structure of friendship because, without it, friendship is flaccid, unstable, and dependent upon a person's whims. It is not creative and not a true friendship. And as a counterpart, friendship is the kernel of the humanization of history, its catalyst, for the whole historical process tends to form the community united in peace. Yet we can never reach the ideal, and thus history constitutes the whole internal dynamic of friendship.

In regard to friendship the theme of poverty arises again because the growth of a friendship is often stunted unexpectedly by the interference of a concrete and static material value which attracts a person's attention and demands his dedication. A religious community cannot be a community of friends—and therefore cannot be a community at all, but merely a form of living together—when the dynamic ideal that should be directed toward the person becomes statically centered upon a structure. The teaching-sister/pupil relationship, the nursing-sister/patient relationship, the sister-of-charity/poor man relationship, is mediated by a structure that belongs to the sisters or the community: teaching-sister/school/pupil, nursing sister/hospital/patient. The relationship is "thingified" and is not personalizing or liberating for either party. It is certain that structures are purely instrumental and should foster this personal encounter which is creative of the person. But in practice they end up by being the primary and direct relationship, the sister/pupil or sister/patient relationship thus becoming secondary. This spoils everything because, despite all the good will in the world, the sister is identified with a power structure and the relationship becomes one of power, which is the opposite of friendship.

A power relationship is dialectical: Someone has something which belongs to me and I do everything I can to get it from him. A relationship of friendship between a person living within a religious structure and the group of persons whom he is dedicated to serve and love is made enormously difficult for many reasons. There is the difficulty which everybody experiences of the differences between generations, and added to it is the difficulty of different existential experience. If the difficulty is aggravated because the relationship is a relationship of power the case is desperate. Does poverty solve everything? If the sister encounters the group she is to serve and love through a structure that does not belong to her, she has not automatically solved the problem of friendship, but she is liberated from the major obstacle to its solution. Perhaps this is the profound meaning of this passage from Matthew: "And a scribe came up and said to him, 'Teacher, I will follow you wherever you go.' And Jesus said to him, 'Foxes have holes, and birds of the air have nests; but the Son of man has nowhere to lay his head' " *(Matthew 8:19-20)*. Is a friendship between two rich men or between a rich man and a poor man an impossibility? A true friendship is impossible unless the wealth is instrumentalized, humanized, and personalized in the personal encounter. We shall never fully understand the epilogue of the parable of the unjust steward: "Make friends for yourselves by means of unrighteous mammon" *(Luke 16:9)*. It can be understood superficially as indiscriminate distribution, as if handing out a package of candy to a group of children resolved the problem of friendship. But it is not so. Possessions must enter into the structure of friendship, which is an affinity that is formed and renewed within a co-creative union directed toward the historical process of liberation.

I have in mind the objection of a businessman. He spoke of a business which was handed over to the workers. They prospered for a time, but then became a closed group and more selfish than the first owner. The mistake was probably in the very beginning, because the owner did not love. He surrendered the reins out of fear or exhaustion or anxiety about the future, and everything that is not done in love sooner or later comes to the surface like a blemish. And therefore this kind of almsgiving is certainly not the foundation of a friendship. The initial mistake was carried forward and perfected by the group of successors who did not unite co-creation with the liberation of others. They became closed within themselves and circumscribed economic growth within the circle of their established society; they thus became "thingified." They cannot escape being "thingified." They are one block of stone placed against another. They fight and hurt one another. It is clear that yesterday's poor who become today's rich treat one another worse than the owner treated them yesterday. Previously, the power relationship united them among themselves for the purpose of liberation. The relationship with the owner was not one of friendship, it was very similar, but it was not authentic friendship. It was a diplomatic relationship. For this reason, the man did not rend his garments when he discovered this: Friendship has its inexorable laws which condition man, even if he is not conscious of this.

Today the nouveau riche workers seem unexpectedly to have changed their nature within the same friendship structure. They are like little lambs, huddled together in the same fold and sleeping pressed up against each other, who wake up one morning as wolves. They begin to bite at one another and if anybody approaches, all he can expect is the claws and teeth of the wolves. When somebody tells me that the poor do not love one another while the rich are extremely kind to each other—and experience is enough to convince one of this—he would seem to be right. All who are interested in the poor always remaining poor or who do not wish to appear to be playing an unfavorable role in the age of the exaltation of poverty say no, the poor love one another very much. But this is a lie. Common suffering is not the foundation of friendship. It can be so only in the case where it is dynamic, a protest tending toward liberation. A group of old people in a home do not create friendship because they see no liberation other than death. And yet, they are poor.

The structure of friendship is one. All other forms of association are not friendship and therefore reveal their nature at every step: They are groups characterized by "diplomacy," deception, hatred, fatigue, "thingification." And it is most important that we see the bare bones of friendship, independently of an affective, psychological schema, or, as we have often said to conceal a failure, independently of a "supernatural" schema. Friendship has an inexorable law.

A Little Sister of Jesus, who works as a nurses' aide in a large hospital in Chile, told me that the sick girls used to read romance and movie magazines and then talk about them among themselves. When least expected, someone would whisper, "Here comes the sister!" The magazines disappeared under the blankets and the conversation changed. The aide noted that the supervising sister was not mean, moralistic, cranky, or anything of that sort. But she was the supervisor, identified with the power structure and not united with them in their search for liberation. She was the rich person and they the poor; consequently friendship was impossible. Her role was to give and not to receive, and each girl did all she could to get as much as possible, with sweetness, force, or guile. In every case, they shunned the person-to-person encounter which is friendship.

On the other hand, the Gospel is truly the book of friendship. It is the story of the encounter of a group motivated by the building up of a kingdom which was nonexistent, although very concrete and in a certain sense already present. Their poverty, their search, and their responsibility with regard to the kingdom united them. Yes, poverty, for although it is true that Jesus has the wisdom of the Father, that he has everything to teach and to share, it is also true that he is powerless before the free acceptance of love. Man is capable of accepting or rejecting love. This is the kingdom; and Jesus must construct it by begging, pleading with man not to reject it but to accept it. His joy and his affirmation are in man's hands. No one depends as much as he does on man. The essence of his person, his name, like that of everybody else for that matter, is contained in a relationship: "And you shall call his name Jesus, for he will save his people from their sins" *(Matthew 1:21).* This salvation depends on whether or not we are willing to be saved and on our discovering the need for salvation. Jesus is the poorest of all men because he is Truth and therefore he cannot "go out of himself" into things.

Outside of truth, there is nothingness and only one who is not identified with truth, like man, can escape into nothingness. Christ cannot do this, and therefore his being coincides with poverty and with the supreme truth. No one is poor in the way he is, because no one is conditioned by man as is he, who is infinitely free. His collaborators will never fully understand this total powerlessness, a poverty that for the Lord is the very essence of his being the Savior of man: " 'Lord, do you want us to bid fire come down from heaven and consume them?' But he turned and rebuked them" *(Luke 9:54-55)*. And in another instance: " 'Master, we saw a man casting out demons in your name, and we forbade him, because he does not follow with us.' But Jesus said to him, 'Do not forbid him; for he that is not against you is for you' " *(Luke 9:49-50)*. And to Peter who saw avoiding Jerusalem as very easy, he responded with unusual harshness: "Get behind me, Satan! You are a hindrance to me; for you are not on the side of God, but of men" *(Matthew 16:23)*.

This creative relationship is not arid and inhuman. On the contrary, it is enriched by all the vibrations of a warm, human friendship. There are passages in the Gospel that shed light on the intimacy in which this little group lived: "Privately to his own disciples he explained everything" *(Mark 4:34)*. "The apostles returned to Jesus, and told him all that they had done and taught. And he said to them, 'Come away by yourselves to a lonely place, and rest a while.' For many were coming and going, and they had no leisure even to eat. And they went away in the boat to a lonely place by themselves. But many saw them going, and knew them, and they ran there on foot from all the towns, and got there ahead of them" *(Mark 6:30-33)*.

Friendship which is substantial, solid, and vitally committed to history must get its vitality and its constant renewal from outside. But it also needs concentration, separation, and revision. We have become too afraid of being closed off, of separation. It is certain that the mania for separation made us fall into a ghetto from which we are only now emerging with difficulty. We are discovering the importance and the beauty of pluralistic dialogue. There no longer exist the Christian and the non-Christian, "the barbarian and the Scythian." Man exists, his destiny, his culture, his exodus. And every separation from the human condition seems to be a betrayal and a failure against love. The Gospel gives the Christian the responsibility to bring hope to this world, without changing it: "As you enter the house, salute it" *(Matthew 10:12)*, that is, proclaim peace to this house. Peace cannot be proclaimed without giving a message of hope.

For centuries the Christian has thought too much about "having to give," and now we are discovering that we no longer have anything to give.

It is the paradoxical presumption of the kingdom, which authorizes the two positions: It is and it is not, it is of this world and yet it is not seen. For many years we have supported a kingdom that was incarnate in institutions, a very visible kingdom present in the world, and now our preference goes to a presence of the kingdom that is obscure, silent, and discreet. However, this message of freedom is not nothingness. It is a value which goes discreetly into the events of history, almost unnoticed, and gives them a completely different and at times opposite sense. They become events of hope, steps forward toward the encounter with the eschatological Christ, a stage in liberation. Most of the time this is not seen. Hope is not an easy virtue, because it must be rediscovered at every moment and saved at every moment from the opposition of the event itself.

Every event includes hope within itself and at the same time covers over and obscures this hope. The event must be read, and it is certain that it cannot be read from without, but only "by doing the truth in love." Truth opens up to us only if we do it in love. But to understand it we need an attitude of watchfulness, that is, that withdrawal in private "to understand the parable." Everything that happens is a parable, and everything is a symbol of a reality deeper than this visible reality. This depth cannot be reached without patiently passing these events—which in themselves are depersonalizing—through the humanized and personalizing filter of friendship. In this encounter of friendship, the person rediscovers the hope of being loved and therefore that love, the love that builds a person, is in the world. He discovers the mysterious presence of Christ, who has guaranteed his presence when two or three are gathered in his name. The Christian community must be preserved from the temptation of the ghetto through its vital insertion in history. I use the word "vital" because it is operating, not with history crystallized in its technical expressions or customs, but with history on the move, history that searches, history as a process of liberation.

The community is saved from indeterminateness and depersonalization through opportunities for encounter, friendly, affective relationships, mutual giving, the constant rediscovery of the community's vocation. "Even the hairs of your head are all numbered," the Master said in one of those intimate encounters. "Fear not, therefore. . . . He who finds his life will lose it, and he who loses his life for my sake will find it" *(Matthew 10:30, 39)*. It seems to me that it is as if he were touching, believing, and seeing the person in order to discover all his dimensions, that intrinsic power and immanent strength, in order that the person not lose courage before the imposing conspiracy of the world and that he know how to be humble and strong. This appears to be the special grace of friendship lived and enjoyed. A person without friendship and without the possibility of availing himself of friendship as a value in itself, as a gratuitous encounter, is like an implicit person or like a house filled with valuable objects which has not been opened.

Friendship opens up the person, makes him explicit, and frees him by discovering hidden capacities, strengths, and unsuspected values. Only in a warm affective atmosphere, in a complete integration on the personal level, in a fortunate circumstance in which all the best conditions for friendship are present, only then can a person become open to everything and draw out from his inner treasure the fullness of his being. It is very true that we must be in the world and in history because a history "apart" is necessarily false by the fact that *there is only one history.* "You are the salt of the earth," you were made to be mixed with the earth. "But if salt has lost its taste, how shall its saltness be restored? It is no longer good for anything except to be thrown out and trodden under foot by men" *(Matthew 5:13).*

Mixed with the earth, lost in the event, participants in the exodus, ordinary men but disciples of Christ, those who have listened to the Gospel, not a race apart, not separate. No, they are salt, rich with that hope that gives savor and meaning to events, preventing their alienation, saturating them with a message of liberation and personalization. They are capable of being friends because only a friend can resurrect a person from alienation, solely by the force and exigency of his person. "Take no gold, nor silver, nor copper in your belts, no bag for your journey, nor two tunics, nor sandals, nor a staff" *(Matthew 10:9-10).* And then again: "Enter the house, and salute it." We are reminded of the passage from the first chapter of Luke: "[Mary] entered the house of Zechariah and greeted Elizabeth. And when Elizabeth heard the greeting of Mary, the babe leaped in her womb" *(Luke 1:40-41).* The fetal man, enveloped in his past, closed within tradition, immobile within the comfort of another or of others who live for him, in his name, rejoices in the womb of his mother and awakens as a person. In this greeting of peace there is the whole richness and emotion of an encounter in friendship which awakens a person from lethargy.

7

POLITICAL LOVE

"But one of them, Caiaphas, who was high priest that year, said to them, 'You know nothing at all; you do not understand that it is expedient for you that one man should die for the people, and that the whole nation should not perish' " *(John 11:49-50)*. Jesus' death is looked upon as the liberation of the whole people. His death certainly had a significance and a power that transcended absolutely the death of any ordinary conspirator or guerrilla fighter. It had all the characteristics of a gratuitous sacrifice for the salvation of a people. Jesus entered into the human rhythm that he proposed as the rhythm of freedom, and he lived it fully. He gave his life for others with the purpose of improving the world and making it progress toward freedom and love.

In Christ's sacrifice is contained the whole promise and the whole reality of the freedom and love that reach their fulfillment only in the ultimate encounter when he will come again in glory, although they become gradually explicit in historical time. The relationship between Christ and the world, between Christ and history, is described in the well-known passage from the fifth chapter of the Letter to the Ephesians: "as Christ loved the Church and gave himself up for her, that he might sanctify her, having cleansed her by the washing of water with the word" *(Ephesians 5:25-26)*. And all the events of political love can be read as a continuation and a reproduction of the rhythm of Christ toward mankind.

Certainly man is not pure, and it is impossible historically that his self-giving be not contaminated with pride, a desire for revenge, the wish for self-assertion. The rhythm of this self-giving is never totally intact because man never totally coincides with his vocation: Man is never his own vocation. Jesus *is* his vocation; he *is* salvation.

87

Che Guevara, Camilo Torres, or others who lived the same rhythm, desired and worked for freedom. But they are not all, completely and definitively, saviors or liberators. Thus all liberations leave some void, a nothingness that must be overcome in the successive *creation* of freedom. Political love is the complement and the richness of the love of friendship, because only this reaching out toward the world in a responsible and involved way enriches friendship by giving it value and dynamism. And it is friendship which makes possible this dedication of oneself to the world. We cannot think of political love outside of a community, and a community cannot be thought of outside of this political love. The whole Gospel invites the disciple to take a position of watchfulness and concrete search in the historical situations in which the values of freedom, charity, and hope are to be incarnated; it invites him to become involved concretely and dangerously in history. The timid servant who does not want to commit himself because of fear is deprived of everything: "You wicked and slothful servant! You knew that I reap where I have not sowed, and gather where I have not winnowed? Then you ought to have invested my money with the bankers, and at my coming I should have received what was my own with interest" *(Matthew 25:26-27)*.

The three great problems related to the theme of political love are these: To what point is commitment in the world valid? With what criterion should we commit ourselves politically? And what is the boundary between evangelization and political commitment? The first question runs throughout the whole history of the Church, continually rephrased and disquieting, because, on the one hand, the ambiguity of the world and history obscures the presence of a Providence, and therefore the hope of a redemption. It would seem that to consider redemption would be to take refuge in faith and hope, in a metahistorical or eschatological world. On the other hand, the worldliness and political approaches of some who claim to be Church members would seem to counsel a separation from politics.

The whole Bible, however, gives the picture of a world to be saved and presents time as the *kairos*, the time of salvation: "Behold, now is the acceptable time; behold now is the day of salvation" *(2 Corinthians 6:2)*. Time is enriched by this value of salvation, by this opportunity for salvation, through the prophetic mission which discovers within it God's plan of salvation. The prophetic and apostolic missions complete one another because the former has the function of uncovering the terrain, the acceptable time, while the latter is the sowing. It is true that political liberation will always be ambiguous and will always leave us with a vacuum—and hence the temptation to take refuge in an apostolate that prescinds from political activity. The temptation against faith, however, is a constant threat as long as we allow to subsist alongside of us a world that is opaque, absurd, and not penetrated by faith or hope. And it will not be penetrated by faith and hope, as if by a ray of light from on high, unless we are within it with a lifegiving function. We can preserve the value of faith and love only from within. The world left outside the process of salvation and redemption becomes absurd and thus is fertile ground for absurd existences.

The talent was taken away from the slothful servant and given to the one who had ten, because with the former it had become absurd, useless, and inhuman—a cause of alienation. And the servant had to be thrown outside because he did not really belong to the community. He was afraid! Fear, irresponsibility, worked to "thingify" the talent when it should have become an instrument of a relationship. He could have done this only if he had known how to discover the *opportunity* which the others discovered. In the Gospel the children of darkness are praised, because—having no need to dedicate their attention to the Eternal, to the Absolute—they can concentrate all of their attention on seizing the opportunity. They have no other vital guiding criterion than this search for the acceptable time. The revelation of salvation is made through a history penetrated with the signs of salvation. They are flashes, mere moments, but they are enough to give vitality and continuity in the faith.

The mistake made by Catholic Action militants was that they proposed an evangelization that was outside a political commitment. By doing so, they created a terrain that was propitious for identifying more with the political power than with true politics. This resulted in a government that did not have the support of the masses and was therefore antihistorical, even though it sought the support of the Church with every possible means.

First of all, this was because the Church is a power factor and second, because in her message there is a doctrinal content that serves men of every age and place. A kind of affinity is discovered between political antihistoricism and religious ahistoricism. One foments the other, and one helps the other in solidifying the structures of alienation. An antihistorical political structure will not give a dime for an activity promoted by the Church that is directed toward developing an awareness of injustice or of the possibility of securing justice at a given moment. What moment of salvation is this? What day of salvation can we expect or, in a certain sense, *create*?

On the other hand, such a structure will give millions toward initiatives and activities that help to perpetuate religious alienation. I told some Catholic friends from Latin America who feared the election of an anticlerical candidate that they could rest easy, that no one would give economic help to the "works of the Church" as he would, because, unlike the other candidates, he had to be pardoned two sins instead of one: He was antihistorical—and thus did not interpret the real demands of the people—and he was anticlerical—that is, he went counter to an inclination of the people. This fatal alliance cannot be avoided except with a religious vision that fosters a dynamic commitment in history, a permanent attitude in the Christian of searching in history for the "day of salvation" and of discovering in time the *kairos* which is the "acceptable time of salvation." And this means that the Christian must be in a permanent position of interpretation and challenge. The Church senses this and the constitution *Gaudium et spes* is the inspiration behind this attitude: "Men are not deterred by the Christian message from building up the world, or impelled to neglect the welfare of their fellows. They are, rather, more stringently bound to do these very things" (*Gaudium et spes*, no. 34).

To achieve this, it will be necessary for the Church to lose her political structure completely. I do not know how this will be possible, because it is clear that the Church as an institution will have to have a visible, earthly structure, and therefore a certain economic power and a juridical structure—in a word, power. But this necessity causes the Church to fall into a political crystalization which is of necessity antihistorical, because it is not informed with a specific political doctrine, but only shaped as a factor of power. "See, I have set you this day over nations and over kingdoms, to pluck up and to break down, to destroy and to overthrow, to build and to plant" *(Jeremiah 1:10)*. It should never be forgotten that these words were directed to a prophet who was poor and had nothing. He was not the representative of one state threatening another. He did not represent little Israel threatening the imperial powers of the East. No, he is emptiness. He is a word, a look, a penetration of events. He is the pure revelation of these events which are called to salvation and liberation.

In God's eyes, what is the meaning of aggression in Vietnam, the occupation of Czechoslovakia, the march of the blacks, the guerrilla warfare in Latin America, the student rebellion? How can we find within these events the true concerns of God? Since the Church, as she is today, is an antihistorical political structure, it is very easy for churchmen to accept only those solutions that come from the leaders of antihistorical structures, whose criterion is the preservation of a static order rather than dynamic justice. There is no doubt that "popular opinion" will always be on the side that is the most comfortable, the most secure, and will therefore give the Church the impression that it is the consensus of the masses. But the illusion would immediately disappear if reality could be perceived with a qualitative criterion that seems to be that of the Gospel, and if we found ourselves at the epilogue. There are always epilogues in history, and they confirm for us that the prophetic minorities have always been right, those minorities who have dynamically understood—through a genuine involvement—the signs of the times.

The Church's insistence in *Gaudium et spes* on "understanding the signs of the times" gives hope that there will be an important and decisive turning point in the Church's position with regard to history and political institutions. Words of threat or encouragement, the functions of "uprooting" or "planting," are ridiculous—especially in today's world with its ever more gigantic structures—if they are expressions of a political power as such. But they can stir the very foundations of the earth if they are a prophetic voice that resounds throughout the world. And this ridiculous power must necessarily borrow strength from other political powers, and thus the tragedy of an alienating religiosity and an antihistorical politics is perpetuated: In both camps, man, the poor man, the man who must hope if he is to live, feels betrayed and no other alternative remains for him but rebellion or opportunism.

Opportunism is not fidelity. It is a provisional and hypocritical adherence disguised to look like fidelity. It is not long before facts prove very clearly that it is equivocal. How the Church is to empty herself and become a pure prophetic voice, I do not know. Perhaps even those most highly placed do not know either. I am consoled by the thought that the Church is of the Holy Spirit and that she has no limit to the means of achieving her goal. At this point it may be asked whether or not the Church has the right to promote or to welcome structures of militants without a precise political commitment. The answer is certainly affirmative if by this we mean that these structures are not essentially political in nature and are not oriented toward a direct political commitment. Indeed, all of us agree in acknowledging that the Church, out of respect for the autonomy of politics, must not become a promoter of political structures.

But if it is meant that these Church structures are created as an instrument of an evangelization emptied of political content, the answer is *no*. How can there be a message of progressive justice, of brotherhood, personalizing love, and fellowship among men, conceived outside of and without the political instrument?

Still, can a Christian get from the Gospel general guidance which would help him to make concrete political choices? Can he get guidance from the Gospel for existentially activating political love, which would be nothing else than a translation of the precept given by the Master to all who follow him? From the crucible of time, the Church has culled some guidelines that may give some direction. Men today "thirst for a full and free life" (*Gaudium et spes*, no. 9). Cultural revolutions of youth indicate that this thirst for freedom, respect, and communication, which is a permanent characteristic of man, has reached a frantic stage of desire and opposition. Man today tends to form a "universal community" (*ibid.*, no. 9) and the Council states that "the promotion of unity belongs to the innermost nature of the Church, since she is. . .a sign. . .of unity" (*ibid.*, no. 42). This freedom and unity can be achieved through a dialogue of cultures. And therefore a Christian who today closes himself up within an exclusivistic nationalism or a timid integralism is outside of the spirit of the times.

And, finally, a word about creativity. Ours is a world in full gear toward scientific and technical conquest. This has immediate repercussions on our way of life and makes our lives extremely provisional. In expressing her optimism about man and his conquests, the Church does not have in mind the superficial satisfaction of someone who feels favored by progress. Rather it is the discovery of the work of redemption, which is going on in the world under the sign of ambiguity and is hidden from the earthbound eye of technology. Salvation prolongs creation. The more man is a creator of the world, the more he is effecting his own salvation. Without knowing it, man often collaborates in accelerating the encounter of creation with its Omega point, which is consummation in the risen Christ. Theology must rediscover this Christian vision which has as a consequence the discovery of the autonomy of the terrestrial realm. It moves us toward desacralization, that is, toward a unification of the plan of creation with the plan of salvation.

These guidelines, which come to us remotely from the Gospel and proximately from the prophetic function of the Church, are very imprecise and are no help for man who must make a commitment in history. I am acutely and continually aware of this when my young friends call upon me as a churchman to direct my message to choices that are more concrete. But it is a temptation, because I would be betraying that freedom and that right to autonomy which I am defending with all my might. It is very hard to find the patience to create new inventions, new techniques, and new political structures. We are continually assaulted by the temptation to use the pressure of power, but without this patience there can never be inventiveness, the free working of the imagination, or creativity.

The people I knew when I was young will remember that I used to say, jokingly, that one should never listen to the clergy when they give advice on concrete political choices, the choice of a fiancée, or a business affair. This conviction has become firm and serious. The priest is also a man and a citizen. And therefore for him too the problem of making specific choices remains open and challenging. If he does not make these choices, his talks on politics—without decisions—on economics—without financial risks—on love—without the face of a woman—make him into a dilettante, a superficial man. He becomes the classic prototype of a person interested in everything but committed to nothing, who takes what is beautiful in life and history, but does not involve himself in what is difficult and risky. And these assaults against priests, with which we all are familiar, are based on multiple experiences.

Is the Christian a revolutionary or not? Is he violent or nonviolent? We are continually beset by the temptation to bring the Gospel out of its *emptiness*, which is not an emptiness of content or substance, but the emptiness of salt that wants to be eaten but cannot be eaten by itself. It is the emptiness of the leaven, which is nothing without the dough. It is the emptiness of light, which is nonexistent for us without the atmosphere. It is like accepting chastity, which is an emptiness. And no one likes emptying himself and taking the form of a servant (Philippians 2:7). Therefore we do everything to get out of the emptiness. In the case of chastity we fill it with passions similar to love, or with apologias or self-exaltations. In the case of politics, we fill it up with power or an ideology. And this is what Paul means when he says forcefully: "the stumbling block of the Cross has been removed" *(Galatians 5:11)*, with the appearance of bringing forth fullness. I do not believe that the Gospel can be decanted into a theory, not any theory, not even the theory of nonviolence, which in other respects can be inspired by the Gospel. For all the more reason, it cannot be exhausted in a theory of violence, which might seem to be authorized by the invitation to take up the sword or by the radical step taken by Jesus against the money lenders in the Temple.

Now we can make some specific remarks about the general lines we have uncovered. The Christian must be an artisan of peace and unity, without sacrificing hunger and thirst for justice, which constitute the principal characteristic of his person. This he brings about through dialogue, which to be genuine and fruitful must be pluralistic. If not, it is a monologue, even if a number of us are speaking or if one person speaks for many. Therefore it would seem that democracy is the ideal structure for the Christian, insofar as there would be freedom in this structure, as well as dialogue and a permanent search for justice stimulated by the desire to move everyone to participate in the political dialogue. In fact, many countries that appear to be democracies are not because they permit a freedom that is confined to what is suitable for the power groups and do not effectively promote dialogue. A great number of people are destined to remain marginal, and therefore the sense of distributive justice for all practical purposes is lacking.

Concretely speaking, which are the democracies? Democracy was and is the ideal political structure of "liberalism." But it is a democracy that does not work for the advancement of the people, and therefore it is in no way—as is intended by the very definition of the word—a government of the people. It gives a seeming freedom of expression, which is in fact denied by the economic strength of small groups of people who, with money, are able to manipulate all the instruments of propaganda. It gives an apparent freedom of association, but this too is restricted and destroyed merely by calling "subversive" everything that challenges it or protests against it. It lays down as a policy the equality for all citizens before the law, but this is then denied shamelessly by the economic, cultural, and affective inferiority in which the majority is kept (which in the Third World means the indigenous majority). To call this political cast of liberalism a democracy is in my opinion a lie and contrary to the Gospel.

Democracy is not anarchy, as certain power groups try to demonstrate. Democracy is making and holding fast to political decisions from the viewpoint of the people and not of an oligarchy or of money. It is a problem of perspective, which completely changes the substance of decisions. It is to make a decision about the people, the poor and the workers, not in an arbitrary fashion from on high, but along with them. I am deeply humiliated by conventions and meetings of intellectuals, bishops, and priests—all those who in the Middle Ages were classified as *clerici* in contradistinction to the *plebs*—which discuss violence or nonviolence, evolution or revolution, as if everything depended on a consultation of physicians standing at the bedside of some gravely ill person. "Come on, old man, take your medicine." By this very action they deny what they intend to assert, that is, the people's right to freedom and their duty to win their rights. Above all they deny trust in man. We shall never fully understand the tremendous trust Christ has in man. Not in the "learned one," the secure and proud man, but in the poor man, the illiterate, the poor little Canaanite woman who did not even know the terminology of the sons of Israel. The learned Nicodemus did not understand, but the woman did. If all the conventioneers, scholars, and specialists put themselves in the service of the people so that the people might become aware of their rights and on this basis make their choices freely, we would be taking a great step forward. But if everything having to do with the people is decided by those who "are not awaiting the liberation of Israel" because they have no need for it, everything done is a waste of time and an offense to the poor; and for the learned ones it means becoming increasingly closed up within their robe of pride and self-sufficiency, that dreadful shell of cement which even Christ's pick-axe cannot break. On the other hand, we want the people to discover their rights, to be able to make choices, to operate politics from the viewpoint of the grass roots, from that of man himself, and not from the viewpoint of economic profit or planned schemas. But then we think for them, decide for them, and oblige them always to accept the benevolent concessions that are handed down to them from our lofty cathedras.

The scandal of the century is the estrangement of the masses from the Church, and it continues and will continue until we, the "intellectuals," the "scholars," the "elite" decide to start a revolution, until we begin to look at structural reforms from the viewpoint of the masses, the poor. This is the very marrow of the question. If democracy means the power of the people, then the people must take this power and oblige me to look at things from their point of view. Jesus looked reality up and down, and the venerable personages, who with their noses in the air walked majestically among the people, were transformed into caricatures through the simple look of the poor man. "The scribes and the Pharisees sit on Moses' seat. . . . They do all their deeds to be seen by men; for they make their phylacteries broad and their fringes long, and they love the place of honor at feasts and the best seats in the synagogues, and salutations in the market places, and being called rabbi by men" *(Matthew 23:1-7).*

Everything would have changed if Jesus had seen things from the other side, if he had looked at this attitude from "on high." A kind of anti-Gospel could be imagined: "Your masters sit on Moses' seat. See what seriousness, what holiness is written on their faces, how stately is their walk. They give forth the odor of knowledge and spiritual unction." This would be possible. But it is not the perspective of Jesus.

Those who love the Church must fight for this revolutionary change of perspective. Thus the political love of a Christian should not be distinguished from that of a non-Christian except in this: the preservation of Christ's perspective, his point of observation. He must never lose his solidarity with those who weep, with those who hunger and thirst after justice, with those who ought to have this hunger and thirst for justice. I take the liberty of adding "ought to" to the Gospel, because the situation of injustice often does not reach the level of consciousness and does not become concretized in hunger and thirst for justice. We must have solidarity with the humble, the weak, those who suffer violence, and not a paternalistic solidarity, not merely an affective fellow-feeling. No. This solidarity must be with their decisions, their choices, and their slowness. We must not precede them, but follow them. We must not impose ourselves on them, but allow them to impose themselves. And this should be done not out of a spirit of false humility, but because our decision is awaiting theirs.

If we call upon a philosopher for a lesson in philosophy or a physicist for a lecture on physics, obviously he will take the professor's chair, speak to us, and be the leader of the group. But liberation is the problem of the oppressed, of those who are suffering violence and live on the fringes of society. And we should rejoice if they call upon us for a helping hand, or ask us to give resonance to their voice or strength to their choices. We should be happy that our psychological enslavements, the violence we all suffer on the affective level, the humiliations that deeply wound our sensibilities hidden beneath the appearances of affirmations, triumphs, and receptivity, can open up to this vast historical liberation and be accepted and appeased in this great thirst for justice on the part of mankind. Let our personal suffering become political suffering and our existential pain be broadened into the immense pain of human existence as in the pierced heart of Christ. When I think of the pain of the world, the words of Psalm 69 cry out to me: "Save me, O God! For the waters have come up to my neck. I sink in deep mire, where there is no foothold; I have come into deep waters, and the flood sweeps over me" *(vv. 1-2)*.

When I speak of the suffering of the multitudes of the poor, even sisters and priests object: "And do you think that the rich don't suffer? Perhaps more than the poor. Don't the rich need us in order to understand, be converted, and become Christians?" These are often the objections of people who do not want to change, who pretend to be deaf because they do not wish to hear. We are in agreement with these objections, which are too obvious to need demonstration. But do you believe you can help the rich with any other formula than Jesus' own? Jesus looked with the greatest sympathy on a young man from the upper class, with his fine clothes. He did not chase him away: *"And Jesus looking upon him loved him" (Mark 10:21)*. How beautiful and how human! "He loved him." He loved him, he did not fawn upon him. He did not think how he could use him, how he could get him to give money for the kingdom. He was a person who suffered from the anguish of man's eternal problem, the "why" of existence: What must I do to gain eternal life?

Life, living, existing with others and for someone, will always be the sole question man proposes to himself, hardly freed as he is from the primordial need to subsist, to eat, and to have a roof over his head. And Jesus answered: "Go, sell what you have, and give to the poor . . . and come, follow me." This means taking the side of the poor, making one's self poor, putting oneself in a position to see things from their perspective. There is nothing else to do, my friend. The young man could not say to him, "Why don't you begin to do so yourself if this is the path to take?" This is why we ourselves cannot say this to a person who asks us what life is, what it means to live. We cannot tell him and therefore we defend ourselves with syllogisms, with a scholasticized Freud or an inoffensive Marxism, with the socialism of the drawing room.

However, for the rich like Zacchaeus salvation is not only "Behold, I give half of what I have to the poor." The old and static formula must be modernized with watchfulness and historical experience. How today, in our own time, can we become poor and enter into the number of those who hunger and thirst after justice?

The Christian must continually break the successive crystallizations of justice with love. And this he must do by being faithful to the Gospel, because the Gospel fills us with the anguish of bearing witness to love in the world at any cost and in every circumstance. In our time the notion of rights and justice has come out of a positivistic and deterministic concept. Certainly some love is to be found in this schematization, but only after a great effort.

The norm is based on objective reality, just as the reality of the seasons determines the growth of plants, prevents them from growing in a haphazard fashion, and limits their creativity. I cannot go out to pick a rose when I see from my window that it is snowing.

This law is corrected by love because, basically, it permits the rosebush to produce roses and the cherry tree to bring forth cherries in the springtime. But Jesus saw through the positivism of his time. Indeed, the Sabbath allows man to find himself as a person by returning to his deepest being, as a contemplating person, but only on the condition that he does not do so without love: "The Sabbath was made for man, and not man for the Sabbath" *(Mark 2:27).*

This "objective" and "realistic" view of justice lends itself to enormous injustices and to tragic codifications in the conscience. Every day we meet up with violent oppressors, people directly responsible for our brothers' hunger, who will tell us, and truthfully so, that they give all that is due to those employees, that they keep not a penny for themselves, and that what the law has set down for them is sacrosanct.

I remember a woman who during the course of a conversation kept repeating over and over again, like someone in a trance, "My husband is upright, upright to the point of being scrupulous." This good woman was trying desperately to have her conscience assimilate an uprightness that was only one side of the coin, an uprightness as seen from outside and not from within.

It is very sad that this positivistic notion of justice has often been assumed by the philosophy of being and defended as realistic and objective—without a thought to the fact that it could be the cause of monstrous injustices.

As an alternative, its defenders posit a subjectivism that defends an idea as the basis of a right, a feeling enclosed within an isolated conscience. Is there no alternative between legalism or the dictate of a conscience unable to succeed in formulating a pluralistic justice?

Justice today germinated from an anthropological reality. The subjective and objective aspects flow together in this view, not in a kind of static concordat but in a dynamic vision. Through historical progress, rights of man are discovered which tend ever increasingly to humanize and personalize him.

Justice must be watchful to see that they are rights that are proportionate to man and not mere expressions of his insatiable greed. And once the validity of these rights is acknowledged to be in line with fuller being, they must be established and accepted as milestones, sure steps on the road of man's advancement.

But, with the pressure of love, the Christian must make these formulations of justice explode. Justice offers a secure platform for love; it is the tranquility of love, its provisional security, the hypothesis which is a point of departure. But love is restless. It has no firm ground, it cannot stay at home. It needs to move and it leaves behind its safe base to move forward in its search.

People who trusted in Russian justice, as in a definitive liberation, were deeply shaken and embittered by the invasion of Czechoslovakia. The alleged motives of the capitalistic countries are more or less the same when they decide to occupy a country: the country's self-defense, or its immaturity, or internal weakness. This sad episode, however, should help a Christian to sense that whatever the "order" may be, it becomes rotten if it is not tormented from within and opened out to the world by the irreplaceable function of love.

We must never lose the watchfulness spoken about by the Gospel. The Christian's duty is to keep justice open with the pressure of love. He must take care not to negate justice with the excuse of a love that is antihistorical, eschatological, the object of pure hope. The basic formula is to live the present stage of justice with impatience, with a desire for fuller being, with the humanizing force of justice, and with a thirst for more, for the new creation.

Without this justice of today, nothing of love is preserved. Every love, even the most vibrant kind, spills out on the ground like water when justice is not present. But love trembles within the fibers of justice and sighs for freedom.

Love—as we have seen on the more personal level of the intersubjectivity between man and woman—wills that the other person be, and that he be with others, in a world that must be modified by accepting him, by allowing everyone this possibility of being and living together, not as objects but as persons in dialogue.

Love is always felt to be "an exile on this earth" *(Hebrews 11:13)* and looks toward the promised city, searching for new heavens and a new earth in which to set up its tent.

The real Christian is not a man of order in the sense that he accepts an established order. He is a man of order in the sense that he does not preach violence, but rather a demand for justice and love which can burst out into violence. He is not a conservative because he is fighting for what is new, for fuller being, for the new arrival of justice.

The kingdom of God must come, it is at hand, it is on the verge of being among us. This trumpet call kept the first Christian generations awake and watchful. They translated it into apocalyptic terms and the Lord had continually to disabuse them of this notion: "It is not for you to know times and seasons which the Father has fixed by his own authority" *(Acts 1:7).*

Ours is a time of change, and this change can happen only radically, not as change for change's sake, getting rid of a Tiberius to put a Nero in his place. It must be a change in perspective *by looking at things from the viewpoint of the poor.*

Why is this the correct perspective? Because in it man is the subject and not money or things.

Latin America is a continent of political change, which is taking place at a most accelerated rate. These changes, however, are not really changes, but rather successions, which is something quite different. They are changes of turn and not revolutions of perspective. They therefore produce only frustrations and deteriorations within the system. Only constant watchfulness can protect us from illusions and naive infatuations.

A true Christian must respect the juridical order so as not to be a utopian, but he must represent an element of rupture, of re-creation, of re-thinking which keeps eyes open to the growth of human awareness.

Jesus died because of a curious paradox, because of obedience to the law and because of rebellion against it. The death on the cross is historical and symbolic. The transverse arm could signify the continuity of tradition, obedience to the law: "For truly, I say to you, till heaven and earth pass away, not an iota, not a dot, will pass from the law until all is accomplished" *(Matthew 5:18).* The vertical arm could represent the break, a violent interruption that comes from on high, the Spirit, and from below, from the earth, which is from time, represented by the lower half of the vertical arm.

Christ died to obey the law, but into it he introduced a force which continually opens it to new ruptures and to new incarnations of love. "Justice," says Madinier, "is the product of charity and if it constitutes a body of rules they are the rules which charity has set down" (*Conscience et amour*, Paris, 1947, p. 128). The force of Christ which explodes justice and continually makes it obsolete, as the Letter to the Hebrews emphasizes *(8:13),* is constituted by the Spirit and by time. It is the presence of the Spirit which reveals the successive appearances of man's existential truth in time. It is in this light that I have understood the phrase from the Gospel: "Therefore every scribe who has been trained for the kingdom of heaven is like a householder who brings out of his treasure what is new and what is old" *(Matthew 13:52)*. This is not meant in the sense that he must make a hybrid mixture of old and new, or put a modern varnish over something that has become worn out, as so often happens. Instead, it means that love, the same political love, brings us to accept the old aspirations of love which have now been made static within a juridical system, and to aspire to the new forms which love is earnestly seeking in its doing what is true.

A way has opened up to us that enables us to have a look at natural law, which the Church so strongly defends and to which it continually appeals as a basis for dialogue with people who believe in God even if they are not Catholic. She thus seeks the support of men of good will when she painfully seeks peace in the world, grounded in justice.

Before everything else, it is clear that the Church, experienced with men and faithful to her personalist message, does not intend to confuse man and nature by seeing man as a part of nature enclosed within nature's laws and therefore a participant in its fixed state. The Church aims to defend the eternal and permanent right of man to fulfillment in accordance with his essence. Let nothing and no one seek to violate his essential structure established by the Creator, under any pretext. Evidently, this eternal, fixed right of the person to be what he should be, to become what he should be, in line with a vocation that is for all men and special for each man, is not reflected in a fixed juridical order, in a static structure of justice.

There is no need to transfer the perpetuity, the fixedness of this right onto two levels. I have the right to live like a man and like a person. But my home is one thing in the Stone Age and another in the year 2000. Today we are increasingly discovering that man's nature is dialogical. The "thou" and the "others" are for the "I" a call to come out of itself, to seek to make the relationship ever more perfect, to be with the others. The natural law is the expression of a person who is progressively growing in the awareness of his being in dialogue, of his being in relationship to others.

Teilhard de Chardin was right when he saw the coincidence between the growth of the conscience and an increase in man's awareness of community. The discovery of what I can do for others, what others can expect of me, what I can do so that others can become fuller persons, modifies the natural law. Yet the law still retains its fixed essence, which is what guarantees man's right to be what he ought to be. This will never change even to the end of time.

If the Church has combatted certain physico-biological and political theories, she has done so to defend the innermost essence of the person as a subject of rights. The Church defends this essence fiercely so that man might not be transformed into a robot or a rabbit. Science advances without being intimidated by these S.O.S.'s of the Church. Sometimes science is right, and many times it is not.

Science must make its tests and often plays with the human person. In one of Clark's books I read that before *Humanae vitae* Malthus's ideas had seemingly already been refuted; it had been proved that progress is parallel to the increase of population and that a very low and almost nonexistent rate of growth in population was characteristic of primitive peoples (*Population Growth and Land Use*, New York: St. Martin, 1967). But the Church is not anti-Malthusian for scientific reasons, but out of faithfulness to man, to his right that no one, from the outside, may limit his right to procreate since this would betray a basic aspect of his essence as a person. A scientific hypothesis can lead to a further liberation of the person, to a step forward in the direction of fuller being. The Church cannot stop science's progress. The Church is mistrustful of novelty out of fidelity to man's essence and it can happen that her zeal may be somewhat exaggerated; but most of the time her cry of alarm, as the epilogue of a scientific hypothesis, is just.

The defense of the natural law does not prevent it from evolving as progress is made in the knowledge of the person. It is a knowledge of that mysterious center of the world which we one day shall know and which continually opens out in the dimensions which Saint Thomas defined clearly as *nos–infra nos–supra nos. Nos* is the "I" with others, the "I" in the family and political community, in the unceasing and dialectical search for justice, the "I" that seeks itself in its total reality; it is not only the conscious "I" that emerges from the deeper and hidden subconscious, but the subconscious itself, which influences the decisions and attitudes of the emerging "I" to the point of distorting and directing its choices. The *infra nos* is the line of the person's relationships with nature, of which he is a part and which is associated with his destiny, as the eighth chapter of the Letter to the Romans shows. The *supra nos* is the world of the metaphysical relationship of the person, his contemplative activity and the field of investigation of the true consistency of his being. The knowledge of this permanent being which the person is progresses continuously and demands a change of the natural law. What is fixed and perpetual is the person who has the right to live his reality as a son of God with freedom and in fullness. And this reality must be created and won in these basic relationships. It is at this point that the changeable and the historical enter in; they are not synonymous with the capricious, the arbitrary, or the subjective.

We are dealing with a real right, a reflection of a reality which continually presents itself as new to our investigation. In this discovery of the person concur the learned, the poets, the heroes, and the saints, and the world can do no less than they. The world is ruled with justice, but justice works in what is old, it accepts what is already past, it stands upon ground that is already secure under the conquistador's flag. The conquistadors are no more, they have gone on ahead, and are not to be seen in the terrain of natural law. It is a right of natural ownership, an eternal, immutable, permanent right of the person, surely. But what are the juridical norms whereby each person enjoys this right so that no one and nothing may attack and limit this right?

The right to ownership does not and will never change. But the number of those who are becoming aware of the right to ownership and discovering that they are surrounded and threatened by wolves is continually changing. The juridical norms of ownership are springing up from within. "There is no objectively conceived human dignity," says Madinier. "The progress of justice consists precisely in inventing a human dignity that is always higher and richer. There is invention in morality" (*Conscience et amour*, pp. 51, 58). The jurist is afraid of invention, of fantasy, but man is continually changing before his eyes, and if he does not accept this change, he finds himself shut up in a "sabbath" that was not made for man. The defense of the natural law is evangelical, because it is the defense of the person, of what the person must be in the world. But this does not authorize man to fall asleep and no longer to rethink the person as the center of history and creation.

"The form of this world is passing away" *(1 Corinthians 7:31)*, and with the world the person too is changing and passing away. How can we see man in the framework of the natural law of pagan society when he discovers his new reality in Christ?

"Therefore," says Paul, "if anyone is in Christ, he is a new creation; the old has passed away, behold, the new has come" *(2 Corinthians 5:17)*.

It is a calumny to define the Church as juridical, legalistic, since this is not to see the whole Church. The Church is the Church of law, but it is also the Church of prophecy, contemplation, poetry, and invention. Polemics, incomprehension, and nearsightedness notwithstanding, I am sure that the Church is the organ of synthesis and the humanization of the world, in which all the lines of seeking, with much effort and pain, converge around the person, the center of creation and history.

Political love might seem to be the layman's love. Why? The freedom of political involvement on the part of a clergyman is a problem of canonical discipline and does not concern us at this time. I am anticipating the assertion that without obedience there is no liberation, but two points must be clarified. The first is that there is no serious love, a love that truly frees men, that is not political. Our ascetical education has taught us to distrust too much the emotional and the sentimental. But let us go to the limit, let us be consistent. At times the Catholic lacks daring because he lacks depth. He has a great will to love, but in what way? To what extent? Love which does not become involved in fighting or changing the structures which oppress or limit man's freedom and dignity is a fake.

We cannot allow a person who calls himself a militant not to become involved politically. This is allowed only up to the age of seven or after the age of seventy.

The second point is that the person we call an ecclesiastic cannot be limited to giving platonic advice on political love. That would be too comfortable and we would not be listened to. The position appeared clear to me in an episode I experieced in Arequipa, Peru, in September 1967. All the workers there had gone on a general strike to protest against a raise in salary unjustly disproportionate to the monetary evaluation which the government had unforeseeably decided upon. The tension was dramatic. Barricades were set up in the streets, and a clash with the army was feared on the morning we were to have a "pastoral" meeting of the clergy. It was clear to us that our duty was to go out into the square where the people were gathered and to share the lot of those whom in our meeting we would have called "our sons and our brothers." This was the pastoral decision we made at that meeting. No other was possible.

8

VIRGINAL LOVE

The Church seized upon Jesus' invitation to virginal love: "He who is able to receive this, let him receive it" *(Matthew 19:12).* Paul accepted it enthusiastically: "Now concerning the unmarried, I have no command of the Lord, but I give my opinion as one who by the Lord's mercy is trustworthy" *(1 Corinthians 7:25)* and the whole life of the Church is an uninterrupted tradition of praise for virginity and witness to it.

But what purpose does it serve in today's world? Is it a witness for present-day man? This question continually troubles me because I hear it posed so frequently.

The answer is Paul's, "one who has received the Lord's mercy." A person who is called to virginity has no logical motives; he feels within himself that he cannot be anything else. When someone has discovered this vocation, he does not find convincing answers, and all kinds of polemics are leveled against this mystery by which one lives and which one cannot explain. At times we are almost tempted to rebel: Why me and not somebody else? Why? Sometimes, on the other hand, we discover this call as a joy, with profound gratitude. Why? It is the great self-emptying of the Gospel, and the mystery whereby the Gospel is salt, light, and leaven.

From a biological point of view, a theory called "fetalization" is proposed today (Cf. Gozzano, *Civiltà delle machine,* no. 3, 1968). It is as if man were a frustrated, premature, and "fetalized" animal. The more he evolves, the more he tends to perfection, the more violently and powerfully is his animal evolution held back. In the sphere of his biological being, the less animal he is, the more profoundly do the forces of the intellect and the spirit develop within him.

Did Jesus want to make a superman? Or did he wish to reveal to us the *New* Man? If we should think that the eunuch *propter regnum Coelorum* is a person who looks down from on high at the poor creatures who are tormented by sex and exposed to the temptations of the flesh, the road would be extremely perilous. Perfectionism, the "vestal virgin" complex for the nun and the "pure man" complex for the man, have given rise to ridiculous, not to say tragic, deformations.

What did Jesus want to achieve with his mysterious invitation? I think he wanted to discover where the deepest root of love is, and he wanted that discovery to become a permanent sign in the world. But this was no masochism or exhibitionist victimism. It was not to please a kind of Moloch who awaits the torture and sacrifice of a man, but to manifest that the true encounter, that which makes the person be and gives him substance and Truth and the capacity of loving in Truth, is the encounter with God. The person with a vow of chastity is a hope in the world; he is a witness that love is possible because deep within us there is a secure anchor, a "rock" upon which we can build our house. Virginal love ought to bring security and joy by saving man from the continuous disillusionment which is the most painful of all. This self-emptying is a receptivity found in the deepest part of one's being, and no one has the right to touch it because it is the center of the heart. It is somewhat like the emptiness of the Gospel, continually assailed by ideology. This emptiness of the heart is assailed by things; and it is necessary to block their passage.

The Pharisee can boast of not having allowed a person to come into his heart, but he is unaware that he has allowed objects, "things," to come in: money, possessions, ambition, vanity, his own self. Narcissism is the pathology of a person who *thinks* he is a virgin: The emptiness is filled up with the "I," not the true and essential "I," but the image of the "I." It is that "I" that is longed for and created as a pure type, the exalted role player, esteemed and placed upon a pedestal, honored with incense, decorated with flowers, enshrined and idolized by pious women and by the habitués of churches and sacristies. This "I" stands in the place of God. It needs money, prestige, a whole sacred wardrobe in order to be seen, idolized, and worshipped by its courtiers. And this "I" becomes profoundly bored in its solitude; it needs distractions and they last only a short time. It needs movies, trips, deluxe furniture, the latest model equipment. Its whole court bows down before it, praises it, consoles it, seeks to bring some joy to its tragic loneliness.

It is not difficult to find the court. The courtiers do not need to be paid because there are many people who need this fictitious ideal, this untarnished model. It is a living projection of what man seeks because of an immanent temptation, his self-deification. It is that "you will be like God" in the devil's tempting of Adam and Eve: "You will not die. For God knows that when you eat of it your eyes will be opened, and you will be like God, knowing good and evil" *(Genesis 3:4-5)*. This man or this woman has succeeded in being like God without dying: It is true that they are neither living nor dead. But they are walking, they are moving. They are a little pale and are not carnal, but they have succeeded in surviving and in seeing God and being like him.

It is worth keeping at a high price this sign of victory which the common man cannot achieve and which was announced to man's primordial ancestors. I have often noticed this sad conspiracy to keep alive this walking personification of the human desire to be like God and to prevent the emptiness of boredom from destroying it. It is somewhat costly because desires beget desires, things call for things. But expense is of no concern since the outcome is too important and too imposing for it to be given up.

And this "thingified" rich man, this hieratic being who has placed things in the place of love, wavers between pietism and clerical arrogance, as he uses others to achieve his own goal which is identified with God's goal. God, the true God, is not served: He is used, and this seems clear as crystal since it is not to God, that is, to an encounter with God, that the influence over others of this "rich man" is directed. His is no influence at all. Real influence is the gentle and liberating effect of the witness of a genuine example which others receive without the chaste or consecrated person even noticing it. Instead, this is a power aimed at worship, the temple, good works, the structure, the external expression of power. The role player does not truly love, nor does he lead others to God, because he does not know God or touch him. He organizes and builds, is "thingified" and "thingifies."

His small or vast court is not directed to the search for and encounter with God; it collects money for altars, it embroiders altar cloths, gathers gold for tabernacles and ciboria. At best its efforts are directed toward a sewing school for lower-class girls or for their recreation. "See," a "consecrated" religious once told me, "we don't have an empty room in our houses. They are for the servant girls [however unpleasant, this was the word used] who come here to learn how to write, embroider, and cook. The poor dears are preparing themselves for life." Leaving aside the word "servant," I do not want to cast discredit on all of this. But my attention was struck, even in this superficial conversation, by the narcissism revealed in the nun's tone, a narcissism expressed in a violent and ill-concealed maternalism, in the "I do everything image"—translated, of course, into the obligatory plural, "We do everything"—and in the notion of the "poor dears, without us whatever would become of them!" I do not mean that there was any contempt in her voice, but there certainly was no love.

God was certainly there, but as someone from the outside, as someone who had to be frequently recalled with ejaculations, who ought not to be forgotten before and after work. He is the one who governs the magic castle, he is the guarantee of this whole economic and logistic organization. He is the hypothesis of the role player of the narcissistic "I" of pietism or power. And as such, he is the one who is beyond. He is represented in enormous plaster statues, in wretched oleographs in every room with an astonished face that seems to say, "What am I doing here? Can't you get along without me? You have turned me into an object, put me 'outside,' 'represented' me. But I am not a representation. I am *Being.* I am a Person and I cannot enter where things are, where the individual 'I' is, a satanic and angelic 'I,' a demon camouflaged as the angel of light." Therefore, as one great perceiver of the human heart says, let no one be deceived when these ministers disguise themselves as ministers of justice: "Their end will correspond to their deeds" *(2 Corinthians 11:15).*

If we look at things on this human level, chastity is contemptible and no matter how you look at it, it cannot be a witness to anything. To give up a husband in order to be the "bride of Christ" seems not only mad, but grotesque. And what of the man who gives up a woman in order to choose Christ as the "chaste bridegroom"? Face is not saved by saying that he is the "bridegroom of the soul," because we have discovered that the soul is not feminine in gender. In this area anybody who loves God can only rejoice at this demythologization. We have finally cleared away the sacred that is not really sacred and a vocabulary which was ridiculous, even if the greatness and authenticity of some persons had purified and ennobled it. Even Charles de Foucauld, who speaks of his love for his beloved Lord Jesus in a sweet and tender language, does not preserve this superficial "literature" from bad taste and from all the ridiculous overlay that covers one of man's deepest and most serious commitments.

When for myself and for those who asked me I sought to discover the logic of chastity, I found three main lines. First, Christ in his *emptying of himself*: the *exinanivit,* the *humiliavit semetipsum,* which Paul so strongly stresses. The second is, "It is not you who have chosen me, *but I who have chosen you.*" And the third: "I have chosen you, that *you might go and bring forth fruit.*"

As far as I know, we have not yet understood Christ's emptying of himself. And there is nothing strange about that because much time is necessary for discovering God. We find the Word in the midst of us and *"we do not know him."* If we did know him, we would not keep saying, "I speak to God and God never answers me." Christ is the Father's whole response, but time illuminates and gradually explicates this response. We understand it more and more until he comes and shows us "his countenance" in all its clarity. "For now we see in a mirror dimly, but then face to face" *(1 Corinthians 13:12).* Thus I believe that we have not yet understood Christ's *exinanivit,* his emptying of himself.

This is a notion taken from both Protestants and Catholics. The former saw Christ struck down by the tremendous wrath of the Father and saw the self-renunciation of the cross and the flesh wounded and annihilated in revenge for sin. In their desire to preserve Christ's divine nature, the reality of his Person, Catholics stressed this will to give in crucified love. In the first view Christ seems almost "thingified" in his hour of darkness, crushed by that satanic power that turns history into the history of wolves. Like all men, he too has been beaten by sin. In the second view we cannot escape the image of a great monarch, of a sovereign lord of the universe who deigns to come and live among us, poor and faithless as we are. Either the kingdom of the earth is seen as a kingdom of Satan in which God has no part, a kingdom which is and will be merely chaos, evil without remedy, the permanent extermination camp from which we can be saved only by escaping through faith to the invisible. Or else it is like the kingdom of France or Spain, populated by people living in misery, a bunch of ragamuffins, who are visited by the monarch who comes down from Versailles to sit at the table in one of the most wretched hovels of his kingdom. The prayer books of the past always brought this image to my mind. And these devotional projections of the monarchy of Louis XIV or Charles V have come down right to our own time.

But couldn't Christ's *exinanivit* be something analogous to the Gospel, which is empty in order to be the channel through which all liberations pass? The word of God is everything and nothing. It is full, it is empty. It is the content, the support, the essence of all human progress, of every road to man's advancement. It continually generates ideologies of freedom and hominization, but it cannot be confined in an ideology. A Christian who reads, who meditates upon the projections of human culture and events, must cry out at every moment, "But this is an explanation of the Gospel!" And cannot something analogous be said about Christ's emptying of his Person? He arrived at the deepest recess, at that depth to which man today more than ever aspires without being able to reach it. It is being the Person in the emptiness of innocence, of total purity. "If you will not be like children, you shall not enter into the kingdom of heaven." But a one-day-old child, a one-hour-old child is no longer a child in the Gospel sense. At birth he is already harassed by monsters, monkeys, spiders, birds of prey, and by that whole grotesque and horrible multitude of Bergman's *Hour of the Wolf.*

Many years before Freud, Saint Augustine in the *Confessions* gave an extraordinarily sharp analysis of the voracity and ferociousness of the unweaned infant. He is not a vacuum, he is already full and inhabited. Truth will indeed enter there, but it will not be the whole truth, nor the truth alone, the free and liberating truth. The great emptiness of Christ in his Person is the great emptiness of the finally pure Being, totally receptive to the Truth and totally open to it. "He grew in age, wisdom and grace," the Gospel says, because just as there was a physical growth in him so also, in a mysterious way, was there a growth in experience; the field of his acquisitions grew larger. In growing he knew more people, more places, more facts, more things. He enlarged the surface of his knowledge, but no aspect of this knowledge reached him deformed, nor did he deform any of these acquisitions of experience, because the Truth completely possessed him. To be born again, to be like children, to become a new creature is the message that runs throughout the whole New Testament.

But we can never be born again down to our roots since we are born old, burdened with lust, avarice, and violence from our ancestors. We cannot be new creatures except in Christ Jesus. Consecration to virginity seems to be this to me: an occupation of the deepest part of one's being. It is God who goes down to the roots of being, to that deepest point where being empties itself in order to receive him. It is God himself who has emptied it; it is the miracle of love. I spoke about this with a married woman and she understood me. Even she felt that her affectivity, her friendship, her love for others, did not touch and never reaches this closed garden, this "sealed fountain" which is one's own and which suffices. At this secret point, this root of the person—it seems to me—we are beyond sex. I would even dare to say that we are prior to sex and deeper than it. It is naked being, being in truth, without fantasies, and prior to choices or outside of concrete choices. It can be compatible with a concrete choice as long as it is not a fantasy and is in the truth.

Paul speaks of a "marriage in Christ," which does not mean, I believe, getting married in the basilica of Our Lady of Lourdes. No, it means marrying in this Center of Truth, becoming one in this free ground, in this tiny cell deep within us where monsters cannot enter because the Word, the Truth that liberates, is already there. Since Christ is not a utopia but a real Person and the incarnate Truth, he can enter there and occupy that space. Here I see the difference between virginal and conjugal love: Chastity can be solitary, availability for him alone, or it can be the chastity of a couple. Human love can remain in the Truth only if it gets down to this level. Here Paul stammers a bit: "Whoever is married must please his wife." He can speak only from his own experience. But a person who has married well has reached this level of truth and discovers this immovable center, this foundation of security, this exclusivity which at times is so far removed from what the person is living on the surface that it is difficult to recognize it. However, it continually sprouts forth like one of those piles the tide constantly covers but which is never overturned or carried away by the current. It exists because Christ exists. This deep center of security does not free the whole being at once; it does not definitively immunize it from temptations and wavering. It tends to liberate the whole being, to occupy the whole "castle," but this comes about slowly. It is slow and painful like all human liberations.

In the Middle Ages, people who made a promise of chastity rolled about on thorns, tortured their body cruelly, took ice-cold baths at night. Modern psychiatry would call them masochists or something worse. Their history is a common one and can be psychoanalyzed and criticized because they did what they could to bring into control their poor person disturbed and tortured by specters and fears. Within them was that awe-inspiring call: "Remember, you are mine"; "Thou shalt have no other gods before me." If this seems to be an overbearing edict, characteristic of an absolute monarchy, within it is a loving violence, the revelation of exclusivity. This basic exclusivity requires vigilance because time is needed for renewing one's whole being. Paul felt that we "bore a treasure in vessels of clay." And if he speaks of a thorn "in the flesh which assails him," he also speaks of an interior security about which there is no longer any question: "Who will separate me from the love of Christ?" Is this not the mystery of chastity which each of us must live?

But this emptying of self on the part of a person is one of joy and achievement. It is the supreme liberation. An honest psychoanalyst would be delighted if he could succeed in emptying a person to such an extent that all of his choices would be in truth. Can we identify this *exinanivit,* this self-emptying of Christ, which is presented as a humiliation, a suffering, with the total liberation of the person? I return to the analogy of the Gospel. The Word of God never allows itself to become enclosed within an ideology; it acts as a channel for everything we think or do in the light of liberation and reconstruction, the integral redemption of the human person. To enclose the Gospel within an ideology is to betray it. It is total, an absolute "fullness" insofar as the Word includes in itself all words, the whole meaning of the true words or fragments of truth which men succeed in discovering in time. To be filled with God, therefore, the person must empty himself in the center of his being, at the vital point of his being. The person continually lives the mystery of this "emptiness" and of this "fullness," which is ineffable and untranslatable.

How can this happen? Nicodemus' nocturnal question to Jesus comes to mind. How can this be? And Jesus answered: "To you it has been given to know the secrets of the kingdom of heaven, but to them it has not been given" *(Matthew 13:11).* "You did not choose me, but I chose you" *(John 15:16).* It is this tremendous mystery that a "chosen one" lives and experiences in a curious mixture of joy and suffering. God's choice, if it is true, if God is God, always elicits astonishment and pain. It is always a loss of freedom, of independence, to which man clings more than to anything else in the world. "Before I formed you in the womb I knew you, and before you were born I consecrated you; I appointed you a prophet to the nations. . . . Ah, Lord God! Behold, I do not know how to speak, for I am only a youth" *(Jeremiah 1:5-6).*

No longer is there any place for the glory of virginity, for the vestal-virgin complex. It is a terrifying choice. And when one preens himself and looks at himself in the mirror, delighting in his white robe and white stole, it means that he is not living the mystery of virginity to its deepest. And if a person does not understand this mystery of a deep emptiness, it means that he is not made for virginity. It is not a decision made from the outside. It is not a choice to belong to a club of the perfect, nor is it some clever calculation to win the adulation of the people. It is the violent and absolute entrance of the Lord into the person. And this determines a whole life within a particular framework, with certain renunciations without which the person becomes divided, frustrated, and mad, or else he enters into the depths of boredom and despair, which will be visible in everything he says and decides to do. Once it has succeeded in becoming humble and scientific and has given up the idea of becoming a metaphysics, it is very likely that psychoanalysis can supply valuable and valid assistance in dispelling the specters, the monkeys, the spiders, the owls, that continue to dwell in the castle. But let it not pretend to decipher some depth choice. It can never reach this point.

Pius XII several times warned depth psychologists to stop before reaching this closed door. Psychoanalysis can be of help in discovering that the closed door is not there, that this secret, intimate corner is empty of God, that the choice is a choice on a level that is not the true secret level of the person. It can help a person to "empty himself" by freeing him from illusions, from the superego. But what then? If God is God, and if it is true that "we shall come to him and shall be with him," this secret room, this center in which God dwells, must exist for everyone. Man either does not find himself at all or he cannot help but find himself in the Being of God. Alone or as a couple, but always in God. Like virginal love, when conjugal love is true, it too must be in God.

In Bergman's film, *The Hour of the Wolf,* the painter troubled by demons lights one match after another, a tiny flame to light up the night which envelops him; the woman who is beside him awaits in terror the coming of the dawn, identified with her terror of the world. She is powerless to save him precisely because she is identified with him. She discovers this herself: "I was identified with him." They were not able to go down to the roots of Being, of the One that is found at the basis of everything, where phantoms, bogeymen, and monsters cannot enter. Both remain outside and above, lost in darkness. And the new being in the womb of the wife will not be born to prevent suicide: A love that is not in God cannot save. Bergman's message may seem pessimistic, but it is not; it is prophetic. In this hell two lonely beings walk along beside one another seeking liberation. They cannot attain it because love does not save if it is not in the Truth. This is what Paul means when he speaks of "marrying in Christ." The woman carries within her, in her flesh, in her psyche, in her spirit, the demand for exclusiveness, for unity. The man carries within himself the demand for plurality, which is basically the call of creation, the invitation to possess the world. If this entering into plurality were not in some way alluring, the man would not accept his role as a man.

But the pathology of exclusivity produces the possessive being, and the pathology of plurality the promiscuity of the male. Either they save each other or both are lost. The same Christ who invited *man* to "become a eunuch for the kingdom" said to the Samaritan *woman*: "Call your husband!" With this phrase he redeemed her from the promiscuity into which she had fallen with the five men who had possessed her. He restores her to her mission of making a "husband," that is, a man responsible for her. However, this responsibility-exclusivity is not the result of good intentions or of decisions made out of fear. It is the result of the new man reborn in Christ. I believe that we do not know or see how, where, or when the redemption of Christ will come. The whole of revelation comments on this point with extraordinary emphasis. "The prostitutes and publicans will precede you." However, I cannot accept the idea that redemption should be looked upon as a hand helping me to get out of the boat at the landing, a kindness and a facilitation. No, without Christ we are lost.

Exclusivity, which is the marrow, sense, and discovery of love, is the sense of God, the discovery of God in us: It is communion with God. If exclusivity does not mean this, then it is not to be found in the deepest recess of being. If it is not a coinciding with God, thought and lived on other levels, at the very least it is degrading. The woman can reduce the man to a baby, turn him into a son instead of a husband, and a forty-year-old adolescent is as sorry a spectacle as that of a mongoloid baby. The person who has not found exclusivity in Christ wavers between sexual promiscuity—which continually alienates him and makes him poorer and more of an animal with every sexual act—or an idiotic infantilism of a second childhood, which lacks even that poetry which is the explosion of the baby's originality. Exclusivity is the gift of Christ. It is redemption in the concrete.

Did not John say that Christ died "to gather into one the children of God who are scattered abroad" *(John 11:52)*? Is this not the meaning of redemption, the meaning of Christ himself? That men deeply sense the tragedy of the diaspora and the nostalgia for unity, for intimacy—like the members of the Dallas Parachute Association who feel the need to take one another's hand in the air while they are falling before their chutes open—is the discovery of the redemption. It is the rediscovery of the sense of Christ. God is One and is refracted in the plurality of men and things, a plurality oriented toward unity. But this unity must be made over again in the center of the person because this is the center of the world, the gravitation point of the whole of history and of all things. And this unifying center that the person is can be preserved and unified only by Christ.

If exclusivity and unity come from Christ and not from us and if it is a gift rather than a difficult conquest, then it is a gift made by God to a man and a woman independently of their characteristics, even if the woman accepts and lives it with a particular intensity because it is less contradicted by her makeup. This does not mean that the woman's suffering is any less. On the contrary, perhaps she suffers more because the plurality of creation is more cruel for her. Horace spoke of "wars hated by mothers" and in its depth this verse is quite beautiful. The woman is ontologically the enemy of division, fracture, plurality, and promiscuity. Her ultimate disgrace is to be made a commodity, a thing, an object among other objects. And perhaps there is no demonstration of the tragedy of the world, of the fierce division among men, like prostitution, which is plurality brought to the center of unity, division effected within the heart of communion.

Christ's mission is to create communion and unity. Everything in him is a return to unity. Matthew's genealogy tells us that Christ descended in flesh and blood from a line of adulterers and murderers, victims, and conquerors. But this tormented and divided line became exclusivity, integrity, and One in Mary's womb. And on the cross, Jesus' body was dislocated, divided, "thingified," and pluralized in order to recreate integrity and unity in the world of history: "For he grew up before him like a young plant, and like a root out of dry ground; he had no form or comeliness that we should look at him, and no beauty that we should desire him" *(Isaiah 53:2)*. Only Christ creates exclusivity and unity in the innermost recesses of the person.

"If the virgin marries, let her marry in Christ." A eunuch is not only one who gives up marriage. In the Gospel sense, the person who marries "in Christ," is also a eunuch because the married person must defend this interior integrity, this deep center of unity which is the solid ground for the reconstruction and redemption of man. It is superficial to think that this integrity is threatened only by sexual attraction. This is a mistake. The woman is often satisfied that she does not have rivals that are blonder, younger, or more appealing. But there are other pluralities, other promiscuities that threaten this "unitary" center of the person: things, the alienation in things. In the customary verbosity of the Bible the directive "You shall have no other gods before me" is commented upon and expanded. "You shall not make for yourself a graven image, or any likeness of anything that is in heaven above, or that is on the earth beneath, or that is in the water under the earth; you shall not bow down to them or serve them; for I the Lord your God am a jealous God" *(Deuteronomy 5:7-9)*. There are other idols, other demons, other alienations. Sexual and erotic plurality is a symbol of them that acquires meaning insofar as the other alienations are present or not. When they are, the integrity is betrayed. If the priest who thinks he is observing the vow of chastity and lives in a pluralized, "thingified" way could see that he belongs to the same fraternity, the same club and stripe, as the businessman who has a lover in every town in which he does business and seeks amusement; if the nun who thinks she is the spouse of Christ and is bogged down in things would discover that she too has the prostitute's identification card in her handbag, because she too has broken the integrity and interior exclusivity—perhaps then the horrible leprosy of Pharisaism, which deforms the face of Christ, would diminish. Integrity is an interior value, immanent in the person. It is the center of his being and cannot be formed from without by a series of precepts and norms. There are attitudes and forms of life which resemble one another but which are actually in opposition. This is the case of an integrity that is imposed and one that is discovered from within. The Gospel sees this and distinguishes the "eunuchs made so by men" and the "eunuchs for the kingdom of heaven." For this reason there is often in this area a curious confusion of language, because one person is speaking of juridical chastity and another of prophetic or charismatic chastity. A pedantic priest, against whom I was trying to defend youth, told me, "Ah, there are two chastities? I didn't know that!" I answered that in Matthew 19 there were not only two, but three.

Charismatic chastity is characterized by a profound interior suffering which is not the suffering of the flesh. It is a self-emptying. This interior unity must be lived in a world that is atomized to the fullest. It is no longer vertical or horizontal, but circular, a place where the logic of principles does not help, because the logic of the event, which often appears to be the logic of the absurd, holds sway. However, it seems marvelous to me that the unifying force and the only hope that can save our culture is the Person. It is no longer theories or the law, but the Person. Unknowingly and unwillingly we are coming ever closer to Christ, who is the Unifying Person, the *logos* and therefore reason. He is the Word. Insofar as he is the Person, he is the principle of illumination and logic. And man today has but one defense: the integrity he bears within himself. What can be said to the despairing painter in Bergman's film who lives as a soul lost in an absurd world? The only saving logic is that of the love his wife could give him if the truth had made her free, not before him or outside of him but with him, in the concrete situation of their life together.

This integrity must be expressed in life. It must become a sign. It must convey to man something of that love of God which "has been poured out into our hearts through the Holy Spirit which has been given to us" *(Romans 5:5)*. It is certain that God loves everyone, but he does not love all men as a mass like a plate of beans. He loves each person by himself as if he were alone. I have never forgotten those long conversations on a rolling hill in my province of Lucca which I had with Mariù Pascoli, in the shade of a quiet little house where we listened to the sound of the bell tolling the hour from Barga. "Our Father," she said to me with that unforgettable voice of hers, looking at me with those eyes that attracted so many artists. "Our Father, no! I should like to be able to say 'my Father!' " She had been reminded of her father who had been killed when she was a small child: "My Father!" And I tried to make her understand that our Father was perfectly compatible with my Father. "Our Father, the common Father, says nothing to me. We people from Romagna are stubborn," she said when she intuited that I was losing patience. My father: The person wants to feel loved as a "thou," not as a number but as a person. And I believe that a great obstacle to chastity today is this depersonalization which is the most common result of making ourselves eunuchs outside of the context of the call to fuller Being.

The young generation is no more sexual than ours. It is more authentic. It cannot accept a chastity that deforms man into an inhabitant of a barracks, depersonalized and depersonalizing. Flight from a woman or a man is not integrity. How does that resemble Mary's integrity? Jesus loved everyone, but the Gospel does not miss the opportunity of saying, "the disciple whom Jesus loved." It emphasizes that he loved Lazarus, Martha, and Mary very much, but "when Jesus saw her [Mary] weeping . . . he was deeply moved in spirit and troubled" *(John 11:33)*. This is certainly not a depersonalized love. Integrity must in some way become a sign of the fact that God has truly entered into the center of the person and for always. It is he who is Being, the basis of every personalization, without whom unity in the world would be sought in vain. I know that it is difficult because all the juridical deformations and all the demons that prevent sex from being a liberating function cover this sign with suspicion, mockery, and ridicule. The courage of the cross is truly necessary. But if chastity does not mature in fuller love and in integrity, which is the capacity for loving the "thou" and for making it exist as a "thou," it cannot be a sign of God in the world of today.

Paul points out a shade of difference between the married person and the person called to virginal consecration. Perhaps we have not yet fully understood it. "But the married man is anxious about worldly affairs, how to please his wife, and his interests are divided . . . but the married woman is anxious about worldly affairs, how to please her husband" *(1 Corinthians 7:33-35)*. He has put his finger on the wound of the great hazard of love. I do not think that the time factor enters into this text, but rather something much deeper. Paul speaks of a life that is not his own, but this does not prevent his inspired intuition from being true. The profound integrity of the married person is dynamic, but it is not something that has been won once and for all. For that matter is there anything that exists that man has won once and for all? Everything in us is in the state of becoming and we possess it only if we live by searching for it day by day. A profound level of relative security does exist, but absolute and definitive security never exists. The couple's integrity is preserved only by being receptive to God, a receptivity that is continually renewed in a vital and dynamic commitment. "Marrying in Christ" means living by collaborating in the building up of the kingdom. The couple is threatened by a crystallization of love, by an identification of one in the other.

The integral giving of one to another is certainly consummate communion. It is wonderful in itself, but it is a contemplative moment which must be broken off and recreated continually by a call which is outside of the couple itself. In the transfiguration something similar happens. In the supreme communion with Christ in the joy of contemplation there is introduced the temptation to be static: "Master, it is well for us to be here" *(Mark 9:5)*. But the Master dismisses this desire. Luke's Gospel adds: "He did not know what he was saying." "The wife wants to please her husband and the husband wants to please the wife," and this seems to distract us from God. This is not because there is anything wrong with this endeavor to please one another, this renewal of a conquest that is continually being broken. Yet the two must not remain fixed, contemplating one another, and thus becoming a kind of narcissism *à deux*. Love is the projection of the two outward. It cannot grow if the desire to be identified with one another causes each party to come out of the deep reality which is his or hers alone. It is the tremendous mystery of love that it is a permanent exodus, an assimilation but not an annihilation of one's self or of the other. It is the giving of one to the other, a transfusion, but at the same time it is the preservation of the profound integrity of one's own self. The danger is in the perfection of love itself. There is no other salvation. Man must lose in every way everything that is nonbeing in order to be saved; he must "lose his life." This is an absolute formula. And all of us are entrapped by staticness. But Paul uncovers the point where this temptation is hidden.

This love between two persons must have a rivalry if it is to be saved, because rivalry is what creates the dynamism of the encounter. When the rivalry of another person or even of objects is no longer present, we must discover the rivalry of God—not as a personal rival, but as a commitment to others, as faithfulness to a vocation which every person has structured within himself, a vocation that is unique and incommunicable. God can hide himself, he can disappear between the two, and the rivalry will disappear. The couple will become enclosed within a circle that seems most beautiful, but in reality is fatal. In genuine virginal love the painful and total gift of self, the complete emptying of the person for God, leaves no room for this kind of temptation. The rivalry of God, who is everything and the sole reason for living, can make a deep communion mature, but it does not permit the quest to "please" one another in the sense we have just mentioned. Therefore it does not allow an identification that would be static and indolent. I would say that the origin of a friendship in virginal love is the opposite of that of conjugal love. In virginal love it originates from God, and a person may encounter a companion along the way. The encounter takes place not in pleasure but in the coincidence of two vocations, that is, in God himself. This is the encounter between Francis and Clare, between the other Francis and Madame de Chantal, between Teilhard and Marguerite or Teresa of Avila and John of the Cross. In conjugal love it is the mutual endeavor to please that is at the beginning and remains at the basis as one of the motives for the encounter. It is perhaps the strongest motive and it continually has to be sacrificed.

The freedom of virgins to "think on the things of the Lord" is not a problem of time or a problem of greater dignity. It is a kind of integrity and exclusivity that is discovered at the beginning. Integrity, I repeat, is a gift of God, of the One. In the case of virginity, it is discovered as fidelity to a personal and solitary vocation, while in the couple it is discovered by the man in the woman and the woman in the man. In virginity the temptation to become static is found in *perfectionism,* in making virginity a state and not the basis for a movement of self-giving that is always new. The "eunuchs for the kingdom of God" are those who are gathered by the Lord and those alone. In marriage, the temptation to become static is hidden in *closing oneself up* within the circle of admiration or identification. In both cases it involves closing oneself up in man. It is the temptation to "be like God," to overflow in the superego, precisely because the temptation is based on an essential structure of the person.

For thousands of years, since the time man's consciousness emerged on the face of the earth, man has been running away from himself; he has been afraid of himself and has been looking for ways to escape. In the couple it is the juxtaposition of person to person, and both make each other afraid. In virginal consecration, the person can fall back into himself and reproduce his double in the role player. Man is afraid of himself, because he is nothing more than a desperate and irremediable loneliness. All the pluralism of things is unified in him who is being and nothing. The person cannot help feeling the responsibility of creation, of things. He is the poor king of a kingdom that is annulling and emptying itself within him. It becomes an empty rind and less than a rind in his hands. This "nothing" is man's fear.

The famous picture Paul paints for us could be called a panorama of fear: "For the creation was subjected to *futility,* not of its own will but by the will of him who subjected it in hope" *(Romans 8:20).* Man senses this void in creation, the being that vanishes before his eyes, and this is his terror. He is pursued by this nothingness that aspires to be filled: "*Creation awaits with great desire.*" Our trembling and impatient history could not be more forcefully pictured, with all the richness of its searching, its experiences, its desire for knowledge. Indeed, there is an immense desire in all that we live and an immense emptiness. *Desire* and *futility* are the two laws which appear in our history. Perhaps there is but one law because the void becomes hope and desire. But man senses it as an emptiness, as irremediable loneliness. "Man will always be alone," Michael said to me the other day. "There is no cure."

But there is a cure, although it is not in us. Closed within ourselves, whether we are alone or in twos or fifty strong, we shall only discover *loneliness.* In John's first letter we have the statement: "There is no fear in love, but perfect love casts out fear" *(1 John 4:18).*

I read and reread this splendid letter and I am afraid to quote it because we can make it a formula that consoles our loneliness. For the act of contrition that I was taught to use at the close of the day, I have substituted an apology to the Holy Spirit for not understanding him, for emptying him, for "grieving" him. I am not sorry because I deserve hell and punishment, but I repent bitterly every day for not being able to understand and bear witness to the Word of God. And I ask forgiveness not because I like to. It is something that strangles me and is too painful inside. I have to beg to be freed so that I may sleep. Is that cowardice? I don't know. I know that God is good.

I had to say this in order to be able to continue writing with this letter of John before me: "No man has ever seen God; if we love one another, God abides in us and his love is perfected in us" *(1 John 4:12)*. If we "commit the sacrilege of speaking as a man from on high, teaching people to pray in order to make God a party to our affairs, the sacrilege of giving religion by the same means of propaganda used to sell soap," as Fromm says, we are acting against God's Word. The Word of God is so dreadful that either we stop reading it or else we allow it to cause all the devastations it wants in us. "For the word of God is living and active, sharper than any two-edged sword, piercing to the division of soul and spirit, of joints and marrow, and discerning the thoughts and intentions of the heart" *(Hebrews 4:12)*.

I hope that each of us can say to God, I do not know if I am converted; I know that I have pain, great pain within me. "Let us love one another" seems simple and attractive because each of us seeks only this: to emerge from our loneliness. Yet each of us also knows how difficult this is. To love in truth, which is the only true love, is difficult. If a person is not to suffer the horror of loneliness, he must suffer the horror of love. The human condition is not blessed, it is a wounded and crucified condition. "So we know and believe the love God has for us. God is love, and he who abides in love abides in God, and God abides in him" *(1 John 4:16)*.

Chastity is not a sign if it does not become love and a love that builds and liberates the person. It must be a total love and therefore a crucified love. We must renounce vanity—the man "pleasing" the woman and the woman "pleasing" the man, the consecrated person's "complacency" in himself or herself and in creating a role player to be put on exhibition. Fortunately, iconoclastic youth has broken the windows of this exhibition and has thrown the grotesque mannequin of the virgin out onto the street. But there still remains within the deep need for communion, the profound suffering of loneliness. In this context, chastity is either the sign of integrity and exclusiveness in love, or it is nothing. In the world's eyes virginal consecration has but one possibility: to discover essentially the secret whereby two persons can come in contact with one another, and walk along together without destroying or emptying themselves, without falling into the chasm of loneliness, but rather in an indefinite progress toward fuller being and progressive enrichment.

Only in this way can our generation find any value in virginity. And through this integral, truly virginal love, it can rediscover God. "No one has ever seen God. If we love one another, God abides in us." This is not a utopia, because I have at times seen the radiance of virginal love when it is authentic. Rarely, it is true, but I have seen it. If it were not so rare, the groaning of man and of nature which sighs for integrity would not be so tragic in the world. Our generation, however, has the advantage of having discovered "emptiness," the pain of loneliness. And perhaps no younger generation more than this one, which is emerging from the taboos of sex and which sees no attraction in the vow of chastity, will discover the authentic value of virginal love. "We have known and we have believed in the love which God has for us." It is a Corpernican revolution. It is no longer I who move, it is God who moves toward me and impels me to the basis of being where there is truth, that is, deep fidelity to myself, to him, and to the person. It is a painful fidelity, however, betrayed and rewon at every moment. If the horror of loneliness is dreadful, no less dreadful is the horror of being nailed to the cross of truth and fidelity. It is so difficult that man constantly flees toward plurality.

"Because he was God," Pascal points out, "Christ did not come down from the cross." The alternative between accepting the horror of loneliness and the tranquility and sense of satisfied well-being of the person who knows what it is to love one's neighbor and who handles all the techniques of love is a false one. It is outside of the perspective of the Gospel. The person is crucified either on the cross of his loneliness or on the cross of love. If there is no sign of the cross there is no sign of the Word, which is the sign of the truth.

9

FREEDOM THROUGH THE CROSS

The crucified Christ has done good and bad to men. This is not strange because all values are values insofar as they have two poles. "Behold, this child is set for the fall and rising of many in Israel, and for a sign that is spoken against" *(Luke 2:34).* The crucifix portrays the image of pain, humiliation, and death, and it can give rise to feelings of horror or kindness, both of which are negative reactions. Most often we are indifferent to it. We are so used to seeing it from our childhood. The only adoration of the cross that impressed me deeply was what I discovered among the miners of Sardinia, who were neither practicing Catholics nor alienated. They were fighting hard for justice and discovered through very simple words the crucified Christ as a brother, a companion in a suffering they did not want. I have seen too often at close hand an unhealthy love for the cross which is a kind of necrophilia or masochism in disguise, a means of exalting the ego, a pretext for escaping a confrontation with life's responsibilities. And it makes me wonder whether the image of the crucified Christ is healthy of not. Perhaps it is necessary to ask this question and to spend some days of discontent and doubt in order to discover the answer.

How much time have I myself spent at Assisi in front of the crucifix which Saint Francis had embraced, asking myself what this image meant. As a child I used to see an immense Byzantine crucifix in my parish church. It did not make me afraid because it seemed that the figure was not suffering very much. What I especially liked was the antique gold background and its hieratic gravity along with the two serious men who stood on either side and who reminded me of two of my teachers. It was always a pleasant surprise to find a good man with a serious and dignified face. At the university I read the medieval mystics, who were the passion of a Jewish teacher who openly professed his lack of religion, and in them I discovered the joy of the cross. Jacopone da Todi pleased and terrified me. And finally, I discovered joy through the cross. I remember that my whole adolescence was concentrated on the problem of living and of living with joy and fullness. Certain phrases made a permanent impression on me: We have but one coin to spend, and it must be spent well; It is better to die once in death than to die a hundred times in fear.

At the age of nineteen, I was deeply struck by a chance encounter, the result of library research, that I had with a humane and most joyful old Carthusian. He did not smile and had a hairy and scraggly beard which put me off. But he had a power to simplify problems which I thought miraculous. I have always been bothered by the insulting self-sufficiency of adults who refuse to see the problems of youth. "Smile and be happy!" has always had the same effect on me as the rich man saying to a poor man: "Play your banjo or drink a glass of whisky, and you'll see that everything will be all right." And then there are the wise counsels of the ancients: "The young should jump and dance, have a good time, and be happy"; "When *I* was twenty. . . ." Even today I am nauseated by this kind of advice, although I too have white hair. I thank God that I still have this reaction. This Carthusian simplified things for me without insulting me. He did not satisfy my desire for self-assertion in a world which is a tangle of contradictions by telling me to go out and play football or find a girl. Everything was dissolved and clarified not in his logic, but in his person. He was a liberated man who liberated. And even today, when I look at the past, my opinion remains the same. Perhaps it was through him that I undertook the way of the cross, seeking through the cross a liberation that I hope is not far off.

I am not speaking of physical death, which does not depend on me and is therefore a useless problem. I am speaking of that liberation of the being from everything that threatens it, deforms it, and turns it into nonbeing. Probably had I asked my Carthusian friend to write down his contemplations on the cross, he would not have been able to do so. I think that if today I were able to write about the cross I would perhaps be quite far from liberation. But I know what I should write: "For if I preach the gospel, that gives me no grounds for boasting. For necessity is laid upon me. Woe to me if I do not preach the gospel!" *(1 Corinthians 9:16).* To catch hold of an outline and attempt to convert the ineffable into speech I go back to the symbolism of the wounds of Christ in which, as the medieval mystics said, we must hide ourselves.

The first freedom is from aggression. This is the whole powerful charge of our energy to live. We exist and we live because we have wanted to. God has placed in being this "spirit of life" which makes it emerge and exist against all the forces that continually threaten it. Aggression, however, destroys being. It is a powerful form of energy under the sign of alienation. We project onto things the history of our person. We use atomic energy, a liberating force, to destroy ourselves. The whole problem is the liberation of this force in meekness, so that we might be "good neighbors" to one another. Isaiah said: "With his stripes we are healed. All we like sheep have gone astray; we have turned everyone to his own way; and the Lord has laid on him the iniquity of us all. He was oppressed, and he was afflicted, yet he opened not his mouth; like a lamb that is led to the slaughter, and like a sheep that before its shearers is dumb, so he opened not his mouth" *(Isaiah 53:5-7).* Mildness, gentleness, nonviolence are qualities looked down upon by men because they often mean destruction, renunciation, prideful compensation. Perhaps now that depth psychology is exploring the subconscious we will succeed in discovering the meaning of this.

Mildness and gentleness that are not in the truth are deformations. If gentleness is a conquest, a virtue, a height that has been reached, then it is a camouflaged form of aggression, it is a wolf in sheep's clothing. But if it is the genuine result of a liberation, then it is liberated energy. As long as they continue to talk about atomic energy at the peace table, we must be afraid because this continues to threaten the world. When it is talked about on the level of technology and is no longer a subject for the peace conference table, then it will be a cause of fear for no one. It will no longer be an energy that is contained or repressed, but a liberated and therefore liberating energy. Peace conferences are war conferences until they have arrived at the ultimate point of deciding that there is no longer any need for meetings on peace.

Gentleness is a liberation when we arrive at peace in truth, when we succeed in accepting the basis of being which coincides with vocation, which is the metaphysical structure of a being who suffers in peace, without protesting, without attempts to escape. He is not enclosed within his own being as an unavoidable fate. He is freed in his own being as in a meadow of flowers. And liberation from aggression must reach into the pulp, the heart of being, where man has become duality and must return to unity, that is, it must reach into the man-woman division or person-creation division, two elements which should be one.

Chastity and communion are the symbols of this achieved unity and, like hope, they represent the prophecy of union. For this reason they are two signs of something that takes place in time, although it is more a promise than a reality in time. They are security for the future. Integrity, exclusiveness, and friendship are the hopes toward which mankind is directed, and they are the ultimate meaning of history. Virginity and the Eucharist are the two signs that the Christian community has been saved through fire.

Freedom from aggression does not come about in a vacuum, but through accepting group encounters in the history of our life as providential and by achieving freedom in them. Perhaps someone may see a trap in this, because I could seek out those events or those persons who have a value of freedom for me or else direct these encounters toward freedom. But in fact I cannot do this because there is freedom from aggression only if I accept and suffer what happens. The moment that love is freed from aggression is precisely the moment that we lose ourselves and give ourselves completely, the moment of total acceptance of what we have encountered. "Like a lamb led to the slaughter and a sheep before its shearers." And this is understood of a hostile event, of something that threatens me. But if it is a question of a personal encounter, this state of being a victim would seem impossible. And yet, how can I lose aggression without there happening in me, an aggressive person, that moment of surrender, of passivity, which I surely look upon as an obstacle, a loss of myself?

A mother whose extreme maternalism and aggression was visible to the naked eye, without any need for a microscope, once said to me, "I cannot and will never be able to ask forgiveness and admit my mistake. I can show I am sorry through kindness, attentiveness, and affection, but not by acknowledging that I was wrong." And she calmly jumped from one side of the chasm to the other, from affective aggression to offensive aggression, taking great care not to fall in. A lost cause! Here words are of no use. Or perhaps I am not skillful enough with words to be of help. "All we like sheep have gone astray" is a vivid picture for me. We are living cheek by jowl like sheep in a sheepfold, and each of us is enclosed within his own loneliness, incapable of bringing about unity: "To each his own." However, in his stripes we can be healed. If we knew how to contemplate at length, in quiet, the wounds of Christ and to let ourselves be pervaded by the peaceful force of liberation, by the flow emanating from his wounded person, we would find within ourselves the way to freedom. We cannot transfer our conflict to him, nor hope to overcome it cheaply: This evening I am ill; tomorrow morning I shall wake up healed or resurrected like Lazarus. From Christ's wounds, however, emanates the strength to accept the chasm, death.

I return to writing these lines with a great deal of emotion, because I have just had a long talk with a German priest who asked me where to find the strength to accept the emptiness of liberation. The only advice I was able to give was "to dwell in the wounds of Christ." Standing in quiet with him, with Christ who often has no face, no tangible presence, is an emptiness. Yet how can we be human, not aggressive, not wolves or lions, but men, if we do not allow this emptiness of the person to live within us?

The sign of this freedom is a strong and humble serenity, which is very far from security and self-sufficiency and at the same time from the despair of doubt. There is but one root to aggression: the richness of the person, his right to exist in the world among others and among things. The feeling that this right is impeded or denied by someone makes us aggressive. There is aggression of assertion and that of negation, the arrogance of force and the arrogance of weakness. The peace of being is a true triumph of the spirit. Not the peace of the cemetery, of nothingness, but the peace of being. It is found so rarely that when we do find it, it is an epiphany of the face of Christ. It is peace in faith. No one and nothing can take from me what I am. They can take from me what I have, but not what I am. Therefore what is the purpose of being in a state of armed defense?

Not everyone succeeds in freeing himself from this aggression, and I would even say that no one frees himself from it definitively. The wolf always lies dormant in each of us. But it is possible to arrive at a certain stability in the peace of being and to be able to give the love that causes growth and personalization by avoiding self-destruction and the destruction of others. There are some who cannot do this without therapy. Why? For the same reason that there is cancer, tuberculosis, and hemophilia in the world. God does not free us from these things from on high.

The second wound of Christ on the cross could be taken as a sign of freedom from the *fear* that is in us as a residue of ancestral horror, a fear which paralyzes our courage and our constancy. In the third of the songs of the Suffering Servant, Isaiah says: "The Lord God has given me the tongue of those who are taught, that I may know how to sustain with a word him that is weary.... I gave my back to the smiters, and my cheeks to those who pulled out the beard; I hid not my face from shame and spitting . . . therefore I have set my face like a flint, and I know that I shall not be put to shame" *(Isaiah 50:4-7)*. This is genuine personal courage, not the courage of assailing others, but of facing up to what assails us.

Often "turning the other cheek" is looked upon superficially and encased within a juridical terminology. And many question whether it is the best tack to take in freeing the world from evil and evildoers. Christ's famous phrase, however, does not do away with justice or lay down arms in the fight against evil in the world. A theory of nonviolence as an absolute cannot be founded on this phrase. It seems to me that the viewpoint of the Gospel is synthesized by Paul when he says "speaking the truth in love" *(Ephesians 4:15)*. To be faithful to this program, courage is necessary since continual oppositions to truth and love present themselves. More than at other periods, truth today is the desire and the defense of the younger generation. It is a resolutely antihypocritical truth, but one that is projected outside of the self.

Each person's truth is the identity with himself sought through an emptying of the self by conquering the constant temptation to other identifications. It is true that Jesus spoke of losing oneself, of losing one's own life, of going into the earth like a grain of wheat. But he spoke of all the superpositions on the true self, which are so profoundly identified with life to the point of shaping the image we make for ourselves of our own person. The confusion between the role player and the person, between identification and identifications, is the cause of many mistakes not only among the youth, but also among people who feel venerable and secure. On the cross Christ gave up his own life out of faithfulness to his true Being, through identity with himself. It is certain that he lost his life, but he did not lose his "self." Indeed, it was by being himself that he lost his life. In this sphere there is a permanent state of ambiguity because there are conservative egotists who do not want to "lose their lives" and think that they are saving their person. They give nothing and end up being totally lost. There are also the prodigal sons who give themselves in search of a truth and an authenticity in giving, but without concern for fidelity to their true being.

The directive "love your neighbor as yourself" is much more profound than the words would indicate, especially in a dynamic perspective. Love for man means wanting man to be what he should be, not by instrumentalizing him so that he will be what pleases me or what is comfortable. It is wanting him to be what he must be in accordance with the structure of his true vocation. I cannot love man if I do not live this kind of love in myself, do not seek the truth in the event, in the situation presented to me, and have no identity in me to which I must be faithful.

At this point arises a discussion of man's vows, definitive promises, and eternal involvements. Can a person living in the permanent fluidity of time commit himself eternally to a fidelity? I would say that he can and must if he discovers that this fidelity is identified with himself. Christ "had to die" because he was a prophet, messiah, and savior. Identity with himself and faithfulness to his mission brought him to death. It was impossible for him not to die, and his repugnance and that of his friends toward death represent a continuous temptation and scandal. He encountered death precisely as a contradiction, as an ambiguity of the world and as man's incapacity to see the truth.

For him to have obeyed Peter and to have consoled his friends who wanted him to remain with them would have been a lie; he would have been contradicting his profound identity. Not to die, to have escaped to some other place, not to have gone back to Jerusalem to go to Lazarus' tomb, would have been the truth of the moment, the objective truth, but it would not have been his truth; it would have been the love required at the moment, but not the love in truth. Faithfulness to the law, to a particular stand, to something external from us, is certainly not in the truth. But faithfulness to one's own truth, to one's own being, to identification with one's self, is love in truth.

How many times this choice presents itself in a person's life, especially in the relationships of love. It is the deepest point of a person's history. In love there is always a truth present because love is the sole force that we have to emerge from our role and to reach identification with our true self. Peter is in the truth when he strongly protests to Christ who is predicting the persecution that is about to befall: "God forbid, Lord! This shall never happen to you" *(Matthew 16:22).* He is in the truth because he loves. At that moment it is Peter's true self that is speaking. His outcry comes from the depths of his friendship, which is true. But this is not Christ's truth. The answer is not cruel. It is deeply human: "Get behind me, Satan!" Christ's heart is in pieces and he must react with all his might, he must say a definitive "no" in order to go counter to his friendship and be faithful to a true friendship: to love Peter in the true love that is his own. This is a profound mystery which touches the vital point of our lives.

Too often these denials of self have been motivated by self-preservation, formalistic obedience, or taboos, because they can be attractive and seem to be a sign to a generation in search of truth. "I prefer to be lost, to go to hell," Michael told me so often, "than to deny a person's demand for love and be cruel." There is no answer. These are two frequencies, two different levels. A person has to succeed in discovering for himself that love is "in truth" and that truth is identity and integrity. I have great hope in the youth and I pray God to give me the patience of the cross, not to come down from the cross, and to make my own that mystery of patience and expectation, that poverty of the cross.

In a report on the still timid and therefore pure hippies of Latin America I read recently: "We are for free love! What do we mean by free love? Not that which is the complete opposite of love, namely, licentious- ness or animal love. Free love is love without barriers, without ties, without the need for artificial documents to give it certification. Not only the love of a couple, between the sexes, but love in the fullest sense of universal love. Love is what nature has given us to live and to coexist with her." The path of love will bring these young people to the truth. Identity with one's self is not taught or learned; it is lived. But it is important that they recognize a love that is not love. Faithfulness to one's self which is fidelity to others demands courage; "I have set my face like flint." It is the courage that the martyrs had. Like all heroes they had the courage to reject a love out of faithfulness to love, to reject the other person in order to be faithful to him, to refuse consolation in order to console. It is not only the courage of the believer in God, for Che Guevara knew perfectly well that in order to be faithful to the revolution he had to sacrifice being a husband and a father. He denied love for genuine love. I remember saying to a friend who died for freedom that prudence dictated that he think of his wife and children. He answered that it was precisely because he was thinking of his wife and children that he had to die for them.

These self-denials are a radical contradiction of atheism and the existential act of faith in Being, because "faith" is the affirmation of something which subsists within the mutability of things. They are like the amplification, the schematization of what we must live obscurely every moment in our choices, which have nothing heroic in them to be told to others, but which have the same value as those acts of courage recorded by history. Today, the courage to live seems to be the courage to accept mutability, time, the loss of identity. But here and there signs of another kind of courage are appearing: a courage anchored in fidelity to Being. The first is essentially atheistic, even if it is covered over by an affirmation of

God's existence, while the second is essentially religious, even if it is lived with a denial of God. "I gave my cheek to those who pluck out the beard." It is the courage of man against man, of the person against the person, which can make man irremediably inhuman or genuinely human on a higher level. The coming generation will reach this point. At a round-table discussion of scientists, this observation, which to me seems very optimistic, was made: "It seems to me that there are at least two aspects of man which, although having many consequences, may be considered basic and will accompany his continual elevation in the future. First, his consciousness, even if it is constantly becoming more universal, will become a consciousness that *above all deepens itself.* Second, pain and therefore suffering—the discussion could be expanded even to include death—is a fact that is interior to man, something permanent, and will be even when science and society will have succeeded in eliminating, externally, both its causes and effects" (Gozzano, *Civiltà delle macchine*, no. 3, 1968).

Man will increasingly find himself faced with his own consciousness, faced with the identity of Being. This discovery cannot be put off because we cannot survive for long without it. It is the sole motivation for living. And when we discover this, we discover pain and the cross not as a "mortification of the person," but as an immanent category for achieving this identification with our own consciousness. There is no longer any room for masochism, for the performance of the cross, because the cross is lived in depth and in obscurity and in itself it is a kind of antitheater, an antisign, and therefore genuine. The cross is a "scandal," not a performance. A scandal is a painful and therefore contradictory sign.

When I find this out, I try to flee from it rather than seek it. Peter is true when he tells Christ: "No, this will never happen to you." And Christ is true when he rejects the temptation: "Get behind me, Satan. You are a scandal for me." Both are faithful to the truth and are therefore in opposition. To create a friendship it is at times necessary to break it. For this reason the paradox of the Gospel is true: "If any one comes to me and does not hate his own father and mother and wife and children and brothers and sisters, yes, and even his own life, he cannot be my disciple" *(Luke 14:26).* There is a very profound sentence in the Gospel: "Blessed are you when men hate you, and when they exclude you and revile you, and cast out your name as evil, on account of the Son of Man!" *(Luke 6:22).* We who have such need for community, for coming out from our loneliness, and live tormented by this thirst for communication: "Blessed are you when men exclude you and revile you" for the Son of Man. This is not out of some formal fidelity, but for the Son of Man. It is out of faithfulness to the Messiah, who in biblical language is the Son of Man. But where is he to be found if not in the deepest root of our being, in our making ourselves small and poor, giving up everything that is not ourselves and that is outside of ourselves? This is the courage a man needs in order to rediscover himself, to be a man and to humanize the world.

The third wound can be taken as a symbol of *loneliness,* which is the great suffering of man today. Growth in awareness seems increasingly equivalent to growth in awareness of being alone. This sickness of man makes a deep impression on me because I am discovering what *pain* is: It is hell. Someone who has not passed through this pain knows merely approximations and figures of pain. He does not know the ultimate point to which man's awareness can descend.

The symphony of this pain I always find in Psalm 69: "Save me, O God! For the waters have come up to my neck. I sink in deep mire, where there is no foothold; I have come into deep waters, and the flood sweeps over me" *(vv. 2-3).* It is a pain deeper than poverty and like death is common to rich and poor. It is a real death, because it reaches the root of being. When we feel "inhabited" in the core of our being, we are never really alone, even if we are by ourselves. On the other hand, someone who does not feel this indwelling within the core of his being is alone even when he is in the company of others. The theologians of the Middle Ages, who were fond of abstract definitions that were sometimes quite graphic, said "God *alone* but not *lonely*" because they saw him immersed in substantial Love—inhabited and inhabiting in love.

Man today, however, is not alone, but he is lonely. The more he lives with others, the more he feels alone. I continually fall into the temptation of wanting immediately to overcome this moment of anguish, of nothing-ness, of pessimism, especially when I discover it in my friends, in the people whom I love and whom I do not want to suffer in this deep mire where there is no foothold. I see then that I fall into that smiling and facile apologetic which I myself have rejected. I seem to be like those who scoff at witchcraft but who run off for the witch doctor when a child is sick and on the point of dying. Man lives in time and we cannot eliminate its stages. If the darkness of the mystics at times lasted for forty years and more, how can we claim to anticipate artificially the outcome of these hours of darkness of our generation? We cannot from the outside, with cheap optimism, deny this darkness and this nothingness which is loneliness.

Neither an external moralism, which seems to be merely authority's prohibition, nor a facile hope can hasten the dawn. How often have I recognized myself in the impatience of Christ's friends to whom he gave the response: "But of that day or that hour no one knows, not even the angels in heaven, nor the Son, but only the Father" *(Mark 13:32)*. It costs us a great deal to come down off our pedestal of prophet and teacher, of "healer," and accept this stage of nothingness in the world. But there is nothing to be done. We can merely hope.

I open the Bible and come upon Jeremiah: "She weeps bitterly in the night, tears on her cheeks; among all her lovers she has none to comfort her; all her friends have dealt treacherously with her, they have become her enemies. . . . Is it nothing to you, all you who pass by? Look and see if there is any sorrow like my sorrow which was brought upon me. . . . From on high he sent fire; into my bones he made it descend; he spread a net for my feet; he turned me back; he has left me stunned, faint all the day long" *(Lamentations 1:1, 12-13)*. We are not prepared for all this because for us God was a theorem, joy a corollary, love the air we breathed, hope the telescope of our observatory. Everything was easy and clear, in this world of objects. We felt like masters. But everything has been turned upside down. Everything has become a problem. It is only the contemplatives and the prophets who can understand today's world, only those who have had personal experience with the darkness of nothingness and those ready to die in order to anticipate the vision of the future. People who are neither contemplatives nor prophets are inevitably overwhelmed amidst the ruin of their structures. Jeremiah did not say: "No. It's nothing. Be calm. Everything will be all right." He wept over bereft Jerusalem, which had been betrayed by all her friends: "How lonely sits the city that was full of people!" *(Lamentations 1:1)*. We know there is a God. But God is difficult and far off. We can see tiny lights in the night. We see that we are painfully advancing in the line of the knowledge of man. But for the moment this knowledge serves only to give evidence of emptiness and incurable loneliness.

We move toward the discovery of society, but we do not discover the techniques for organizing it in peace without suppressing thousands of men and without bringing death to the very marrow of the person where freedom abides. It seems that there is nothing left for us to do other than sit and weep over desolate Jerusalem, as Christ himself wept. He wept and allowed himself to be swallowed up in the darkness waiting to cover the city. It is hard to accept this powerlessness. Yet if we knew how to give the free gift of ourselves to this solidarity of powerlessness and poverty—as Christ did for Jerusalem, without wishing to see more clearly than others—we would certainly enter into the rhythm of Christ. We are not successful in helping man in his tragic loneliness if we offend him by speaking of another earth, of another hope.

This bewilderment, this losing of self, this acceptance of the nothing-ness that can make us friends of man, seems to be a heresy because it is thought of in theological, intellectual, or juridical terms. The Church has always tried to give certitudes and does not accept doubt, shades of meaning, or wavering. For this reason today's rationalists cannot understand youth. Only the mystics and prophets understand young people. The mystics understand because they go beyond the sphere of knowledge, passing through the valley of the shadow of death, of doubt, of the feeling of being swallowed up "in the deep waters and the depth of the mire." It is not they who bring obscurity and doubt to the truth through processes of intellectualistic logic; it is the truth that abandons them. The prophets understand because out of fidelity to the message that surpasses time, they remain entrapped in time. I see this in my contacts with youth; in them I see the lines of demarcation of ideologies are disappearing in the creation of a community united by this same anguish and this same search, the search to escape from loneliness.

Bernanos' country priest is really a precursory sign. He is a poor and haggard man who drags over useless paths his poor body wracked by cancer; he lives in the church and senses there his own revulsion to prayer. Yet he is a man who maintains a deep faith rooted in being. Faith, however, does not seem to dwell in him, in this poor existence wavering on the brink of despair. We find faith in the priest of Torcy, who is almost the first man's antithesis: a healthy body in which faith has become blood, health, security, balance. It is really an intuition of genius that the two generations meet and accept each other instead of being at odds. And the generation of security discovers beneath the ashes of this destruction the sparks of life. "The people who walked in darkness have seen a great light; those who dwelt in a land of deep darkness, on them has light shined" *(Isaiah 9:2).*

Our time mercilessly dismisses facile certitudes, formula faith, and dilettantism. Either faith is discovered at this depth, in the deep mire, "in a land of deep darkness," or else nothing is. Man is truly passing through an experience of himself, and while he continues the exploration of nature, he cannot resist the call of this at once fascinating and dreadful depth that is his heart. And the deeper his insight, the more he feels alone. He has denied the God who is outside or above and does not find him within. "My God, my God, why have you forsaken me?" The only guide for our generation is one who has gone down into this deep place and who therefore can no longer be a guide but only a witness and a sign.

Christ's fourth wound could be taken as a symbol of *antihypocrisy*. The total poverty of the man on the cross laid bare before men gives the image of that total revelation of the self from which we try to escape at all costs. The Gospel of John adds that the soldiers came to give the *coup de grâce* and when they reached Jesus, "one of the soldiers pierced his side with a spear, and at once there came out blood and water." And another passage says, "They shall look on him whom they have pierced" *(John 19:34-37)*. Hypocrisy is certainly not the temptation of the coming generation, but rather that of my own, because hypocrisy supposes certitudes and a certain internal security. A generation without certitude and without security is preserved from hypocrisy. It will not be long, however, before they invent one of another kind, because hypocrisy is man's eternal temptation.

Just recently, speaking with a community of priests that represented both generations, I came to think of the profound transformation that has come about during these last twenty years. The men of my generation know perfectly what a priest is, what he must do, and what the world expects of him. In other words, what the world wants to see in him. The dreadful temptation of the role is too easy and too superficial not to fall into it. The priest of the new generation does not know who he is, what he must do, and what men want to see in him. They have done away with clichés one by one. The young priest's temptation is that of not accepting his priestly existence, which seems to have dissolved away. The content of the polemic between the two generations was basically this: The past generation defended these certitudes, these solid objectives which allowed them to live and to create their roles. We are reliving the history of the appearances of Christ, naked, defenseless, not involved with anyone or anything, in a structure sure of itself, well organized, united by fear, vanity, and self-interest. All ages have seen Christ appear, but to me it seems that this is the appearance before the tribunal, the last appearance before he went down to his death. It is extremely difficult for the men of my generation to accept this stage in which man, after the transition from magical behavior to rational thought and behavior, must take a further step: that of adapting to today's technological civilization.

"But can we think it possible to modify man in his entirety so as to enable him in a short time to adapt to the demands of technological life and to erase the difference resulting from the very rapid advancement of technology? I think not, at least not in a relatively short period of time" (*El Mercurio,* Santiago de Chile, November 3, 1968). How can we be seekers, groping our way along? The hypocrite needs solid bases, objectives upon which to rely. People who have built up their own role see it being pitilessly destroyed. They are aware that they cannot hand it down to the generation that follows.

It is true that the new generation is pitiless and cynical. But with pity nothing is destroyed and nothing is rebuilt anew. People who have only a role are left with nothing: "Behold, your house is forsaken and desolate" *(Matthew 23:38).* A doctrinal encounter is no longer possible; today theological duels are unthinkable. All of existence is involved. And the priest once again turns to man because his sacramental and doctrinal certitudes have disappeared. The bond of obedience to the institution loses motivation if the motivation for existence is not discovered. The priest is a condemned man like all other men if he does not have in his deepest self an undemonstrable and inexpressible certitude, an inner support. It is stronger and more solid than the theological demonstrations contained in all the libraries of the world; it is so intimate that it cannot be objectified, but it gives consolation in the dark hours through which we are passing. Without this, he has no motivation for his life. At times, in those wretched reception rooms of religious houses and seminaries, my eyes chance to glance at vocation propaganda. I don't know what amazes me more: that they were able to arrive at these "motivations" or that they accepted them as motivations.

We can no longer debate. We must give our lives. We have to read and reread the twenty-sixth chapter of Matthew. "And as they were eating, he said, 'Truly, I say to you, one of you will betray me' [The great loneliness]. And they were very sorrowful, and began to say one after another, 'Is it I, Lord?' " *(Matthew 26:21-22).* The sadness of being alone. For this loneliness, for this sadness, there is no other cure than this: "Take, eat, this is my body." This is the response that came out in the conversation with the community of priests: They expect nothing of us, exactly nothing. They don't expect us to be the teacher since there are no certitudes, nor the pastor because they can manage for themselves, nor the father since they have broken with the previous generation. Perhaps they expect us to be a friend, but they mistrust facile friendship because they have already had long experience with loneliness in a crowd. No other way is open for us than that of Christ: "This is my body, which is given up for you." There is no longer any room for hypocrisy. We cannot construct the role of the hopeless one by putting on the mask of Greek tragedy, because the hippies wear flower shirts, orange or pink trousers; and we cannot "disfigure our faces" like the hypocrites Christ saw parading about the squares, because this generation has learned to hide loneliness in rock music or to escape with LSD. "What's your program?" a journalist asked some young people in San Francisco. "Free music in the park," was the answer. There was no place for sour faces. The only thing left is to die for man. Hypocrisy is definitively conquered with death through fidelity to man, because until death we have the right and the duty to doubt ourselves, to be role players.

I discovered this while searching for the traces of a man who attracted me very much, even though I felt so different from him. It was the Curé of Ars. This extremely simple, almost ignorant man, living his existence intensely as a giving of self, found himself in a dreadful state of doubt which was always with him, the feeling that he did "everything badly," that he was role playing. His frightful anguish was assuaged in his giving of himself, and he said, "I do not love because I have not yet given my life." The only really serious thing we do is dying. There is no longer any structure there to defend the priest, just as there is no structure that defends man. And without external defenses, we are also without ground for hypocrisy. Perhaps before resolving the great theme of the future, which is the organizing of the community, man ought to suffer his own loneliness deeply and for a long time. In order to become integrated, we must first of all discover ourselves. Fellowship and communion are not reached without first cruelly suffering individualization.

Only the Christian can live this suffering intensely as his way of participating in the cross. Patiently, he agrees to stand on the brink of the great lake of despair without falling in. "The elders of the daughter of Zion sit on the ground in silence; they have cast dust on their heads and put on sackcloth; the maidens of Jerusalem have bowed their heads to the ground" *(Lamentations 2:10)*. This difficult hope can be lived only on the level of contemplation. On that level, there is no longer any room for hypocrisy because structures and spectators are lacking. Narcissistic hypocrisy is no longer possible because there is no longer even the possibility of being a spectator for oneself. And only this difficult hope can be accepted today by the poor and the youth.

We are about to break another sound barrier, not the one over our heads, but the one that is within each one of us. We can do so not by putting on the brakes, but by courageously accelerating our speed like the first pilot who succeeded in breaking the sound barrier. What does the world expect from a priest or from a Christian? That he have the courage to accelerate and break this barrier. Turning back is impossible. Like childhood memories, certain images out of the past cause us to smile today. We can no longer play the role. We know that beyond the barrier there are new spaces. We know this, but we cannot say it because it is so much inside of us, it is the innerness of our self, which we can objectify only at the moment that we offer our whole being.

Christ's fifth wound can be taken as a symbol of the *triumphalism* that has harassed us like aggression. All of us look for power as a means of making ourselves superior to others and of dominating them. Politicians seek the power of force, businessmen economic power, a woman the power of beauty, a man the power of aggression, the priest the power of the glory of God. There is a clever way of projecting on the saints and on God something that we want men to discover and venerate in us. God and the saints can be useful for the projection of our most subtle desires. We want God to triumph, truth to win out; we want God to be acknowledged. But very often behind this God and these truths are hidden our own self and our own truth. How easy it is to make the transfer from the triumph of God to the triumph of man! To the Romans Paul wrote, "For Christ did not please himself; but, as it is written, 'The reproaches of those who reproached thee fell on me' " *(Romans 15:3).* This is the exact opposite of triumphalism: "Not glory, but the reproaches of those who reproached thee fell on me."

The polemic between triumphalists and defeatists has been going on for several decades. (I do not know what happened in the past. I am speaking of what has happened in my own lifetime.) The triumphalists throw out accusations of defeatism, of Protestant or Kierkegaardian pessimism, of weak faith, and of denying the resurrection. The defeatists accuse the triumphalists of Constantinianism, that is, of connivance with the political power, of superficiality, of superstition, and other choice compliments. At present the defeatists are certainly the more numerous. As always, there are dangerous substitutions because it is undeniable that we can also be defeatists out of a lack of deep faith, out of despair, laziness, a kind of envy of God, or out of protest against the Church. The triumphalists augment the joy of the world, inspire optimism in an adolescent or superficial individual, preserve in the world a smiling picture of God, a projection of people who have no serious problems to resolve. They are the people who say, "Smile and you'll be happy," and for this reason they can count on the protection and the propaganda of many followers of a folkloric religion, of a facile faith, and of a hope that is the "happy ending" to the whole human adventure.

I think that the formulation of the polemic is superficial and inaccurate because it is formalistic. It takes on more a liturgical aspect as a sign, rather than the substance of the matter. In the Gospel there are certainly moments of apotheosis and moments of obscurity, of total defeat. In the sixth chapter of John, we have an account of the vibrant enthusiasm of men who see the "magic" figure of Christ. Having seen the miracle done by Jesus, these people say: " 'This is indeed the prophet who is to come into the world.' Perceiving then that they were about to come and take him by force to make him king, Jesus withdrew again to the hills by himself" *(John 6:14-15)*. And to the Pharisees who were arguing about the triumphal entry into Jerusalem, Jesus answered, "I tell you, if these were silent, the very stones would cry out" *(Luke 19:40)*.

We cannot read into the Gospel either a triumphalist orientation or a defeatist one. Christ's desire was that all men should arrive at the truth and he identified himself with the truth. He asked that the Gospel be "preached to all men," and that "there be preached on the housetops what was whispered in the ear." However, he also spoke of a "little flock," of the "few chosen ones," of "taking up the cross and denying oneself."

No one is authorized, even were he able, to compel great crowds to believe, nor to drive away the crowds in order to reduce the number of believers to a small group. Man cannot make a biological selection of the faith. If the defeat of triumphalism is the result of fidelity to the truth, of a qualitative search for the essential, it is certainly in keeping with the Gospel. If it is the search for an "in-group," for the reduction to a few in order to be in good standing, for a religious purism decided on by one person or group, then it can be the eternal temptation of the ghetto and a new Pharisaism. In the same sixth chapter of John a selection is made automatically, because Jesus does not mince words with the truth. "After this many of his disciples drew back and no longer went about with him" *(John 6:66)*. However, when his disciples were tempted by purism, he reproached them: "Master, we saw a man casting out demons in your name, and we forbade him, because he does not follow with us." But Jesus answered: "Do not forbid him; for he that is not against you is for you" *(Luke 9:49)*. The consistent viewpoint of the Gospel is that of a constant search for global truth which becomes life, that is, for a profound and absolute consistency.

The world lives tormented by alienations, which are discovered to be ever more numerous and more dreadful. There was a comment made in a meeting I attended that "the populations of the countries that have remained backward have primarily a hunger for food, while those of the developed countries are hungry for an ideal." This is the great hunger and thirst for justice which history is in the process of clarifying and amplifying in its search for a solution. We have often asked ourselves what was this justice the Gospel was speaking about. Was it eschatological or historical? At the moment, the horizon is broadening and the idea is becoming clearer. And this broadening of the scope of justice is uniting more men, and especially more young people, in a single and frightening hunger which is exploding in protest, in what has been called the "rage of the poor."

Present structures, whether cultural or political, merely augment the potential of this rage. For this reason leaders look with apprehension to the future. We can bear hunger and thirst only if we know that tomorrow or the day after tomorrow we will be able to reach a place where we can satisfy this hunger and thirst, at least enough so that we can continue along the road. We can live without bread and water, but not without hope. Triumphalism is insulting when it denies this hunger and thirst for justice. Jesus was able to say without insulting: "Blessed are they that hunger and thirst for righteousness" because he allowed all the alienations of the world to flow together over him and permitted his person to be rent into pieces to that point of identity and of essentialness, to that nucleus of Resurrection without which destruction would be total destruction, the end of history, chaos, the denial of truth and of God, the irreversible fall into nothingness. For us this is unthinkable and inconceivable since we are in the state of being. Jeremiah's lament seems like the fabric for a Bergman film, the plaint over all the alienations of man: "I am the man who has seen affliction under the rod of his wrath; he has driven me and brought me into darkness without any light; surely against me he turns his hand again and again the whole day long. He has made my flesh and my skin waste away, and broken my bones" *(Lamentations 3:1-4)*.

Jesus bore the alienations of man upon his shoulders. He allowed them to pierce him like a sword and to flow into him like a violent torrent of water, like a rage that reached to the very place of hope, to that center of being and life that always triumphs over death, that wins out over all dissolutions and corruptions. We continually see the triumph of love and life over death and all human generations will see it. But death will be the permanent challenge, the constant provocation to creation, history, and man. Till the parousia, the final coming of the Son of Man in glory, man the spectator and actor will live out the great drama of the cross, wavering constantly between fear and hope. Triumph exists, but it is hidden beneath the cross, and well within the darkness. It is a hidden hope.

At this point I cannot help but think of Saint Dominic in the San Marco museum, seated beneath the cross. I think it must be one of Fra Angelico's paintings which I have contemplated on the most. Dominic is seated. He is neither sad nor happy. He is in contemplation. In the painting there is neither the desolation of Calvary nor the gaudy holiday atmosphere of Venetian and Flemish painting after the fifteenth century. I have often thought—and perhaps the experts will laugh at my analysis—that after the "fearsome journey" in the medieval wood and before becoming "carnal" in Renaissance Florence, between the alienation of the spirit and that of the flesh, man stopped under this particular Tree to rest a while, to be himself. It seems to me that there he found the deep and painful joy of being himself. So many times, and still today, have I tried to sit beneath the cross in silence, without words and even without feelings. If only from the wounds would come down on me something of that quiet and deep force which would help me to live with the men of my time: "As dying, and yet behold we live; as punished, and yet not killed; as sorrowful, yet always rejoicing; as poor, yet making many rich; as having nothing, and yet possessing everything" *(2 Corinthians 6:9-10)*.

10

POVERTY AS FREEDOM

"Blessed are the poor in spirit, for theirs is the kingdom of heaven" *(Matthew 5:3).* It is not only the Gospel that has discovered the coincidence between poverty and happiness. Every philosopher, at least since Socrates, has discovered man's relationship with nature. It is a polemical and dialectical relationship and posits an alternative: dominate it or be dominated by it. Or for those who are less strong—often considered the most wise—escape from it. In its process of mutations, in its perennial state of becoming, nature involves man, while man has an intimate experience of his identity and his place in life. For man to "exist," to reencounter his identity, he has to detach the pulley that connects him to the machine of nature.

This problem that has confronted man for twenty-five or thirty centuries—to speak only of our own culture and the age that we know—has been handed down to us. And I think that we will also hand it down to future generations without any definitive resolution, because it is part of the structural problem of man and his history. The whole Gospel is an invitation to poverty as a rediscovery of the self, of the new man, of the genuine man who is to be reborn "in water and the spirit." It is therefore a call to man to become liberated from all his alienations.

Seen from the outside, this is a message from one poor man to other poor men, the marginal people of Israel, those toward whom the prophetic preaching was directed by preference, leaving aside the rich and the self-sufficient who awaited nothing and no one. Taken out of its context, the message can be interpreted in contrary senses: as resignation ("Do not concern yourselves with time that quickly passes, and prepare for the kingdom which will come"); as a provocation ("Blessed are you who are to bring about justice, and therefore you will be the hungry and the thirsty who perforce must take a step forward toward a greater justice"); or in a personal sense ("Blessed are you, because you are freed from the concerns of the world and can be about the things of God"). However, this last sense can be understood in a dangerous way because it is authentic only on the contemplative level. And it must include the love of nature; the contrary would be pathological and a psychological deformity.

When we look at poverty as a "virtue," we place it outside of its Gospel context because poverty is not a virtue, but rather an emptying. The conquest consists in being master, cultivator, and guardian over the earth. "I will give this land to your descendents after you for an everlasting possession" *(Genesis 48:4)*. "The Lord God took the man and put him in the garden of Eden to till it and keep it" *(Genesis 2:15)*.

If we see poverty as something separate from man and his history, we cannot avoid Pharisaical casuistry—as we try to define its content—or the temptation to write books on poverty, thus insulting the poor. What the poverty of the Gospel is, and therefore what its limits are and how it must be lived today, are themes for discussion, round tables, conventions, chapters of congregations, and meetings on every level. The Gospel is used to defend the most diverse and even contrary conclusions, because it is true that the "Son of man had nowhere to lay his head" *(Matthew 8:20)*. The poor Son of Man, however, went to the house of Zacchaeus and of Lazarus, accepted invitations from rich publicans, and wanted a more comfortable place to sit down and eat for the last time with his friends. To put it in a proper perspective, we have to speak of poverty from the viewpoint of wealth, just as we must speak of antimatter from the standpoint of matter or of nonexistence from the standpoint of existence.

The Gospel proposes to man the courage to live by *overcoming the challenge of time.* In the famous paragraphs on man's cares in Matthew 6, stress is laid not on the sparrow who is happy with what is enough for the moment, or on the lilies of the field who grow in splendor without worrying about their existence. Rather it is on the discovery of a faith made authentic by our being liberated from the fear of tomorrow. Believing in God-as-Providence does not mean uttering his name, which could be false, but rather genuinely and practically relying on the fact that "God knows what we need." The central focus of the discourse is "Seek first his kingdom and his righteousness" *(Matthew 6:33)*. If priests had all been consistent in preaching this as a formula that differentiated the believer from the nonbeliever, or if they began to do so today, we would deal the death blow to capitalism. Capitalism is antireligion because it first seeks profit, the proliferation of money, and then—through this—deludes itself into thinking it is striving after justice. It is essentially atheistic and is not saved from atheism either by a verbal profession of faith on the part of one who accepts it or by all the good deeds capitalists may do. Its product is insecurity, which is the exact opposite of faith. Even though it is shrouded in darkness, faith is security in man's innermost being and the rock upon which "the wise man built his house" *(Matthew 7:24)*. It produces insecurity in the rich person and this is the real motive for his religiosity, a religiosity which is the symbol of atheism. It is a sacrilegious show, genuine sacrilege, the true profanation of the Eucharist, not of the sacramental bread but of the real body, because it is a denial of God, violence done to things, violence wrought on the mystical body of Christ.

Capitalism also produces insecurity in the poor man and is therefore the cause of his profound alienation. If he is religious, it is for the same motive as the rich man. It is an ontologically false motive because he strives to escape insecurity by losing himself in another, more alienating insecurity. In it he loses the basic support of his search for his own identity. If he is not religious, he will never discover the deep root of his freedom and therefore will pay dearly for the social struggle; he will pay with still other alienations. One of Aesop's fables comes to mind. It is about a horse and a man. The horse says to the man, "Why don't you give me a hand so I can avenge the offense I received from the boar?" And the man declares that he is ready to help him: "Let's go." And he got up on his back. When the offense was avenged, the horse said: "Thank you very much. You can get down now." But the man never got off the horse again.

We no longer know how to escape this tragic chain of alienations. If the Gospel actually advised us, as we might superficially think: "Do not busy yourself about what you will eat for your body is unimportant; think of the soul," it would indeed be the book of alienation. This is not what it says, but rather, "Do not have as a motive for your existence eating, drinking, and piling up capital. *Seek the Kingdom of God and his justice.* Seek the kingdom. Don't wait for it. Bring about the kingdom of God and his justice. Strive to be the man God made you."

The Gospel insists upon the eternal theme: "Do not seek just any ordinary justice, one of the many you have thought up in opposition to another, but seek true justice, the first justice which is that of God and which is yours. Seek this justice, which is both structural and vocational.

Think over your true destiny again, and achieve it." Is this possible without destroying an order? If we all thought seriously about this, we would not find the youth revolution of our time absurd but in accordance with the Gospel. It is certainly uncomfortable and dangerous, but it is not absurd. The graffiti scribbled by unknown youths on the walls of France are expressions of the prophetic attitude of young people today, even if they are quotations from revolutionaries or surrealists. They savor more of the Gospel than certain invitations to order that we come up with in opposition to them, or than our complaint about authority destroyed, or authority in crisis. "The passion of destruction is a creative joy." "Don't liberate me, I'm all right by myself." "Once your eyes are open, you can't go back and sleep in peace." Youth is in the process of discovering that our "justices" are not justice, and they cry out loudly to us to have the courage not to call justice whatever project we are involved in. If we stubbornly refuse to listen to them, they will break windows, put bombs under our easy chairs, and tear down our buildings. "The economy is wounded. Let it croak."

Do they know what they want? They do not want anything because it seems they only want to destroy things, we say in our smug wisdom. They confront us, however, with an immediate and inescapable duty, the will for man's integral conversion: "To build a revolution is also to break all the chains that are inside." The justice of the kingdom consists in reproducing the image of God on earth. This is the person who in all his deeds and in all his relationships seeks the bond of love. This is the man who discovers that his own accomplishment can be achieved only in love. He cannot do this if he is not poor, if he does not liberate himself, in his process of becoming, from all the desires that make him turn in upon himself and prevent him from giving himself to others. The rhythm of Christ, the giving of himself to man, the giving of the body as a complement to the giving of the word, is the eternal and unique rhythm of man. Youth's mistrust of authority is a mistrust of the words of the adult generation, because the word is creative only if it is a symbol of the gift of self. Every discourse, even if it is formally sacred and just, is unjust, dissociated, and desacralized intrinsically if there is an existential attitude of selfishness, or the concern for self-preservation. We are becoming aware of this and this is a step forward, a giant step toward the understanding of the Gospel. The Gospel without the Eucharist is one of the many projects of justice which do not save the world. Christ spoke and gave himself. He spoke of his indwelling in man, of his identification with man. To all the wise men who are asking what youth wants, there is only one answer: "They want you to guarantee your justice, your plan, by a commitment to give yourself. And nothing else. All those projects which result in your self emerging economically sound, in your achieving prestige, and in your status being more secure, can only be failures, even if they were well intentioned."

The sign of the liberation of this self is that all our projects are freed from fear: What shall we eat? What shall we drink? What shall we wear? In contemporary terms we might say, "What profit is there in this investment? What is the profit curve that the economists will work out for me in this enterprise?" It is clear that the role of the economist will always be more necessary in an age in which production is no longer on a personal level, a direct relationship between the producer and the thing. But everything must be thought out with an eye on man's real needs. The profound motive of my existence must be to "make friends by means of unrighteous mammon" and not to make mammon my friend, without being concerned whether this friendship is making enemies for me.

The schema we worked out interweaving the relationship between external and internal poverty, the poverty of the spirit and the poverty of possessions, enters fully into this perspective, because it reaches right down to the roots. Man must live seeking the kingdom of God and his justice; he must seek himself in love, which is the equivalent to willing with all one's might that each man should be. We return to the problem with which we are involved. To live we must know how to accept being poor, we must be able to reject what is superfluous, be watchful that desires do not crop up within us, and know how to reject the pressures of desires that come to us from the outside. We must do violence to the violence of advertising, the oppressive strength of capital which forces me to work for it, with its enticements of colors, sounds, and voices. We are living in an enchanted wood, and we are irremediably alienated if we are not liberated by a profound concentration on and a violent fidelity to our existence as Christians, as men of the kingdom.

One of the famous manifestos on the walls of the Sorbonne said this: "A new society must be formed on the absence of any selfishness and self-idolatry. Our way will be the long march of brotherhood." These are old words, but as rediscovered by the youth in a climate of need and therefore of truth, they take on the freshness of hope. If we could attempt a structurization of the Gospel, a message which seems closer to poetry than to mathematics, it seems to me that it could be presented as a fundamental motivation, a call to man at the roots of his being, at the very center of his life. Before making any decision, man must rediscover himself. Out of these deep roots there arise the decisions that are motivated by the truth which man has rediscovered in Being.

These decisions are two. One seems more radical and the other more common, but both converge because if they do not end up in love, they would no longer be in the image of God. Practically they must be the articulation of the structure of the person, which is essentially love. In chastity, the basis is integrity rediscovered in God, the identification point of being, through a renunciation which becomes an integration, or through an integration that postulates a renunciation. The two paths meet in the justice of the kingdom, in the liberated person, capable of relating with a creative love.

In the sphere of poverty, the root is found in the sixth chapter of Matthew, in which man, stimulated by a need to set up a relationship with things, is driven to the depths of himself. It is the fear of things rather than their use that drives him to this depth. But fear always arises when we look for a relationship: "Do not be distressed"; the necessary relationship with possessions produces distress. And Jesus invites us to emerge from this distress above all through the path of the contemplation of Being. These things which fly out of our hands, which seem so fragile and so bound up with contingency, are really not. This seemingly insecure world which threatens your interior security is not as you think. It is assured in Being. "Consider the lilies of the field, how they grow; they neither toil nor spin; yet I tell you, even Solomon in all his glory was not arrayed like one of these. But if God so clothes the grass of the field, which today is alive and tomorrow is thrown into the oven, will he not much more clothe you, O men of little faith?" *(Matthew 6:28-30)*.

Jesus reveals the beauty of the world by freeing it from futility. Our generation no longer succeeds in seeing a creator God who presides over the life cycles of nature and man. But like no other before it, it does sense the beauty and futility of creation. Its anguish comes precisely from the discovery of this futile beauty. If you bring architects, politicians, and technicians together, they immediately begin insulting one another, trying to pass off the blame for the decay of our cities. Men ask themselves, "What have you done with beauty?" The Gospel brings us back to the security of being, liberated from economic interests. Outside of the economic category, an artist or a contemplative is at times able to see things in themselves, as coming from the hand of God. Without this rediscovery of the essentiality of things, the use man makes of them is necessarily altered.

On this basis two decisions are possible: "Make friends for your-selves by means of unrighteous mammon" *(Luke 16:9)* or "Go, sell what you have and give to the poor" *(Mark 10:21)*. Either of these can be made only by the new man, reborn in God, who rediscovers the true value of things. Without rebirth, in man's hands riches become the riches of unrighteousness, and selling what he has and giving to the poor becomes an escape. The control, the sure test, is to "make friends." For every decision that does not result in love is wrong at its very root. "Making friends" means to look in one's use of possessions for a horizontal relationship, because the vertical one, directed from the higher to the lower, necessarily provokes an aggressive response. It seems impossible that such a simple and clear psychological law is still not understood by the rich. Americans wonder why their aid provokes aggressive responses as do the ladies dedicated to charitable causes and anyone else who gives from on high. The United States certainly does not lack psychologists and sociologists who have explained this. But perhaps it is not comfortable to admit it. It is not only money, grain, sugar, and rice which come down from above like alms that provoke an aggressive response, but also teaching and words. The university professors are amazed that the behavior of the students is parallel to that of the workers toward their employers, while it would seem that the teacher-pupil relationship should be completely different because there is no exchange of possessions. However, if teaching is "alms," that is, a relationship of one who is above with one who is below, of the "haves" with the "have-nots," should we expect anything but an aggressive response?

Socrates already intuited this when he defined his method as maieu-tic. He felt that he had inherited the skill of his mother, who was a midwife. A teacher helps with the delivery of the truth that is within. This is a horizontal, dialogue relationship. The whole Gospel is an invitation to go down, to place oneself on the same level, and—in order to correct the deformities that have grown up in the use of authority—to place oneself beneath as someone who "serves." In this sense material poverty becomes the poverty of the spirit and both become united and inseparable. All relationships must become friendship, that is, a searching together. They must become relationships between two who have nothing and who are searching, two bereft people, two poor men, not a relationship between one person who has everything and another who is empty. "Make friends," and therefore wages must vanish, along with slaves and those who work for others. All enterprises must become communitarian, that is, they must be a community in which everything is clear, in which the various responsibilities, projects, and earnings are shared, and in which everything is thought out and put in common. Money, which is a symbol of things in history, is an instrument of divisiveness and must become an instrument of fellowship, a vehicle of friendship rather than a vehicle of war. This demands a community in production, in distribution, and in consumption. If someone produces for another, for someone who is not accountable for anything, if distribution is decided by someone from outside and above the producer, if in the ultimate use of things there are many products that are not available to everyone, society becomes not a friendship but a permanent battlefield.

The poverty of those who have and who cannot or should not give up their possessions consists in using these possessions to make friends—but not in the manner of the Sforzas or the Viscontis who killed and robbed and then confiscated the money of the poor to build pious Charterhouses. This "making of friends" must be rethought in time and continually renewed in its content. It is another case of the empty fullness of the Gospel, of its nontemporality and up-to-dateness. Only fifty years ago this invitation to make friends could be understood as making bequests to hospitals and orphanages and putting one's conscience at peace before death with generous wills that represented the crumbs from the sumptuous banquet served on the shoulders of the workers. This is like that fourteenth-century Italian merchant from Prato who lived for the accumulation of money, thinking that he would devote himself to the things of the soul in his old age. But he was seized by such an anguished fear that he had to leave everything to the hospital in order to die in peace. Today, this "making of friends" enters into the dynamic sphere of psychology, economics, and politics. It is embodied in political ideologies which eliminate as much as possible the vertical relationships and the distinction between the thinking and directive brain and the anonymous arms that move. There emerges a view of money as a symbol of union and not of division. A new view of poverty is also born, which is no longer the classical idea, synonymous with indigence, but rather the renunciation of personal interests in order to achieve a friendship that is understood as co-creation. All landowners say that their farms are a community of friends, and all the great bosses of industry will tell us that they form a great family with their dependents. But we must always transcend the psychological and affective plane in order to see what is structural and real.

Is it a structure of true friendship, or is it an unjust structure, hidden beneath smiles, donations, and acts of goodness like pilgrimages, tours, and Christmas and Easter presents? The person who seeks this real friendship through real structures is not indigent, but he is poor because he is rejecting the cunning of the world, the opportunity that has put into his hands a tradition and an economic theory that have been maintained over the centuries and butressed by tempting experiences. He is poor because this means that he still has the heart to "feel like a man," to grasp the sense and savor of the person and therefore of friendship. He is not yet completely walled up in things. He still wants to discover them in beauty, in a state of freedom. His eye is still capable of seeing things as they are, free from an economic superstructure, as a value of themselves, and of seeing the truly free person among things.

In *Populorum progressio* Pope Paul said that new formulas and new theories had to be invented to save man from this common alienation: the two worlds, one of which is hungry for calories and the other hungry for ideals. In order to invent these new theories, it is necessary that the working hypothesis be the desire to transform. But how can a person transform if he has control over money, which is a symbol that someone has collaborated with him, even if he does not know who his collaborators are? He has in his hands a symbol of friendship, which is either a good—and those who have collaborated in bringing it to him are his friends—or it is an evil—and then he cannot use it. In reality that does not exist. He is in no way a friend of those who have given him their time and a little, or a lot, of their lives for this possession to reach his hands. Therefore it is a sacrilegious symbol, and by means of it he continues to commit sacrileges and to divide the world. Today ideologies are circulating in the world which propose a structuralization of a more just society in which friendship is possible, so that each person can enter into a relationship in accordance with his vocation and no one can attack this personal freedom. But the formation of such a society seems so far off. In the name of the Gospel we must tirelessly preach this truth: Man must be a friend of man and not a friend of money; money must be the sacrament of friendship and not of division, the maker of peace and not of war. The Gospel ought to stimulate this quest and this experiment by its denunciation of any other view of money as sacrilegious, wicked, and atheistic.

All these denunciations, however, are just words without the liberating function of poverty, of the poverty of renunciation: "Go, sell what you have, give to the poor, and then come and follow me." Here the Gospel might seem to be self-contradictory because "to give to the poor" is almsgiving and therefore the opposite of "making friends." A poor man, however, can give alms. In dividing the piece of bread he had begged with the poor man he met on his way, Saint Francis was giving alms, but this almsgiving was horizontal and not vertical. The Franciscans who are sitting around a well stocked table in a monastery, which is certainly not a poor man's hovel, and send via the porter the same bread to the poor man waiting at the door are giving alms vertically. The first provokes a response of loving brotherhood; the second necessarily provokes an aggressive response. This explains the explosion of repressed aggression in mission lands against those who had done only good and the violent and indiscriminate destruction of charitable institutions and even the benefactors themselves. It is repressed anger which almsgiving did not succeed in eliminating, but rather contributed to intensifying. Men are ontologically brothers and the affective, psychological, and political expression of this racial brotherhood ought to be friendship. As long as this does not come about, history will search for it through paroxysms and bloodshed.

The poor man can give alms to the poor, but the rich man cannot. He would be causing harm. A friend of mine suffering from cancer told me that he experienced a deep joy because he felt he was sharing in the suffering of the world. He felt purified and on his way toward his encounter with God. And everything he told me was most beautiful. But it would never occur to a healthy person to go into his room and say, "How beautiful! How lucky you are! You have cancer!" A poor man can find joy in poverty and sing about it, but a rich man cannot preach it to the poor. Almsgiving is an injustice if it comes from a rich man. It is love when it goes from one poor man to another, when it is a vehicle of friendship.

Poverty as institutionalized in the Church has almost always lost its value as a sign. It ought to be a sign of the contemplative state, of the Church that creates a state of security in insecurity, and of the capacity to grasp the true being of creatures. The contemplative state is above all one of *security and vision.* The poverty of "Go, sell what you have, give to the poor and come," the poverty that is called perfect, ought to be recognizable in these signs. Institutionalized, it can give only free rein to a wretched casuistry, which instead of being liberating greatly restrains freedom of action and instead of being a sign is a countersign. Total poverty is not the liberation from the responsibility of possessions. Even here we can speak of three classes of eunuchs. One of the three is the poor, those who are poor because they have found God as an inalienable possession, as true wealth, and therefore do not seek any other riches and do not serve another god. Thus poverty cannot be discovered on an intellectual level, but on the existential and therefore contemplative plane. The sign is this deep interior security that God is truly the being that fills all, that "Man shall not live by bread alone, but by every word that proceeds from the mouth of God" *(Matthew 4:4)*.

The theme of security and insecurity is very relevant today because capitalism makes man insecure. People who are hungry for calories are insecure about tomorrow. They continually ask themselves if there will be work tomorrow and health enough to work and sufficient money to continue to have what their family needs. People hungry for ideals suffer from the insecurity of futility. They see all things and themselves in the midst losing substance. It is the anguish of nothingness. If religious poverty is supposed to provide two securities—an economic one because the religious is assured of his living despite any economic risks, and a psychological one because faith gives him the security that God exists and that heaven is waiting for him—how would this "poverty" be a sign? It is one of the many well thought-out sociological structures which can serve as a model on the political plane, but is in no way a redemptive sign. The security of total poverty can be discovered and therefore transmitted only on the level of poverty. Otherwise we provoke an aggressive response. Poverty is a necessary complement to faith, and it is the sign of faith. Only a poor man can speak of God as Providence and therefore of the Christian God who does not abandon any of his creatures, who has numbered the hairs on our heads.

Many followers of the Gospel today are seeking to become poor in order to discover a poverty that is not to be found in books or discovered at meetings. But they do not succeed in hiding the fact that they are mimics. Not all of them are playing a role. Many are sincere, but they are wrong in their motivation. The *coup de grâce* for capitalism will not come about without uprooting the root of insecurity, which is the true evil of man. Insecurity deforms man's perspective because a world seen with an attitude of fear is not the real world. It deforms things because it makes them futile. Art today is not beauty. It is truth, as always, because it seeks a new relationship with things. Because it is not liberated, the world is not beautiful, and the artist perceives this. When we speak of surrealism, we speak of a true realism which man seeks above and beneath deformity. I think that the motivation of this new striving for evangelical poverty is wrong. If it is an expedient pastoral measure to become like the poor and thereby make religion acceptable, it cannot avoid being vertical and thereby provoking aggression. If it is a tactic to share in the social struggle and to make the poor aware of their condition, it does not go to the root of the evil. It merely adds one or three or four units to the liberation army, and that is certainly something. But by doing this, it takes away from this army the small group which has the commitment to bear witness—at a depth that theories cannot reach—to the fact that security is possible. Saint Francis gave rise not only to a religious movement, but also to attempts at democratic structures within the verticalist and monarchical Middle Ages. And there flourished an art in which the poor man, the man of the streets, not the counts and princes, expressed an immense security. The figures of Giotto are imaginable only in a society which is secure and secure without arrogance. Evangelical poverty must be worshipful. It must be discovered afresh in a direct relationship with God and therefore be a liberation from everything that mediates between God and men, between man and man, between man and possessions, a liberation from everything that engenders insecurity.

If the poor man, according to the Gospel, is not someone who by sharing in the anguish of men discovers love and beauty within, he finds nothing new in the world. "God: I suspect you are a left-wing intellectual," an inscription says, and it is the perfect definition of the rethinking of evangelical poverty. Charles de Foucauld did not go to Beni Abbes to propagandize or to teach, even if in the beginning he had the zeal of an evangelist. He went there to worship and seek God, not "through" or "by means of," not "making use of," but alone with himself, face to face with a Thou. He eliminated the intermediary out of an ontological and existential necessity. He left the road that prevented man from being himself and therefore from being the naked I, the I in truth whom the God-Thou seeks. And he rediscovered man as he is in truth and in a brotherhood freed from categories, from the limitations of race, religion, and culture. Living among the poor is essential. "Go, sell what you have, give to the poor." Making oneself poor is an indication that is valid for all times. But it is necessary to interpret precisely what this invitation requires: "Come and follow me," because there is no other way to evangelical poverty.

I know it is dangerous to judge poverty from the outside, like all decisions of man. Everything can become deformed when meanings are sought. But a serious and authentic person is safe from the danger inherent in this search for meaning, and *this search can serve as a test to decide whether this is evangelical poverty or not.* The test is security and vision. Poverty is the sign of a person who has found a security which is true, which allows itself to be seen because it is not supported by any other means and is in the pure state. A rich man's security is a form of violence, not a value. It is materialistic and atheistic. And the state of poverty of the religious is of this type. The insecurity of the poor man is also not a value. It is violence suffered and therefore the motivation for a violent response. We do not imagine evangelical poverty as a third and nonviolent way: This poverty is neither political nor antipolitical. It does not exhaust man's function nor does it fill his whole space. There was a book written about Father de Foucauld as a politician in regard to Africa. He was a man and he remains a man with all of man's commitments. But as a Christian who felt the invitation "Go, sell what you have, and come," he filled poverty with infinity.

Until the end of history the anguished struggle will continue in the world to discover dynamically the relationship of the person with possessions, a relationship which is a projection of the interpersonal relationship. Basically, and in different forms, it is the problem of love. History is in process. We shall certainly die leaving this struggle afire in the world. We shall hand it on to future generations. No one can escape the responsibility of taking his proper place, no one, no matter what his status. A person who lives in evangelical poverty must announce by his life the victory of man and must indicate the way to reach peace. The kingdom of God is among you, the kingdom in which man sees man without economic indicators, as a liberating relationship, in perfect Franciscan happiness, and finally, in the liberation from the profound anguish of being neighbors yet never meeting. If evangelical poverty is not the proclamation of the kingdom of God in the world, it is a commodity, it is nothing. Happiness must not be announced, but lived. A woman in love does not tell everybody, "How happy I am." She shows them. The poor man in the Gospel sense is only the person who has discovered personal liberation from things. He is one who possesses the kingdom of God, who makes it seen in this world because he discovers security and essentiality, that is, the beauty, the true beauty, of things. Things lose beauty when they become empty, and they become empty because they lose essentiality. Economics empties beauty from within because it takes away essentiality, alienates things, makes them become a symbol of another value. This was discovered by Marx. But his program to save things from alienation does not save them from futility. Hunger for calories is followed by hunger for ideals. Seeking poverty in order to enter into the universe of the poor seems to me to be a praiseworthy step. It can be an act of courage. But it is not complete fidelity to the Gospel unless the poverty is a basis for contemplation and becomes contemplation. When faced with the world today, Christians, whether angry or satisfied, revolutionaries or ritualists, are in both cases traitors to the Gospel.

I note the temptation in the Christian to turn back and separate the religious element from the political element, while the effort to unite them should be constant. For it is clear that if religious poverty were a sign of alienation, it would cease to be a sign in this world. I think it useful, then, to stress the need to fill freedom with the infinite. A contemplative can and must share in the anger of the poor. A sentence of Father de Foucauld's could be written on the walls of the May revolution in France: "We cannot be silent dogs." And perhaps he is a prophet precisely because in discovering poverty in contemplation he had a glimpse of the possibility of living the contemplative life without betraying the poor. Jesus advised a rich man to sell his possessions and give what he received to the poor in order to make himself poor. Therefore he authorized something which appears to be a "camouflage" today, a kind of disguise. And indeed it is when it is a striving after a result, an efficacy, if it is not continually saved by the depth of prayer, which is a continual return to the root of being, a return to my true, essential reality.

Everything that is "virtuous," that brings "merit," that is a means for other things, necessarily produces role players and therefore hypocrites. The poor man does not have the "virtue" of poverty. He is not poor in order to evangelize other poor people. He is poor just as he is a man called Anthony who was born in a particular house. And poverty has deeply marked him, creating this concrete being, with reactions, moods, desires, violent moments, this being of hate and of poetry. Someone who is not poor and is invited by this mysterious voice to leave everything ought not to think that he can become a poor man, because he would be playing a role and would be making a complete mistake. In this case, poverty would not *be* this person; it would be a chosen companion, a suit of clothes he wears. He would still be marked by all the reactions of a rich man, of a person who has power. What is formed, then, is a hybrid. On the deformities of a rich man are superimposed those of a poor man, added from outside, and the result is a grotesque role player who is out of place both among the poor and among the rich.

One cannot make himself poor. He can only empty himself to the roots of his being and therefore achieve that powerlessness, that interior poverty, which is then reflected externally as the love of essentiality, as a profound security that is not a self-security. It is a rediscovery of things anchored in God, in Being, and therefore gives human hope a new dimension. The division between those who hunger for calories and those who hunger for ideals is an unfortunate one. It can be used in a geographical sense to sketch out a map of hunger. Yet everybody is hungry for ideals. A digestive apparatus transported by two legs just does not exist. What does exist is a person who walks around with a full or an empty stomach. The poor man is a person who is hungry for ideals like anyone else. The rich man who becomes poor, going and selling what he has and giving it to the poor, and who stops at that point, sees the poor man as a mouth and a stomach. He insults him more than the rich man, who at least sees him as an enemy, fears him, and therefore sees him as a person. A person who has become poor, but not through the Gospel, sees the hunger of the poor man. But the poor man is more hungry for love, for that love which is a person-to-person encounter, than for bread. The violence he has suffered for thousands of years has depersonalized him. Even he has fallen into the temptation of flight into the superego through the violence he has suffered. If we speak with a night watchman, he will tell us that everyone, from the president on down to the lowliest employee, has to ask his permission to enter his factory. He is playing a role just the way his president does. Only the president does so by other means. In a town in Venezuela, one holiday, almost everybody got drunk. The poor on rum and the rich on Scotch. But everybody was on the same level.

The "selling everything and giving to the poor" of the Gospel was not counseled with a view to the social struggle, nor to evangelization, nor to imitation. It was counseled because only to the extent that man divests himself of what alienates him and seeks identity with himself can he discover God. Just as chastity is the sign of love for the person which is freed from aggression, and therefore the true discovery of the person, poverty is the sign of a relationship with things which is freed from aggression. What is most urgent is saving the poor from their saviors, because both those who want to push them into violence as well as those who preach resignation to them see them as mouths and stomachs and not as persons. Father de Foucauld sought only God, and he was so serious about this that he isolated himself in the desert of Beni Abbes and thought of building a wall that would protect his solitude. But he left it unfinished, because man, the poor man, sought him out, and everyone had the right to seek him out, to sit down beside him and to speak to him. It was not he who was searching. The poor man was looking for him. He could not be anything but poor because prayer is a mockery if things come between a person and God. It is impossible to serve God and Mammon. And it is not really possible to find God if the poor man is offended by a power structure which implies pertrified violence and oppression. Love of God is false if it is lived under the sign of violence to our brother. He is not a poor man; he is a seeker after God.

It seems to me that we can establish certain premises about evangelical poverty, which is so much discussed today. The first is that we cannot seek after and love what is not, and poverty in itself is a nonbeing. A person who is poor is in the truth because he is seeking being, whether he knows it or not—to be more economically, to be more in dignity, to be more in love. His true being is the aspiration toward fullness. The person who becomes poor goes in the direction of nonbeing, of a void. And if this is not done in view of a genuinely fuller being, of an identification with oneself, it is a travesty. The poverty of the Gospel is a consequence of the "Come, follow me." To stop there and to be in nonbeing, to remain resigned to this state like old people waiting for death, cannot constitute any kind of an ideal. A revolutionary, a conspirator, an artist, a researcher, all these are the poor, because they are so absorbed by the ideal they truly live on the level of the person that it is not possible, even if they so wished, for possessions or money to come between their person and their ideals. They can come from behind or from the side, I would say, but they cannot intervene in the dialogue of the true self with the expression of himself. Because if they could intervene, the person could cease to be ecstatic, contemplative, and true. He would become alienated. In the world, there is a secular "Come, follow me," and how do we know if behind it the Word is not hidden? But the interference of the things that exist in the world can mislead man as long as he does not discover the roots of poverty of being. The function of evangelical poverty is that of discovering the depth from which the call "Come, follow me" comes, and therefore how much security of the absolute and how much stability it brings with it.

The second premise is that a person is not poor in order to become a symbol. This truth must also be rethought. A young couple walking arm in arm and looking into each other's eyes with that ineffable smile of young people in love is a sign that fills me with joy and optimism. I am filled with tenderness perhaps because I discovered in a year in the desert what the abyss of loneliness and death was and the culmination of happiness that comes about when one feels oneself loved. But the two young people do not love one another so they can be a sign. They are a sign for me, and I who am outside receive the message with an enrichment of my being as a kind of help given to me by both of them. If I had gone out that morning with the idea of suicide, I could have concluded, "No, life isn't so gloomy. There is still love, youth, and fullness." I am a sign when I do not know it. It is not I who make myself a sign. It is others, people I don't know, who can receive my message. But of what importance is that to me? It is important to me that God is known and loved, because I am convinced that this alone saves man from the unhappiness of loneliness and saves things from futility. Can my neighbor discover God through me? A person who has had an experience of God always finds himself faced with this question without ever getting an answer. There is no unctuous hypocrisy about what the Gospel suggests. It is the truth: "We are useless servants."

A person is not poor because he likes to be or because he wants to be. He is poor out of necessity. Poverty is violence, a necessity, and therefore in it there is emptiness, constraint, the opposite of choice. There is a necessity which is the result of violence and injustice, which is proper to many victims of the permanent delirium of a few. To go back to the analogy of the eunuchs, these are the poor made so by men. They are the real eunuchs, because the violence of a few prevents them from realizing themselves as persons. This is an empty, useless necessity, a privation which is nothing; it is solely the futility of being and is contrary to the fullness of God, the mandate to possess the earth, the great human vocation to transform it, to co-create it in time. The born eunuchs are those who love nothingness and emptiness. There are also eunuchs for the kingdom of heaven, those who are driven to emptiness by the necessity for self-emptying, for being themselves, those for whom it is no longer possible to think poverty, to calculate or define it. Those who are outside it can crystallize it juridically and formally, but those who live it cannot.

For this reason, the state of poverty is exposed to a great misunderstanding. In the Middle Ages, Francis' marriage with Lady Poverty was the cause for a celebration. People sought to make visible what was invisible, that is, the secret that in him had become poetry and happiness, contemplation and security. Even Dante joined the game and wrote of Lady Poverty, to whom "like death no one was pleased to open the door." Francis bore within himself the sign of liberation in joy, which is security, and in contemplation, which is poetry. He permitted a misunderstanding which nourished the art of Giotto and Dante, that of personifying emptiness in "Lady Poverty." But no one has ever seen Lady Poverty. History has not yet forgotten this martyred man in the flesh who rediscovered the stars, the flowers, water, fire, the sun, birds, and all creation—which he saw ultimately liberated from anguish and made truth and poetry.

11

DIALOGUE OF FREEDOM

One day I was driving through Santiago de Chile with a doctor in his Volkswagen. We were on our way to the nearby locality of Maipú, and the doctor, a believer, wanted to talk. He asked me what to pray about and said, "None of my acquaintances prays, or at least in the old traditional way. Maybe we pray without knowing it. Maybe we do better than our parents because we're not looking for peace in prayer. We're not asking for any grace. We don't believe any more in the magic god who solves all problems." In my answer I avoided giving him the tract on prayer—which, moreover, I did not remember anyway—and told him about my own personal experience. And I don't think there is much more to be said, although I said little.

People from my generation are coming out of a cave—to use a Platonic image—in which we saw projected the image of the magic god, powerful in love and powerful in revenge, and our prayer was motivated by fears. That God not punish me, that he be good to me, that he be my ally—these were the motivations of our prayers. We concentrated on the way the prayer was formulated, which had something magic in it.

Was this attraction for magic created by religion, or is it something that is deeply rooted in man? This very morning in Santiago a group of teenagers ripped off the buttons from the suit of their idol, the Spanish singer Rafael, and they are selling them now for 50 escudos ($5) apiece. Despite the impressive cordon of police, the fans of the singer broke into the enclosure where their idol had gone to bring flowers in honor of one of the national heroes. There they fought to grab a petal or a piece of a leaf that had been barely touched by the sacred hands.

161

Statues and images of the saints are less and less venerated and kissed, but the passion for relics continues to be strong. This does not lead us to conclude that it would have been better in this case to have had the image of Saint Aloysius instead of Rafael and to have sold little holy pictures of the saint for $5 apiece. It is worth keeping in mind, however, so that the reaction of religion might be more forgiving or at least more tolerant.

This doctor felt that he had emerged from the sphere of magic and had discovered that there was nothing left.

On prayer lies heavily the whole tradition of magic, alienation, and deformations, through which it passed in its various stages. It is somewhat like language, which has preserved quite visibly all the signs of its various stages of development, from the grunt to the word, from the cry of fear or concupiscence to the cry for the bond of community. Prayer is becoming something quite remote from us because it appears either as a sign of man's inferiority, destined to vanish once he has grown up. Or it appears as a duty—and therefore something alien to life—which supposes a vision of a sovereign god to whom we must pay a toll in order to walk about on the streets of the world. Or else it seems to be something frightfully complicated and metaphysical, and man today feels increasingly less prepared to climb this high ladder since it is quite unclear what we shall find at its top.

It may perhaps be necessary to change the starting point of prayer and to go back with another spirit and another experience to the Augustinian path. We will no longer be seeking a God who is outside and above, but the God who is deep within us. I feel that prayer is above all a seeking, a seeking different from the scientific one, because it is more one of simplification and reduction than of development. It is a seeking in the depths, toward authenticity, toward truth, toward flight from illusion, toward liberation from what is deforming and superficial.

Prayer certainly presupposes faith, since without faith in the renewing and transforming Spirit, it would be nothing but a gross and alienating psychoanalysis. Prayer is the search for the center of liberation. As such, prayer can lead us to alienation because it presupposes the Other. It presupposes that basically we cannot give salvation to ourselves. But it also presupposes that every man should achieve it, even though he is not the ultimate salvation and liberation. In this sense, prayer implies a real, qualitative leap into faith because, as long as there is no renunciation on man's part, no existenial acknowledgment of the fact that he is a creature—a recognition which on this intimate level becomes an act of love—faith is not faith.

The tendency to identify faith with an eagerness for justice is very widespread in the world. And it is true that faith in salvation and liberation is manifested in the vigorous and hopeful acceptance of the struggle for justice. Our generation has become increasingly indifferent to truth for truth's sake, to the static "God who is." It wants to discover faith in a becoming, not the faith that is, but the faith that becomes. This is a reaction against the fossilizing concept of faith considered as a possession that only has to be defended from thieves. In a rich sense that is very much in keeping with contemporary sensibilities, Paul spoke of a truth which is done in love.

In this vision of faith identified with doing, and with doing justice in the world, prayer is absorbed. Involved here is an endeavor not to separate man's speculative or contemplative activity from his action; the Savior is identified with salvation, and salvation is obtained in the concrete effort to pass from oppression to liberation. This view has made possible the encounter between the believer and the nonbeliever, both united by a common faith in liberation, which the believer identifies—without asking too many questions—with the liberator.

This is a noteworthy step forward and a return to the Gospel, to the prophetic tradition in which the knowledge of God was expressed in a commitment to the triumph of justice; a true return to God was concretized in a struggle for justice, to free the person overwhelmed by the unbearable weight of the evil caused by man in the world. But the point that distinguishes the Christian from the non-Christian is faith in the liberating Word, in the Word in whom all prophecies are fulfilled, the authentic force for liberation within liberations. For all liberation, when made concrete and historical, is therefore limited.

We can combat the great cancer that is today called "sacred-secular dualism," a denial through identification. We can drive it to the last piece of earth beyond which is the void, but we cannot deny it without denying the faith.

Marcuse's *The One Dimensional Man* impressed me, because it seemed to be the projection of a culture that is terrified by alienation and projects its terror into the most obscure space of metaphysics, seeking to liquidate the last feeble resistance that comes from this space. According to Marcuse, only one thing exists: *man,* who bears liberation within himself. and this is the first step. In the second step, Marcuse stresses that man *is* his own liberation. Therefore, there is no hope for man: His search for justice and liberation—which should be creating faith—is destined to fail because no faith originates from it. Marcuse holds that the developing countries cannot take a direction different from the one that leads to one-dimensional society, from the one against which youth is more or less confusedly revolting.

The identification of Christ with man ("We will go to him and be with him;" the parable of the vine and the branches; "It is no longer I who live but Christ who lives in me"), which is the marrow of Christian revelation, has in fact remained in the shadows. It is a vision that has not been studied and above all not been lived, on account of theology's concern for defending truth in itself, a God totally distinct and separate from the world and from man. Is it inevitable that the sacred-secular distinction should turn into dualism and that this dualism should be projected in the world, causing the alienations from which we are suffering today?

I think not, and I am more convinced every day that the solution of the problem is not in an intellectual synthesis that a genius like Thomas could work out with detachment and serenity, sitting at a desk. The problem of the human dimension today is at the barricades and can be discovered only at those same barricades.

Consequently, I am anticipating: I believe in prayer as a painful, long, and difficult personal search for this mystical identification of man with God, which is not projected as a dualism in the history of the world. For this reason, I have spoken of prayer as a search, which in order to be serious cannot be a search on account of others but must above all be a search on account of oneself.

If it is a search on account of others, no one and nothing will save it from the contamination of wishing to be a sign, a teaching, a pulpit. In this regard I feel that today's crisis in prayer is very healthy. We cannot shorten the stages of history. There must mature in each of us the anguished sense of being no longer able to pray, the feeling that we have been followed for a long time by the specter of dualism and alienation. God is really found the moment we discover we have lost him.

The image that we have of prayer must be destroyed in order to rediscover gratuitous prayer, as a discovery of the true spiritual dimension.

Prayer is a dialogue with a view to identification. The initiative comes from God, who is at the basis and is perceived as a call away from things toward the center. Everything has been said: If someone has been called, I must believe in the one who does not feel he has been called. And if it is a dialogue, I must be silent before the creativity of the dialogue.

Indeed, we cannot write about prayer, we can only recommend an experience of prayer. The only thing that can be said to a Christian today is that faith comes about in the search for justice, because in this struggle faith in liberation is incarnate. The Gospel never separates love of God from love of man, and I believe that the meaning of this union is not so much the once-and-for-all unifying of the two sources of love, but rather it gives us verifications. There will always exist two moments for man: that of work and that of attention, that of reflection and that of execution, which are the two sides of the creative act. Both moments must be historically based so that man does not become lost in abstraction or in empiricism, but in time and in quality they remain separate. It is true that the love which becomes contemplation and that which leads us to the struggle for freedom are but one love. But the contemplative moment is the moment of clarity and vision and of the discovery of being in love. We must not ask of prayer anything more or less than this. Here we can make a first examination of prayer. When we speak of clarification or light, we must not understand by this that prayer bestows the privilege of seeing the future with clarity, that it frees man from his doubts, his struggles, his bewilderment, that it shortens time or increases one's strength. No, it does nothing of this. Prayer is a discovery of the essential nature of love, the discovery deep within me that I am loved, that man is truly loved.

It is the overcoming of one's essential loneliness and therefore the victory over uselessness. It is not a definitive victory, however, because whoever discovers it must be ready to lose it and regain it at every moment.

The wane of the Constantinian age, of the Counter-Reformation, signifies a decisive orientation toward poverty and authenticity.

To destroy religion as an alienation, it must be destroyed as a power factor. In postulating a Church that is "distinct from but not separate from the world," the theology of Vatican II gave a definitive blow to the Church as a power and therefore to religion as a power. And it was natural that a whole movement should arise that demanded that this new vision be faithfully put into practice: The Christian as a Christian has no right to power, that is, to have means with which he can act externally on society and oblige it to make determined choices. He must share in the power and the powerlessness of man by joining the fray like everybody else.

As a man he will live the drama of political power, economic power, the drama of the power which gives him his status. It is a drama because power is an instrument of efficiency and is at the same time a generator of tensions, aggression, and therefore of deep anguish.

As a Christian I must claim recognition for my freedom of opinion just like the Moslem, the free-thinker, or the Jew. But I must not claim any special power to modify laws, to impose my will, the will of my group, or my faith on others by external force. The problem becomes particularly acute for clergymen and religious, who find themselves in a status that is a power structure and do not know how or to what extent they must disinvolve themselves.

This is one of the reasons, perhaps the chief reason, for the tensions in the Church today. The problem is complicated and heightened by the fact that the person is not free. He is monopolized by being conditioned in a thousand ways and is so manipulated that a religious propaganda which would be capable of competing successfully with these power structures might seem defensible. Perhaps the political forces are not the strongest in this competition, but rather the forces of advertising. These are the normal vehicles today for a philosophy of life which is without human roots and is therefore completely depersonalizing.

For my own part, I think that because of this competition, today more than ever, religion must be able to offer this zone of freedom. Only in this way can it be accepted and understood by man; conversion will have this orientation: liberation from those things that condition man.

Renunciation of power ought not to be a renunciation of the strength which is the profound internal security we have spoken of above. The Christian will always have the task of "conquering the world." The age of the Crusades, of the power of arms, of political, juridical, and economic power, is over; but the view of life as a struggle, the definition of the Church as militant, of the conquering missionary Church, and therefore of the Christian as a "conqueror," will never pass away. We must have the courage not to renounce these images, even if the memory of the Middle Ages, the Inquisition, and political integralism is still fresh and very much with us.

The difference consists in that we now go from outside to inside, from power to strength, from a security incarnate in structures to a security without structures. Here is the real point of division between Christians within the Church. And to this point can be reduced the real meaning of the problems of the "grave of God," of the death-of-God theology, of "atheistic faith." God was made into a power factor; it seems that with the power dismantled the theology which upheld the power will disappear, and thus God, the faith, and everything else will disappear as well.

The Christian must urgently propose another alternative. Between the Christian strengthened by the power structure on the one hand, and the desperate man, defenseless in the face of alienations and lost without any hope for freedom on the other, there must be presented the man liberated in the deep security of faith. "And this is the victory that overcomes the world, our faith" *(1 John 5:4)*.

We must announce the death and resurrection of the Lord, something which dies and which is born, death in hope. Day by day, the motivation for existence is diminishing, and mankind is more than ever in need of a search in the direction of hope. And this search is prayer.

I think it is very dangerous to accept certain convictions that are basically very old: Everything is prayer, time for prayer is a luxury and an alienation, love is prayer, prayer is discovering God's action in the world. I do not argue with this. But I hold that more urgent than popularization of knowledge is the discovery of man's hope. Consequently, knowing how to defend the contemplative zone is already a sign that the person is saved. And therefore it is the hope of salvation.

Even the liturgy may not be a zone of freedom for the person. Of its own nature it ought to be. It ought to be the sign of liberation in love, but it is not always this because it does not always authentically express the liberated person.

Knowing how to discover the contemplative zone in which one continually sees again the identity with himself, the meaning of vocation which is the meaning of life, is a sign of maturity in prayer.

But is not this leisure a luxury permitted solely to monasteries freed from the worries of existence? I told my doctor friend that it was not. Everybody should be able to open the Bible, to allow himself to be penetrated by the Word of God, and to rediscover in this Word, listened to in depth, his own freedom.

It is necessary to rediscover constantly who I am, beyond my commitments, my obligations, and the complexity of things. All of this presupposes that "the Word became flesh and dwelt among us and we saw this glory" *(John 1:14)* and that someone is at the door calling *(Revelation 3:20)*.

I seek this quiet and this separation because "I hear the voice" and believe in this mysterious intimacy, in this living in God. Our culture leads us to consider faith as recuperable and demonstrable only in the terrain of social struggle and involvement with history, since only in my *being* with men am I a man of faith. Another and equally basic dimension in the Gospel, however, is that of God among us: "If anyone hears my voice and opens the door, I will come into him and eat with him, and he with me" *(Revelation 3:20)*. It is a voice that cannot be heard except in quiet. We have to take the initiative to open the door and to listen.

Prayer understood in this light is not the privilege of aristocrats because it lacks formulas, does not demand education, and is simpler than might be imagined. I know this from my own experience. In an extremely poor region of the Argentinian Northwest, I did some research among people of little culture, without any religious education whatsoever, and with certain convictions that came out of the clouds of superstition and magical alienation. In contact with Protestants, these people discovered that "God who is within us," with a certain polemical tinge against Catholic extrinsicism. And I saw how this idea, a very simple one laden with consequences, framed them in a faith-security that to me seemed free of alienations. They expected nothing from this faith. They discovered the error of a prayer and a practice aimed at asking for something and discovered in prayer the need of not abandoning the struggle for liberation.

I think I did not allow myself to become too enthusiastic and to judge too emotionally. I know that the polemical factor can be of considerable influence, but in this case it was of little importance since it was a group of people who were not religious, at least in practice. There was also the factor of novelty. I saw that this kind of prayer and this particular path were possible for a simple man. I touched with my hand the truth of "Come to me all who labor and are heavy laden and I will give you rest" *(Matthew 11:28)*. I discovered the possibility of a prayer for the poor, outside of the structure of intellectual class privilege. I also discovered that prayer belongs essentially to the poor because, if it is the discovery of God within us, it is unavoidable that one have nothing to preserve.

The challenge that the world of today and tomorrow has for the Christian and the believer is this: to see whether he has been able to discover that other dimension, the truly human dimension, which asks not so much for discovery as for the itinerary, not the formula but the experience. In our culture it is not possible to hand on hermetic or definitive values or hidden treasures. Nothing is understood if it is not in a dynamic perspective unfettered from arguments of authority. Since our generation finds separations horrifying, it is necessary to know whether this path is reserved for the few separated from the world, or whether it is practicable for those living an ordinary life, without special privileges or structures.

Predictions of the future say that tomorrow's man will have much time and little space at his disposal. But it is necessary to discover today, in the tightness of temporal and local space, this pathway that leads to interior space. There is no method that teaches it. Only as a witness is it transmittable. Faith always requires courage, and courage today consists in overcoming the barriers of criticism and fears which have been erected around prayer and in setting it on a path on which we might get lost. I should be grateful if the Christian had a little more of that spirit of adventure, that acceptance of the risk of being burned, of being unable to turn back, which is so typical of youth today. It seems to me that our Aristotelian upbringing induces us to avoid risks when we do not see everything clearly and definitively and do not have our return ticket in our pockets. Basically, in accepting the risk of the human condition, in exhausting the problem of faith in the struggle for justice, and in accepting simply the historical sphere there is, if we look closely, a flight from and a search for security. As the clerical structures that protect me fall to pieces around me, I instinctively look to the human community for protection. If fleeing from "religious alienation" in order to be a man like the rest of men can be an act of courage, it can also be a search for security: I am a little terrified by the risk of being alone, of undertaking an uncertain quest, a no-return expedition that probably would make me lose my popularity, my credit, and my small status. Yet it is only at this price that I can gain faith. If God exists, if Christ has truly risen, if it is certain that he lives in each one of us, if this promise to remain with us until the end of the ages is true, I ought to meet him, feel him, touch him in some way, and this contact ought to transform me. It is the verification for which the world is waiting.

Anthropology proposes two problems to be resolved: man's profound loneliness and his alienation in things. He has to have the courage to walk ahead through his loneliness in order to discover the meaning of adoration. If Saint Francis discovered it, will not I too be able to discover it? It is said that Christianity has not contributed anything but alienations and deformations, that Christian culture has been only magic and fetishism from which man must be liberated. Indeed, we should not defend these fetishes, but on the contrary we should be happy that these structures are falling to pieces. If we believe Christ is God, we know that what is collapsing is only the plaster, the baroque decorations which time has added to the original picture. The Christian must seek the true God. Because he sees this God and because he is a contemplative, the prophet is an iconoclast. However, how can we distinguish the destruction caused by prophecy from the destruction coming from desperation? Only time will tell.

But there is a sign that can become increasingly obvious—the courage of faith. This is humility—which is different from the fearful timidity and the resigned masochism with which some people identify it. It is the result of a discovery in the faith, the discovery that it is not I who will save the world, nor is it a thousand "I's" who will do so, even though my mission as a man is to give myself to the task of liberating the world with all my being.

But there is a liberating function which is not taken sufficient account of and which goes to the root of freedom. It is the rediscovery of the true being and true value of things. The person seems insensible to truth in itself, to the metaphysical value of persons or things; the whole truth is in the existential act. Last night, in a conversation with some young people, the discussion settled on a priest who had gone to live with a married woman. She had left her husband and children. The unanimous opinion was that he had done right because this was his truth and because both were consistent with their own selves. Then, this morning, I opened the newspaper at breakfast and was struck by an interview between a journalist and a revolutionary. The introduction to the interview repeated pat phrases: We're sick of dialogue; take care of your weapons after using them; clean them as carefully as possible, otherwise the damage can't be repaired. Then he spoke of youth: "They look at life and see the mediocrity with which we have become accustomed. We are living in a world of lies, of conventions, in which it is at times more important to wear a tie than to tell the truth. The young person is very clear about this. He is fed up with lies and denounces them with great ease. . . ." This is all very true. But how can we put things back in their place? With revolution? Yes, and this is our historical duty, our way of loving one another. I am not the one to decide, on paper or in my lonely meditation, what love is and what decision to take; the decision arises out of a heartfelt, open, and receptive encounter with the community. However, as a Christian, should I not bring a sense of the profound to this revolution? History places in love the flesh, the real, and the concrete, but Christ places *the true* there, without which love is illusory. "Do the truth in love."

I remember the time I spent with some miners in Sardinia. The drillers who went down into the mine to open up the way through the stone had two rubber hoses along with them—one for water and the other for oxygen. These were secondary in regard to the work the drillers had to do; they were accessories that did not open up the rock. In the same way, a person cannot live, nor open up his own path, without knowing the real meaning of things, without this vision. Scholasticism defended the value of being, of the real, of the essence; but it cannot compete with today's culture, which is a search for the phenomenon, an observation of the phenomenon, and the courageous exploration of the unknown; it is the acceptance of "how it is" without concern for "what it is." Yet men feel that there is need in the world for a clarifying function. There is lacking the presence of an Adam to give a name to existent beings: "So out of the ground, the Lord God formed every beast . . . and brought them to the man to see what he would call them; and whatever the man called every living creature, that was its name" *(Genesis 2:19)*.

"Now things have no name," say the youth as they rip up the cobblestones and break windows. "Everything is a lie." There has begun to circulate in public opinion, and especially among the youth, Marx's discovery that merchandise, the thing, "ceases to have value for us because of its concrete qualities, its real properties. This is to say it ceases to have value in itself, in its relationships with life as it is. It is valid only in relation to this abstract object, this impersonal thing which is money." Man is thus incurably altered and therefore alone, profoundly alone, in the midst of altered things that have lost their name. And in discovering that he is in a world of lies, he feels impelled to become involved in the struggle for freedom when hope sustains him—or in drugs when his motivation weakens. The Christian must know how to discover value in adoration, but not as an act of pleading to the sovereign lord who waits upon his throne for the homage of his subjects. No, adoration is the discovery of things in their pure state, as they are in truth and not for what they are worth or for what their use can be to me.

The *Song of the Creatures* is an attitude of adoration. It is the discovery of the proper being of the creature among creatures and therefore an emptying of every right to possess, to take something for oneself. Marx felt the very acute desire to rediscover things freed from the economic value man attributes to them, beyond and outside of alienations.

The poetic expression of this discovery is the *Song of the Creatures*, a lyric expression of a fact recurring in history. It is an act of adoration in which man discovers himself existentially, not on the intellectual level, but on the level of life, as a creature, without the right to occupy a place higher than the rest but a place among the others—horizontally. Here Francis discovered himself among and with creatures, and for that reason he called the sparrows, fire, water, the stars his brothers and sisters. Neither a master nor a despot, he is one among these creatures. I do not see how we can rediscover things liberated from alienations outside of this function of adoration.

If this adoration were man's only activity, then it would be alienating. It is very easy to feel oneself a creature among creatures without feeling responsible for the use and abuse made of them. The moment of adoration must be interrupted, as Jesus abruptly interrupted the contemplation on Tabor. But for a man who has seen things in truth, it is impossible to deform them in a false structure and to give them a value that is not the true one. He will leave them in their proper place with the proper meaning, using them solely for the purpose of an interpersonal relationship of love. He will not be able to lose his horizontal relationship now; he will remain with and among others, not from on high, nor by violence, nor with force, but with love. And in this attitude of adoration there occurs the return to truth, to that vision of the world in truth which precedes and accompanies "doing the truth in love."

The Christian must not be ashamed of this function which is his, nor blush at the Gospel, which at this moment of history has this meaning: to free the world from deception and to rediscover himself and things beyond alienations. He must be able to overcome the "ignominy of prayer," which to many, logically seems to be alienation, a luxury, an aristocratic activity, magic—the scandal of the cross. If Christ is risen, if he is the meaning of things, if it is true that "in him all things were created, in heaven and on earth, visible and invisible . . . . He is before all things, and in him all things hold together" *(Colossians 1:16-17),* then I must discover in him the real meaning of things. If in Christ things find their "reconciliation," that is, their true name and meaning, I cannot rediscover their meaning except in him, the root of all things and the axis around which the whole of creation turns. And since Christ is presented to me in the Gospel as a Thou, I should be able to discover him and to speak to him in such familiar terms as one would to another fellow human being. But to discover him, I have to be sure that I am not seeking him for my advantage, for my salvation, to escape my own responsibilities, nor to ignore a complicated, dirty, and contradictory world, because Jesus came into the world precisely to reconcile it. To discover Christ is impossible without an efficacious desire for salvation and liberation.

Jesus presents his own life as an alternating between an active, militant presence among men and a withdrawal into the desert, into solitude, into the profound search, into the mystery of man and history. Nobody loves men the way he did and nobody is more communitarian than he. But he was not afraid to leave his companions and go off to pray. Man needs continually to rediscover in quiet the truth about himself and about things, because in this truth is the meaning, the motive, of his living. And this continually escapes him in the bustle of life.

Love itself both liberates and delimits. It liberates by possessing and making its own. But it needs a parallel and complementary function of the permanent discovery of truth, and this on the existential level is the act of adoration. In the Gospel we are continually told to "love," but we are just as frequently told to "be watchful." Remain on guard, searching the horizon in the expectation of him who is to come.

It seems to me that only by discovering adoration as gratuitousness will man be able to become "gratuitous" and see things in poverty, outside of economic alienation. I see a deep urgency and need for the function of adoration in the Church, because it seems to me that in the name of the Gospel we are repudiating the profound meaning of the Gospel: "I thank thee, Father, Lord of heaven and earth, that thou hast hidden these things from the wise and understanding, and revealed them to babes" *(Matthew 11:25)*. We shall not be able to discover this humility of the Gospel, this poverty of the Word, if we do not get onto the wavelength of the Gospel. Jesus, the poor man and prophet of the poor, is not discovered at the end of a long intellectual investigation to rediscover the concept of God purified of traditional theology. Nor will we rediscover in this way the unknown God, whom we do not know how to name today because all names and all definitions have been destroyed by philosophical criticism. Jesus, the poor man, is discovered by making ourselves into poor ones, little ones, by rediscovering our poverty before him and by receiving it in the humility of our hearts, in intellectual receptivity, in the serene—but not desperate—acceptance of our powerlessness to contain him in a concept and to express him in a syllogism. We feel insufficient, wavering, and insecure. Is this not the moment, when we will feel enshrouded by darkness, that we should invite the Messiah to come to us with his light?

"The people who sat in darkness have seen a great light, and for those who sat in the region and shadow of death light has dawned" *(Matthew 4:16).*

Despair is the sign of the unaccepted and prideful powerlessness of the rich man, the teacher who feels he has the right to teach, but cannot. We want a poor Church in the service of the poor, but we do not think concretely about this immense mass of poor people who have the sense of God and who possess God without knowing it, for we, the teachers of Israel, have shut the doors of revelation. The poor have felt rejected by the rich in intellect and power, by those who claim to defend them. And they point a threatening finger at those who sit in the chair of Moses. What do these rich actually give the poor? The promise of a liberation—without a liberator. An abstract God who exists and does not exist, who is and who is not, who is not close to man because he is indefinable. We who feel that we are responsible for the Gospel block the way of the one who said that "he came to announce to the poor the Good News, to proclaim liberation to the captives and to give sight to the blind" *(Luke 4:18).* They are prepared to receive him because they are humble, the little ones, the poor. We, however, are not. We no longer know how to discover the moment of "littleness," the moment of solitude, in which our poverty—that profound poverty with which we come in contact in our daily experiences—becomes an adoration receptive to the truth, a tearful cry: "Lord, that I may see." Like the Pharisees, we are convinced of our truth and we fight, teacher against teacher, school against school, theology against theology, and raise clouds of dust in the land of the poor, preventing them from seeing the face of Christ.

The mystery of the Incarnation will always be a mystery of silence, of humility, of availability. There will always be the God for everyone, the God who comes to us, and not the God we win for ourselves. He comes to us without any other demand than our receiving him, our adoring surprise, our faith filled with wonder. "How can this be?" *(Luke 1:34).* Today it is impossible to avoid all the problems of the world. They invade the Church and our theological culture. We must have the courage to face up to them with lucidity. At the same time we must be on the alert to prevent the alienations and infiltrations of power from soiling the Gospel, instrumentalizing it and making it dangerous for the poor, for those very poor for whom Jesus was the Messiah, the angel of the Good News for all those who yearn to alleviate suffering, exploitation, and misery. We must rediscover the center of our poverty, and this can be done only in the quiet of solitude and an entreating contemplation. The poor, who are fearful of the rich, powerful, and materialistic Church, are anxious to feel that we are their companions, poor like themselves. And if we wish to give Christ, we must discover him as poor men and truly on their level. The prophets mercilessly destroyed the idols because they had found the true God, by whom they were overwhelmed and whose violence—"the stubborn creative will" of God, as my philosopher friend Eggers Lan calls it—took possession of their lives and did with them as it pleased.

The signs of the times can be read with historical and philosophical wisdom, but this is not a prophetic reading, that which reaches the depths and succeeds in drawing out the hope that is hidden in time, that which can keep afloat our tenacious will to love God and does not abandon man to his despair. Prophecy is not the reading of historical time, but of the time of salvation. It is the discovery of the firm purpose of salvation, which runs parallel to history and within it, and which secretly animates its contradictions, conflicts, violence, and oppression. Prophecy is the resurrection of hope from the rubble of destruction. It is the revelation of the God who rebuilds and restores the destroyed kingdom. It is the discovery of life beneath the pall that covers man's disillusionment and powerlessness. It is the discovery of God beneath the accumulated ruins of our sins. If the interpreter of history is a man of culture, then the prophet, the interpreter of the history of salvation, is a man of God. He is so possessed by God that he no longer has time or means to ask where God is, who he is, whether he is found outside, within, or above. "I appointed you a prophet to the nations" *(Jeremiah 1:5).* And this voice is heard only in silence, in prayer, in the faith acquired over our pessimism, that is, in genuine humility. What would Mary, in a slum, moved by the disillusionment and the suffering of her neighbors, do today? She would listen as always in silence and in the humility of her heart to the Word of God, pondering it in her deepest self *(Luke 2:51).*

Whoever believes in the Gospel and in its saving and liberating efficacy must live in two times, accepting the terrible suffering of ambiguity. We cannot cease being men of our time and we must also live the vicissitudes of Christian culture, which feels incapable of giving an answer to the man of today. Our duty is a manly acceptance of the provisional, because in it love is incarnated and become concrete. But we must rediscover the Gospel, and we cannot do this without accepting the preconditions in the horizontal dimension and the depth dimension. The Gospel will be rediscovered in this attitude of humility and responsibility, and it is achieved with responsibility in the choices of life.

Man today feels the need to be human, because day by day he seems to be becoming more proficient and less human. The leaders of progress themselves note that the world has grown outside of us much more than each one of us has grown within ourselves. That "supplement of the soul," which according to Bergson would accompany technical progress, has hardly appeared. Or, looking at it from another angle, others say that unfortunately the advance of civilization has been too slow. In all its forms and expressions one can feel the absence of the human, and we realize that we shall not find it solely by speeding up progress. The human is within and not outside. It is not a conquest, but rather a self-emptying. If it were something achieved by culture, the most highly educated people would also be the most human and thus to be "human" would be a privilege. Culture continuously discovers the need to be human, for it discovers and constructs instruments and things which in the hands of a person can be values of liberation and under the power of a nonhuman can be threatening and destructive. What is most human we find on the level of the poor, of those who do not participate actively in cultural progress but who can be its victim when culture is lacking its supplement of the soul. Theirs is the kingdom of heaven, that is, this kingdom of the human where things have value for man and to the measure of man. We must remain in this category, in this group to whom Christ brought the Good News, and not only by seeking a political or economic or cultural "poverty," which itself can be a search for a role. Rather we must discover it in prayer, in which we truly discover our nakedness, our deficiency, our powerlessness, and in which we rediscovered prophecy, and it was a premonition. Now Christians must rediscover prophecy. By inquiring with courage into this mysterious sphere which is sown with danger, we discover faith in Christ, in the Gospel, and in its liberating force.

In the search for this spiritual zone, for man's second dimension, we must have the courage to take out this time of emptiness, of leisure, of silence. If God is God, this zone exists and we have to find it. If God does not exist, "we are of all men most to be pitied" *(1 Corinthians 15-19).* The Gospel is incarnate in a culture, but this does not exhaust the Gospel. Indeed, cultures evolve and each gives way to the following. We are men when we accept the provisional. Being in the eternal, the permanent, without accepting the provisional, is truly an alienation. Religion should be rejected when it is this kind of religion. Everybody sees that it is a privilege. It is out of this vision that have arisen those mansions of contemplation, those castles by the sea or in the mountains where the feudal lords of contemplation live, those who have installed themselves in the eternal. Acceptance of the provisional is part of the human condition, which no one has the right to deny. But at the same time, we must not "empty the cross of Christ." We must seek the permanent, which to be permanent is not necessarily static, because redemption runs like an underground river accompanying history: "And his mercy is on those who fear him, from generation to generation" *(Luke 1:50)*. The act of faith is and will always be madness, a losing of oneself, a true gratuitous act of courage, a folly. It is the moth falling into the flame of a candle.

This appears rather incomprehensible in so logical an age as ours. But clarity belongs to the sphere of science and technology. In the human sphere, man is still groping. Why not try adventure? Father de Foucauld's prayer rings very true today: "O God, if you exist, allow yourself to be seen!" If you exist, I must return more human from this adventure. In any case I cannot remain on the surface, one among the many in this ideological pluralism, trying to hide as much as I can my useless baggage, tolerated by the others—who in order to have my presence endure the ideology that I carry on my back. After a while we see that this is useless. Either I return from the exploration in faith like Moses from the mountain, clarified, humanized, prophetic. Or else this kind of metaphysical prolegomenon to my participation in history is a useless complication, something that must be saved out of pure expediency. How very quickly out of date those old tracts on prayer have become and how this crisis cuts at the roots of the self-sufficiency of certain priests and teachers. This is wonderful.

We all feel ourselves to be in a state of search, without certitudes, without ready-made schemes in our pockets. We are in the same spiritual condition to understand or joyfully receive the faith as the Canaanite woman, Zacchaeus, the woman with the hemorrhage, those who climb trees, or who hide under the table, or who surreptitiously touch the hem of Christ's robe. Before the stupefied look of the formalistic Pharisees, Jesus resuscitates the faith of those poor people who are looking for him outside the door hermetically sealed by the erudite monopolizers of God: "But woe to you, scribes and Pharisees, hypocrites! for you are like white-washed tombs, which outwardly appear beautiful, but within they are full of dead men's bones and uncleanness" *(Matthew 23:13)*.

And what about us who criticize the old Pharisees? Are we perhaps not the new Pharisees who close the doors of the kingdom of heaven? Are we not, without realizing it, substituting sacralism and cultism with an aristocratic illuminism that shuts the door to Zacchaeus, the centurion, the

Canaanite woman, and which makes the importunate blind man from Jericho keep silent? Are the poor truly evangelized by someone coming from the "grave of God"? Jesus too spoke of the "grave of God": "But the hour is coming, and now is, when the true worshippers will worship the Father in spirit and truth, for such the Father seeks to worship him. God is spirit, and those who worship him must worship in spirit and truth" *(John 4:23-24).* Jesus puts the axe to the old Pharisaical tree trunk. He rejects everything sacred that excludes; he rejects the enclosure which makes the Canaanite woman an outsider. But he does this, not to make an atheist, but to discover the true worshipper, the true worshipper "in spirit and in truth." He does this so that each of us will no longer have to go to a well, but will discover the pure water within us: "Everyone who drinks of this water will thirst again, but whoever drinks of the water that I shall give him will never thirst; the water that I shall give him will become in him a spring of water welling up to eternal life" *(John 4:13-14).*

It is true that desacralization has its basis in the Gospel, but under the sign of a more authentic discovery of grace, of the revelation of the true God who lives in the innermost recesses of man, who is rooted in the very basis of the human being to renew him profoundly by communicating his life to him. If Jesus destroys a temple of stone, it is to substitute for it a living temple "whose stones are men" *(1 Peter 2:5)* and of which he is the cornerstone. Every desacralization that is not the fruit of this discovery is not in accordance with the Gospel. The Good News preached to the poor, to those whose hearts are broken, is the news of the God who is near, of Emmanuel, the God with us and in us, who troubles man's heart so that he will wake up and collaborate in liberation. History will try to hide him under all sorts of pretexts, and the power of money and the power of culture will attempt to stamp him out. But he is persevering and remains, a scandal and a folly for the great ones of the world, but salvation for the humble and the little ones who receive him.

12

THE SIGN OF FREEDOM

The Gospel has handed down to us the sign of freedom, and the Christian community has carried it on from generation to generation, covering it with meanings derived from culture, theology, and spirituality. This sign is the Eucharist. In its theological aspect, that is, its meaning in relation to God, it is called "communion," and in its human significance, "liturgy," which is its symbolic face. It is a delicate and difficult reality because it is the center of a choice, the choice between Jesus as a role player or Jesus as the risen Son of God. By extension it is the choice between man animated, sustained, and vitalized by God—and therefore as a real, permanent being—or man as a phantom, an appearance, a moment in the eternal becoming, held to be the only real being.

The choice is between, on the one hand, Christ who emerges in the resurrection from chaos and the power of death—and ourselves risen with him—and, on the other, Christ the prophet overthrown by time and death, who has merely left behind a remembrance, a word, an exemplary death. Either we accept Christ the Truth, who makes true every human endeavor, every step toward liberation, every sacrifice of man for man, or we admit that it is useless and tragic to try to give meaning to history, which then is a continuous succession of irrational acts and unmotivated decisions, a tragic necessity before which our consciousness serves only to acknowledge an invincible adversary and the injustice of having been chosen to control, to direct, and to organize—with the certainty that we shall always lose out. I believe that the Eucharist will be an increasingly controversial sign, because man today is called by events such as the loud protest of youth to clarify the significance of history and, consequently, to establish whether God has anything to do with it or not.

In my daily work, made up of confrontations, clashes, dialogue, discussions, and silent meditation, I have succeeded in clearing up two points for myself. First, my consciousness, emerging from matter, is continually called to search for identity with itself and to an encounter of fellowship with others. Second, this comprises the whole problem of the relationship with things and with possessions.

This is the pendular law of life: Without the continual discovery of my identity, without the return to the root of being which is a return in God, things identify me with themselves, for they find me at their mercy, available, without my own specific weight. And I continue to "thingify" other people and creatures as I am incapable of discovering the dynamic order which is basically the existential adoration of the world. Without losing myself in others, in those others outside of me, my being becomes futile; it goes astray into a sterile and dangerous narcissism. I seem to see clearly where the error of sacralization is. It is having made history futile by freezing the person in his moment of identification with himself and giving body, a phantasmic and apparent body, to the rhythm which is the moment of self-emptying, of the pure return to the I. And this is done before any choices, outside of any stands, the new man, the new creature, Paul would say, without circumcision or uncircumcision *(Galatians 5:6),* that is, before having chosen a people and thus a history, neither the people of the promise nor the Gentiles. In Christ the new creature takes on worth.

When at the moment of turning toward being and the discovery of its roots in God we try to give a body and a history to it, the world loses its meaning; it becomes futile. We thus separate the history of the individual from the history of the world. We make the "history of the soul" into "history." When the man without identity loses himself in history and his consciousness is no longer capable of emerging from it, the world becomes futile.

In this context, we can understand the mistrust on man's part in regard to the Eucharist, which exists even among Catholics. For historically it is true that whole generations of Catholics "thingified" the Eucharist as the center of worship, making it an instrument of a pseudo-identification, of a negation of integrity, rather than a sincere search for integrity. In Christian religious practice, the Eucharist has permitted too facile and comfortable an encounter with God, without a return to the roots, without the painful and exhausting search for identity, without "rebirth." Christians passed from Easter to human life. "Cleanse out the old leaven" *(1 Corinthians 5:7)* and "Put on the new nature, which is being renewed in knowledge after the image of its creator" *(Colossians 3:10)* sounded like symbolic words, like invitations to a Christianity of another age. The Eucharist has paralyzed men more than it has fostered the search for sincerity, for the authenticity of the person, by offering a cheap encounter with God, which required only an effort to find a little time and to accept certain articles of the law.

Today many people are afraid of continuing this same mistake and for that reason think that it might be better to limit its use. The danger hidden in this search for authenticity, if it is undertaken on the level of culture, is that it can end up by forming new ghettos and creating a new Pharisaism. So that this does not happen, it is necessary to pose the problem to the poor, not only the economically poor but also the poor in religion, those who are authentically religious because they have no religious training—like the Canaanite woman, Zacchaeus, the woman with the hemorrhage, the centurion. The rich "proprietors" of the Eucharist do not know how to use it with true respect.

The Eucharist's ambiguity continually displaces its significance for true being, because it is both a real presence and a symbol. To stress the presence too much is to "thingify it" and to permit in its name the repetition of the farce of the encounter with God. To overemphasize the symbolic aspect makes the meaning of God-with-us disappear and replaces the theme of the rebirth of the new man—which is a rebirth in Christ—with an external, moralistic rebirth. Christianity continually wavers between the hypocrisy of the Sadducees, who in denying the resurrection emptied religion of its meaning and thus practiced it out of mockery or juridical fidelity, and the hypocrisy of the Pharisees, who canonized fidelity to the law, which Christ came to destroy. Calvinist rigorism and Catholic superficiality are two ways of emptying the cross and two roads to hypocrisy, hypocrisy that is not peculiar to the religious man. The alienation of the superego is broadly human and the constant companion of the history of consciousness. But in the religious sphere it has received the name of hypocrisy. The difficulty, then, is immanent in the mystery of the Eucharist and in the presence of God in the world, in history, and in man.

The Gospel does not disregard this difficulty. The first theological discussion of the Eucharist occurs in the sixth chapter of John's Gospel: "Jesus said to them, 'Truly, truly, I say to you, unless you eat the flesh of the Son of man and drink his blood, you have no life in you' " *(v. 53)*. And later on, seeing the consternation of his hearers, he adds, "It is the spirit that gives life, the flesh is of no avail; the words that I have spoken to you are spirit and life. But there are some of you that do not believe" *(vv. 63-64)*. The ambiguity of the Eucharist, which is truly a real presence, is found in this: "My body and my blood," but "for others," for something "beyond," for something "besides," something "deeper," and I would say "truer." "You are detained in the flesh, but the flesh is of no avail. The words that I have spoken to you are spirit and life." There is no intellectual response which clarifies the ambiguity. There is only the poor irrational response of Peter: "Lord, to whom shall we go? You have the words of eternal life; and we have believed and have come to know that you are the Holy One of God" *(vv. 68-69)*. The Eucharist is an ambiguous sign because it is the sign of ambiguity which we know today by the name of identity and alienation. Identity sought outside of alienation becomes the "alienation" of the spirit. Unity sought in alienations falls into total alienation, into the loss of identity, into the loss of the subject. It falls into the loss of awareness as the unifying and adoring center of the world, if we understand as adoration the discovery of a dynamic order of the world and, as a consequence, of its meaning.

If we try to examine in depth and without a polemical spirit the reasons of those who wish to "desacralize" the Eucharist—by removing its varnish as an "object of worship" which has been given it in the Catholic world—we must admit that this limitation prevented us from seeing the Eucharist as a need of the world, a historical factor, an authentic value of the liberation of man. All of this is admitted, but it is not sufficiently needed. For the Eucharist is so enclosed within a ritualistic context, so jealously guarded within a sacred precinct, that the world cannot really make it its own and liberation is accomplished outside of this sign. This is an essential problem posed to us at every moment. Certainly there is a way of "eating the flesh and drinking the blood" outside of the religious rite; but, on the one hand, the insistence of the Gospel and the whole of Christian tradition and, on the other, the growing anxiety of men to preserve their identity and to free themselves from alienations reaffirm my conviction that Christ is necessary for the world. I am not scandalized by youth's cry to "free religion from the priests" because I recognize that it is more just than it sounds to our clerical ears. By sacralizing the Eucharist, we have dehumanized it and betrayed the Incarnation by making Christ into someone separate, distant, someone outside.

Rereading the sixth chapter of John, which I am continually studying, I lingered over one sentence: "Perceiving then that they were about to come and take him by force to make him king, Jesus withdrew again to the hills by himself" *(v. 15)*. *Take him by force to make him king.* This is exactly what we have done with the "Son of Man." We have kidnapped him to make him king, raising up thrones of gold and precious stones for him. And we have not hesitated to use the language of monarchies: throne, crown, baldachin. The enthronement of the king demands, consequently, the creation of princes, courtiers, and knights, well dressed and resplendent, so that his retinue might be a court. "The Son of Man, perceiving that they were about to come and take him by force to make him king, withdrew again to the hills by himself."

In a discourse filled with optimism, given on September 25, 1968, Pope Paul VI underlined the value of the authenticity of the youth who oppose the hypocrisy of past generations, their spirit of search for the absolute and for community. I think that the framework of the Eucharist, the liturgical sign, should be rediscovered by the young and the poor. Up to now we have discovered it from an intellectual and clerical viewpoint. And for that reason, it has not been a symbol within the reach of the young and the poor.

In a parish in Latin America I celebrated the young people's mass accompanied by instruments and songs, which, undoubtedly, were in accord with the taste of the new generation. But everything was devised to make the rite of the mass more acceptable and less ponderous; it was like a mathematics or German lesson made up of toys to amuse the pupils. If the young people had been left to themselves and told, "Prepare the Lord's Supper," I wonder whether they would have had recourse to such a noisy, distracting context, whether they would have created this jovial, worldly atmosphere. Or did all this correspond to the pedagogical criterion of the priests who wanted to attract the youth. Since we place various human groups in social categories that are hard to transcend, we reach the conclusion that young people want to be merry, to sing and dance, not to think of serious things, and that the poor who suffer from the pain of an empty stomach have to be given bread before they are taught the Our Father because they are not hungry for ideals.

Clericalism comes from looking at persons and things from our own viewpoint, without letting them look at us and things—which would change everything. Without rebellion and without the wish to be a reformer, but rather as a simple man in the street, I wonder whether in the age of "happenings" and the growing awareness of those who were thought incapable of thinking, there could not be given greater freedom in preparing and celebrating the supper of the Lord. The Church has always maintained rigid uniformity in the mass so that the sacrifice, through this external uniformity, might appear as the unique sacrifice of mankind. Today, however, we are discovering that this uniformity has not succeeded in creating the need or in giving the responsibility for forming the ecclesiastical community.

A Church has been formed in the law, in a rite, and not in love; but formal unity is not substantial. How, I don't know, but I feel that it is necessary to put the Eucharist into the hands of the people, since it is *their* Eucharist, even if the power of consecrating has been entrusted to the small group of ordained ministers.

The Eucharist goes to the heart of three great problems of man and, as a Christian, I feel that these questions are still open. The world has been thought in Christ and by him and cannot avoid moving toward him and seeking him. The problems are the identity of the person with himself; communication with others; and freedom, which is the problem of becoming a person and of growing in relationship with others and with things.

The Eucharist is the synthesis of the mystery of Christ, who is the incarnation of God in the world. "The first act of the Incarnation," Teilhard says, "the first appearance of the Cross, is marked by the plunging of the divine Unity into the ultimate depths of the Multiple" (*Science and Christ*, New York: Harper and Row, 1968, p. 60). The Incarnation of the Word is not a static fact culminating in the formation of the man-God, a being on the throne awaiting our adoration. Rather it is a force contained in mankind and history, which moves it from within. It provokes an increasingly richer concentration in increasingly more complex centers. In the order of matter, this concentration is expressed as a unification of plurality and, on the level of the human community, as a growing socialization, as the need to be together, to work together, and therefore to love one another. The anguishing discovery of loneliness is surely the prelude to an age of intense search for living together, a striving to create small, basic communities that will be the models for the great human community.

To rediscover the Eucharist, it is necessary to blot out the images that a bad theology and Christian customs have engraved deeply in us: the Eucharist as a delegated prayer, as a sacrifice offered in the name of others for the souls of the dead—and here come into play all the statements about

Christ coming down from heaven onto the altar. If the Eucharist, as an act of worship, is separated from the Incarnation, it becomes a limited act, something apart, which presupposes a knowledge of the cultic and the mystical and the capacity on the part of its initiates to understand and enter into the cult. On the other hand, the Incarnation is a universal fact in space and time. The Eucharist appears as an act that is *done,* and it is not well understood why it is done or what its purpose is. The Incarnation, however, is a *being* of history and the world, a being that is so important and essential that if I do not look at the world from this point of departure, I run the risk of never fully understanding it. I leave outside and apart its deepest and truest "why"; I know the plant but not the history of its root, of its living and being nourished in and from the earth. The Eucharist is the sign of this mysterious life that appears and acts on the surface, although its life center is within and in the invisible.

To be a sign, symbol, or sacrament means to bring to the surface and to make visible—within man's possibilities—this life center which is operative insofar as, in time, man freely collaborates. And because there is opposition and resistance from man, the mysterious presence of the Word in the world and his working within it become painful and difficult. They become passion and cross, extreme tension between Christ's will for unification and the relapse into plurality and dispersion. Despite this resistance, the force of unification triumphs because Christ rose from the dead. The Eucharist is a sign of tension and victory, of cross and resurrection. It is the eschatological sign of a victory that will certainly come about because the Christ present is the risen Christ. At present, however, there is suffering, struggle, all the uncertainty and tension of the exodus.

This tension is manifested daily in the resistance brought by nature when man seeks to understand it, to assume it, and to assimilate it. It is seen in the interpersonal encounter, which is dialectic and incomplete so long as the person does not reach the deepest point, the roots of his being, the true identification with himself. At the same time, however, there are signs of triumph and resurrection. There is the moment when man contemplates his victory over nature. This moment quickly disintegrates, however, because one conquest elicits in man the restlessness that pushes him on to another. It is art that fixes this contemplative moment of victory, of man's liberation. A sign of triumph is the enjoyment of being together, of sensing our unity with others, which becomes patent in the ecstasy of a couple. There is the profound joy of sharing with others, which Christ discovered in the pure happiness of sitting down at table with his friends. It is present here more than at other times because it is a moment of poverty for each person, a moment of collective need, of equality before the need for food. It is a moment of love made a sign because, behind the food are the expressions of persons and possessions which bring life and its continuity to each of us. These expressions of struggle, victory, confrontations, and contemplative ecstasy take place continually in the world under the most different aspects.

A friend accompanied me to a dinner at the house of some poor people—the kind of people who don't extend an invitation because it is the correct thing to do or for their self-interest, but out of love, to enjoy the simplicity of the encounter. My friend told me, "This is their mass." Indeed, the mass should be inserted in this reality in order for it to be in place—a sign of a genuine and concrete human reality. It gave me peace to think that there is a relationship between the mass celebrated in the liturgical and sacramental context of a church and this human reality which develops historically outside the Eucharist. It is not foreign to the Eucharist; it is outside of our visibility, but it is substantially united and dependent. No light illumines the world and no energy moves it other than those produced by this Center, unknown to most people and misunderstood by almost everyone. I believe that if men discover this, the acceptance of their own destiny would be freer and happier. And there would be fewer retrogressions, fewer negations of our function as men. For what reason, then, has the Word been made visible, and why has the Incarnation, which liberates in time, been made into a sign, and a sign that is so homey and accessible as a meal? Surely not so that we might hide it.

The Eucharist is the concrete and vital act of faith in the God who is with us and in history. It is the act of faith in life. Just as a person who eats believes in life because he wants to maintain his strength to continue his human journey, whoever eats the flesh of Christ and drinks his blood profoundly accepts life and its meaning. And I would say that this is the true meaning of Jesus' words: "The flesh is of no avail; the words that I have spoken to you are spirit and life" *(John 6:63)*. Eating the flesh of Christ, if it is true, must result in the discovery of the deep meaning of life. Our identification with Christ is the identification with our true self, because man is absurd if he situates himself outside of his true vocation, if he does not identify with it. His vocation is freedom. Therefore, if Christ is our only model, each man must coincide with him and in the different stages of the development of his history be a little of a savior and a messiah himself. Like Christ, he must be king, prophet, and priest. As a king, he has to take possession of his goods. As a prophet, he must discover a way to use them. And as a priest, he has to use them for sanctification, that is, to "sanctify men in unity," to make possessions into instruments of communication and unity. Teilhard would say to "super-center them" so that they might be a means of unification and not alienation. The return to oneself, to one's own vocation, becomes a necessity when the person discovers the temptations to dispersion which continually beset him. "Your life is hid with Christ" *(Colossians 3:3)*, says Paul, and he presents with clarity this return to communion with Christ. For this reason the Eucharist will always preserve a solitary aspect, this personal meaning—in the past exaggerated and separated from the total meaning, which is much richer and more pleasing.

The very concept of vocation relates to doing, to doing with others and for others. But the departure point for vocation is not outside but inside: it is internal. It is true that a vocation becomes clear and specific in a commitment with others and that in becoming historical its motives become enriched. But I feel that the root, the truth of its motivation, is in the intimate communion with Christ, which is the first truth. It is necessary to overcome the fear of loneliness. We agree that we have emerged from an age in which the Eucharist was a private devotion and a kind of "fetish." Once the rite was performed and the bread received, we felt calm, and that was certainly a deformity. But if we leave aside the moment of "concentration" for "superconcentration," we shall never encounter our identity with Christ, our being in him. Being in Christ is not for me alone, as an individual, since the rest of men are also in him together, in a profound and unrepeatable unity in the world, which is the Mystical Body. The human community is the symbol of Christ's victory, the true eschatological symbol, because it will be achieved solely at history's point of arrival. For this reason, the mass, which is the reproduction of the Last Supper, represents a state of suffering, of struggles, and of death, and demands a concrete commitment on the part of believers: that of reducing tensions and working actively for the unification of mankind.

I do not intend to stress here that today the notion of unification has acquired a very profound and broad meaning. We cannot speak of an apparent pacification obtained in our time, or of the kiss of peace, when this kiss leaves intact and unchanged the collective sufferings of men, the situations of contempt for the poor, all of man's injustice and sin, which in practice, in the social and political structures, prevent this unification. For this reason, the content of the Eucharist, the substance of which is the symbol of bread and wine, might seem to look more like a group of trade unionists who are fighting for their rights or a group of persons who are striving for liberation than the image of an inert community, disjointed and conservative, which is congregated around the altar. Before starting out to make war, the Crusaders gathered at mass because they were aware of being involved in a commitment to liberation. This was a liberation that, in time, would give rise to divisions among men. However, perhaps the Crusaders were unconsciously prefiguring the unification of men of faith.

It is indeed dangerous to see love as coinciding with an ideology in which love and hatred, ambitions and authentic desires for unity are mixed. For this reason, it seems well to me that guerrilla fighters or others who have recourse to violence do not ask for masses to be celebrated. However, it is painful to discover that in the Church building we find an empty sign, since it represents a community which is not a community and a redemption which is not being brought about, while outside the church we find the substance, the liberating action, and the effort to make a community, without the sign, without Christ, or at least without the invocation and discovery of Christ.

The community that comes together for the Eucharist could never be the ideal community in which everything is accomplished, in which unity already exists, because such a community does not exist. Or if it exists, it is a small, privileged group, which can fall into the temptation of the ghetto. The true historical community is made up of tensions, desires, struggles, and it is precisely for this community that Christ died. If the human community already existed, this mysterious source of vitality would not be necessary, this hidden force which forms unity. The Christian assembly ought to know that it is not a community and to be aware of the schisms which come about among us. Socio-political criticism is a great help in this area. The schisms have profound and remote origins. They are not superficial fissures in the social structure. They have deep causes that we should not fear to discover and point out. What we call the "liturgy of the word" ought to be the deep and patient search for all the historical causes that prevent this community—present in the breaking of the bread— from being a true fellowship. The act of contrition, the request for forgiveness from God and the community, ought not to be reduced to a form and a rite. It should be real. "For, in the first place, when you assemble as a church, I hear that there are divisions among you; and I partly believe it" *(1 Corinthians 11:18)*. If we go to the root of the problem, we note, especially in today's world, that this dissension has a cause that is more economic and social than dogmatic. With the simultaneous presence of people who suffer from hunger and others that are drunk *(ibid., v. 20)*, how could schisms and divisions be avoided? The difference in economic condition and degree of welcome between the rich and the poor are a cause of schism: "My brethren, show no partiality as you hold the faith of our Lord Jesus Christ, the Lord of glory. For if a man with gold rings and in fine clothing comes into your assembly, and a poor man in shabby clothing also comes in, and you pay attention to the one who wears the fine clothing and say, 'Have a seat here, please,' while you say to the poor man, 'Stand there,' or, 'Sit at my feet,' have you not made distinctions among yourselves, and become judges with evil thoughts? Listen, my beloved brethren. Has not God chosen those who are poor in the world to be rich in faith and heirs of the kingdom which he has promised to those who love him? But you have dishonored the poor man. Is it not the rich who oppress you, is it not they who drag you into court? Is it not they who blaspheme that honorable name by which you are called?" *(James 2:1-7)*. Social tensions and differences are not dismissed by a wave of a magic wand, but they can be abolished by an instant of repentance. The Gospel shows us the example of a renewal in love which is immediate: The adulteress and the crucified thief are persons who skip many steps. There is a time, that of love, which is not historical time, because love is a value that endures when time has come to an end. Repentance is an act of love on the condition that it is efficacious, that is, on the condition that it is concretized in a true and wise commitment. Zacchaeus came up with a very daring project, which was then to be achieved in time.

The mass cannot be understood without this project inspired in reviled love. This is repentance. The mass ought to put concrete projects of social transformation into motion. Everyone should agree at least in acknowledging the lack of collective love and on the necessity of correcting things with adequate means which cannot be left up to the good will of individuals—even if there can be disagreements on the lesser or greater efficacy of the means. No means will bring about complete justice or total community, but it is necessary to choose and decide. Only in a dynamic commitment is the thirst and hunger for justice kept alive and relevant. Without this, it rots. Never has anyone spoken to the Christian assembly like Paul: "I do not commend you, because when you come together it is not for the better but for the worse" *(1 Corinthians 11:17)*. On the other hand, some have stressed that the more consecrated bread the Christian eats, the better he becomes. The religious intensity of the parish has been measured by the number of communions, and not by the communion of fellowship, by the growth in unity and love. It is true that the former can be proved statistically and the latter cannot. But the communions that do not succeed in achieving communion or at least in awakening an anxiety to achieve communion are a waste of time. "It is not for the better but for the worse."

It is obvious that we cannot open up this problem without allowing the laity to share in the preparation of the homily. The words of James on the injustice of the rich man, on the contempt for the poor, have a very concrete historical tradition and context. Certainly this participation by the people will give rise to arguments and conflicts and will look like partisan political haggling, but the risk must be taken. There is no other remedy. The monologue-homily of the priest is, necessarily, paternalistic and obliges the community to see but one aspect and omit all the rest. It can give rise to tensions, as is happening among the youth, or it can authorize partial and comfortable views of Christianity. I took the opportunity to listen to a homily on the beatitudes in which the preacher maintained that the beatitudes were nothing other than the customary commandment of the Gospel expressed differently and that basically all they meant was this: "Blessed are those who love the Lord above all things." Everybody was content. There was no need to ask forgiveness from God or the community because everyone was authorized to think that in his heart, into which no one sees and over which no one has any control, he loved his God above all things.

For these reasons, it is becoming increasingly urgent to remove the mass from its framework of intimidating solemnity and to situate it in history. I recently rediscovered this in an unforgettable encounter with some mothers from a former slum in Santiago. I gave a short explanation of the right of each man to work, basing it on the parable of the workers in the vineyard. This gave rise to a discussion, which shed light on concrete and previously ignored problems. We spoke of the need which the worker has to participate in the struggle to bring about justice for himself. And the women told me that their husbands had protested and taken part in strikes, but for that reason they had been fired and found themselves without bread and without work. "And I," one mother told me, "have fourteen children. What am I going to feed them?" These words of Monsignor Ancel come to my mind: "For the worker, the facts are the context that permits him to concretize the meaning of his expressions without fear of making a mistake." When we theorize, we are the absolute masters of dialectic, but when we get down to facts, to the Gospel as lived and translated for our time, we are surpassed by those who live. I think that giving dignity to the poor and to the worker at mass does not consist solely in giving them seats up front, which is very simple and can well be demagoguery. Rather it is in offering them ground where they can express themselves, be in control, and win out. Our abstract theology and our antihistorical commentary on the Gospel are a violence, which is not corrected by seating arrangements at mass. Nor is it sufficient to put the poor at ease by treating them familiarly. We must accept the superiority of their analysis and their explanation of the facts, which are the flesh of the Gospel, the condition whereby it can be something living and vital in the world of today. In the meeting the oppressors were not there, those who fire the workers and do not want to hear protests, those who ought to be striking their breasts before the offended and humiliated community. The dialogue with the mothers ended with a community resolution: mutual support so as not to weaken their strength and to achieve justice.

The mass is the affirmation of the reality of beings. To look upon the offertory as the offering of the first fruits to God the sovereign Lord, as a form of paying tithes, is for me a pagan notion that contradicts the whole of biblical thought, particularly that of the prophets. For me the offertory is the full acknowledgment that all things, those of heaven and those of earth, visible and invisible, ". . . all things were created through him and for him" *(Colossians 1:16).* By rediscovering their specific meaning in themselves, I also discover their vocation to be concentrated in the deepest area of the consciousness and to be supercentered in order to be integrated into the Mystical Body, in which are included not only persons but also all things redeemed and liberated by Christ. The offertory is the sign of a poverty and a profound respect for things and persons. It is the resolution not to use things for our own convenience, or to humiliate others: "Or do you despise the church of God and humiliate those who have nothing?" *(1 Corinthians 11:22).* Things cannot be rediscovered in Christ if we do not involve ourselves in saving them from alienation by returning their true meaning to them. For me, it is not enough to contribute from what is mine to the Supper of the Lord. I must commit myself not to squander things, not to alienate them and take away their own identity. The mass opens up the problem of poverty, of man's relationship with things, and therefore of the co-administration or the self-administration of business. It would be necessary to find a symbology that would represent all of this. In the hymns or words we use, we repeat the intention of offering our endeavors and our work, but this offering is looked upon statically, for what it is and for its significance within the present structure. Redemption, however, is the liberation of the world and of matter in order to make them converge in the act of worship, in which man and things coincide with their vocation, which is their reason for being.

The consecration and the communion renew for us the mystery of the Incarnation in all its stages, from Advent to the death and resurrection and annunciation of the Second Coming. The Eucharist is the sole hope of the world, since we and things are in God and in some way share in the absolute and eternal and are snatched from emptiness and nothingness. For this, however, it is necessary to give back to the mass its dynamic significance.

In effect, God came on earth to "re-create" continually with us, to re-create man and things by transporting them with himself in the movement of his love. Man must incorporate in himself the living flesh of Christ in order to ingraft into his being this force of concentration of himself and things in love. Therefore it is ridiculous to look upon the mass as a prayer to "get something" in the sense that, for example, we can arrange and pay for a mass while we remain peacefully in bed or attend to our affairs, confident that the soul of our deceased person will go to heaven in exchange for this modest price. The mass commits every man and the whole man. At times we get the impression of finding in the world and in the actions of men broken off pieces of the mass, like the fragments of those fine Roman monuments which during the barbarian invasions were spread over the fields and then degraded by the most diverse uses which were so foreign to their true purpose. Men of taste and patience will have to go out and rediscover half buried in the field these unrecognizable bits and pieces and then rebuild the monument. But success is impossible if we work only with the sign or only with the liturgical act. We must rediscover the human realities that are an integral part of the sacrifice. The liturgy is the gesture, the sign, which expresses the vital and historic reality of man. For this reason "secularizing" the mass does not mean losing the profound meaning of the sacrifice, the placing of things in God, that is, on the path toward true humanization where the Incarnation has placed them. Thus the mass will not be merely a rite to be performed, a duty to fulfill once a week. It will be the axis of history and the deepest meaning of life.

Some might object that this would risk losing the sense of mystery and worship of God, which is the mass's central meaning. I think not, because the hidden mystery is precisely this liberation to which we all aspire and which can come about integrally in the world solely through the Incarnation. The worship of God is this search for a dynamic order, the true meaning of things as they were created by him. "The heavens are telling the glory of God; and the firmament proclaims his handiwork. Day to day pours forth speech, and night to night declares knowledge" *(Psalm 19:1-2)*. This is not a question of human words, nor is it a language of someone whose voice can be imitated; it is the order, the structure of things, which sings God's glory. Man must sense that established disorder, institutionalized violence cannot sing the glory of God, even if voices are loud and the liturgical symbols are proclaiming praises and glory. The whole task of clarification, of harmony and beauty, which can be accomplished in symbols, is of no avail if these symbols are not symbols of a harmony and an order that is sought through man's participation.

Man without the mass seeks an order in the world by investigating ever more seriously structures and by interrelating them for the advancement of creation. But these structures become either futile or else dangerous in man's hands. The mass without man is the music of Bach or Beethoven, Fauré or the Beatles. In any case it is the celebration of a harmony that does not exist and that is not in the process of becoming. Many times the liturgy has been "thingified" and has become almost a specialized discipline, an esthetic passion, the cermonial of an imaginary court. And the tragedy of priestly existence depends in great part on the fact that the symbol has been emptied.

What can be done to put all the parts back together? We must have the courage to go back to the Lord's Supper, that simple and ordinary gesture so charged with meaning, and work out its true significance by gropingly seeking with men the signs of our time. We must find the symbol adapted to our own sensibilities, especially to the sensibilities of those who are excluded from the mass: the poor and the young. The first are excluded because of the solemnity of the rite and the second because it is encased in the law. Ultimately, the mass has to become more an encounter of reconciliation and freedom than a ceremony. Ceremony and rubrics are disappearing in a world that is in a hurry. Through very complicated and tortuous routes, it is becoming like the simple world in which Christ was born and in which he celebrated the Eucharist. We are a transition generation, and we still must bear the weight of vestments and ceremonial which are such a burden to us.

I dream about what the mass of tomorrow will be like among the youth: "I'll see you there on Saturday. We're meeting at Mary Lou and George's house. Mary Lou just had her first baby and can't go out." The priest is a bit like Alyosha Karamazov, a mystic, but very human and very much a friend of youth. The first theme will be reconciliation: "If when you approach the altar, you remember . . . ." Mary Lou and George are not getting along as well as they should. He has a great political ideal that completely consumes him. She shares this idea theoretically and wants to be his companion, but she finds the way to communication blocked. He is entrenched in an abstract love for mankind, a love that is urgent and planned out: "Today, in this country of violence, there is no time for weakness and sentimentality." Mary Lou finds it painful to be treated as a child, or still worse, as a prostitute. She is becoming increasingly withdrawn. Their friends are discovering that the French students are right: "Make the revolution while making love, and make love while making the revolution." But what love? How? The love made up of attentiveness to the other, of self-renunciation, of the search for the other's true happiness. Love one another in Christ? Without the presence of woman, the revolution will not be filled with love. George understands that he must know how to give something up in order for his message to have substance and to be truly human. Mary Lou understands that she must share with George what is vital for him. Here is where reconciliation is brought about, around this table. The priest speaks as one who has experienced the depths. He limits himself to reminding them that there is no genuine personalization, and therefore respect for the other, an encounter, without the love-producing presence of God.

A mass among the poor. Lucy invites her friends to come to her house tonight because the Supper is being celebrated. Everyone will bring what he can, because they will be together for the whole evening and it will be late. The priest is one of the neighbors and has a job. They read the Gospel of the workers in the vineyard. Frances says it is true. Were not her two oldest sons born of the same parents and in the same house? And yet one is kind, behaves, and gives almost everything he earns to the family, while the other is rebellious, wasteful, and selfish. Her husband corrects these impressions, which he thinks are pessimistic, and says that his wife is impatient and irritable. She admits it, but what can she do? There is no money, prices are going up, there is a lot to do around the house. It's natural that you lost patience when you just can't take any more. Christ was part of this kind of a life, and assumed concrete situations in order to help man find his freedom within them. Let the husband become reconciled with his wife as they search together for a more genuine way of living together, with a greater understanding of one another. Let men become reconciled with one another by seeking a more solid and dynamic kind of friendship. Let the poor be reconciled with the rich by seeking justice in dialogue and by offering the rich a possibility of salvation in a genuine friendship that is respectful of the poor and co-creative with them. Christ, who comes among us to be our bread and our wine, the food that deeply nourishes the person and all persons, is with us to sustain us in our weakness. He makes possible a reconciliation that is neither false nor opportunistic, but rooted in the truth. He makes possible a commitment in love and in justice, a joy that arises out of the discovery of the meaning of life.

It is true that there must be singing at mass, because the liberating coming of Christ is proclaimed, a hope shines forth. Paul said, "Be filled with the Spirit, addressing one another in psalms and hymns and spiritual songs, singing and making melody to the Lord with all your heart" *(Ephesians 5:18-19)*. It is the song of a traveller who knows he has not gone off his path. He is on the right road and will sooner or later arrive at his destination. But this song must be genuine, and to be genuine it has to originate in faith, which from slavery to the law has become freedom in the Spirit.

13

OBEDIENCE AS FREEDOM

Obedience is looked upon not as a conquest, but as an expression of temporal or qualitative immaturity, a sign of inferiority. It is seen as necessary protection in childhood, which in adolescence begins to crack up like an eggshell; it falls apart completely in adulthood when it becomes identified with obedience to the extrinsic law, which is truly a form of servitude. But there is a "structuralistic" obedience, which is both the sign and the means of the growth of the person. This is obedience to God, that synthetical obedience on which, according to the Gospel, "depend all the law and the prophets" *(Matthew 22:40).* This genuine obedience is another way of expressing love because there can be no obedience without love.

Obedience is above all a radical love for oneself, identified with faith. It is the desire to live, to do something, not to be destroyed. Being reborn in Christ is this discovery of the intrinsic value of the person, a value which is a relationship with others and with something. Above all, obedience is faithfulness to one's own being, to the will to live; this is not abstract but rather very concrete, because it is identified with vocation. My being in Christ is accompanied by the certainty that I exist for something which is the sphere of love. Conversion is often conceived as a return to practices abandoned in one's youth or to religious practices proposed in this awakening of the religious spirit. Actually it is the discovery of God in the meaning of one's own being and of one's own existence in the midst of others and for them, in a particular history.

This notion is very important. It enables us to discover what possibility for alienation or liberation can be given by faith in a God who is present in man, even to the point of being identified with him. It is undeniable that one's vocation must become historically explicit in actions, options, and structures that have their own inexorable laws. Liberation must be accomplished within this reality. Most men never find their vocation because they are obliged to accept positions that do not help them to develop themselves. They have to submit to structures that demand the total abdication of the person. One of the objectives of the struggle for freedom is to win the right each man has of fulfilling himself in keeping with his own vocation and in a line that contributes to the development of his dignity as a "brother of Christ." Every dignity that comes from outside, that is not structural, that does not originate from an immanent force, like the joy of being or ontological adoration, is false. Man cannot worship God with words if he does not know how to worship him with his life. God is denied and crucified in every person whose essential dignity is denied, a dignity which is the right to self-fulfillment in accordance with one's vocation. The person cannot encounter obedience to the external law when his attitude of obedience is undermined from within. External conditioning, the need to earn one's livelihood at any price and by any sort of abdication, destroys this root.

Yet the people to whom Christ preached the beatitudes—which are the state of the liberated person—were more conditioned than men today. They were slaves, things. Was the revelation that they were sons of God, brothers of Christ, an opiate or was it a true and authentic liberation? I think we must move toward this coinciding of the discovery of our essential structure and its historical fulfillment. If the dignity of the sons of God is an inferior fact centered in a vacuum, it really does constitute an alienation. And all of our preaching on dignity, on man's greatness, on the importance he has before God, will give rise to ridicule, rebellion, or aggression. Where is this dignity? How do we see it? How do we defend it? How does it grow in line with this concept? The answer to these questions has always consisted in proposing an external and individualistic morality: respect for one's own body, not doing things unworthy of our own dignity, discovering phantasmal greatness and dignity within ourselves, believing in opposition to the challenges of history and of structures.

I wonder if man has any other way of defending his basic dignity than through the political commitment to build structures that permit him this personal obedience to his true self. Must it be either this kind of commitment or else taking refuge in religion like a corpse, waiting for the Second Coming of Christ? We learn something in this regard from the instinctive defenses man spontaneously discovers as a compensation for his vocational frustration: superabundant procreation, alcohol, play, that is, escape. In my opinion we shall find salvation only in a creative and therefore personalizing community. And personalization comes about in love. The Gospel invites us to expect the coming of Christ as the consummation of things, the ultimate event. But at the same time it is a message of salvation for our generation. Each man must achieve his own freedom today, and this means that death and resurrection are occurring today. This is the meaning of the Eucharist: a stage in salvation for today, with a content of hope and an impulse toward the total salvation of tomorrow, and this salvation of the person is not individualistic but communitarian. Today communities of freedom and fellowship must be formed. The Church out of fidelity to Christ has always endeavored to make present in the world a being and a doing. The being should be verified in religious communities. But for many reasons, once the prophetic and creative moment has passed, these have become crystallized into static communities which are not true communities at all. Rather they are a kind of living in common which is poorly representative of the human hope Christ brought to the world.

The obedience of many people is not liberating and creative because it is not fidelity to a personal vocation which is enriched as it becomes explicit in its contacts with reality and is discovered in the liberation process being accomplished in history. For many, obedience seems more like a law which keeps everyone in his proper place and confines him there out of fear. The Holy Spirit will inspire the formation of new and genuine communities, cells of the Church that are representative of the authentic plurality of the Mystical Body maturing in the world. Virginity and marriage, contemplation and action, poverty and service, all are harmonized in love. The religious communities are frozen into a specialized group of persons who practice a unique form of life and have thrown themselves into the apostolate. They have two constitutional deficiencies today. The first is that, in fact, they propose but one aspect of the Mystical Body, separated—and often polemically separated because of the growth of the Pharisaical spirit—from the rest of the Mystical Body. The second is that almost all these communities—including the contemplative ones—have developed in line with the Church's mode of *doing.*

Many wonder what is the purpose of a life consecrated to God, since every life is consecrated to him. Often the religious life is reduced to justifying itself with motives of convenience and temporal freedom. However, even well organized boarding houses or dormitories permit their guests to devote all the time possible to study or work. They see to it that they do not waste time preparing meals and sewing on buttons. The Moslems with whom I once worked in Algeria, when they discovered that I was not married, asked me with astonishment, "But who washes your clothes?" They could not understand religious consecration, nor did they show much understanding of marriage. Yet in the Catholic world the sense of religious consecration—the kind of mysterious and rather magic fascination that a religious, and particularly a nun, radiates—has also disappeared. It seems to me that if we were to take a survey, the sense of the religious life would not be much more than: "Who washes your clothes? Who prepares your meals?" Obviously, this question does not offer much joy or courage to people who have embraced the religious life. In these structures obedience necessarily becomes an irrational, vertical game, which provokes an aggressive reaction. "The nuns are mean, they have no heart, they don't love each other," is very often the conclusion reached by young people who spent their adolescence in a Catholic boarding school. Certainly this is not a happy result. We must acknowledge that in this structure a latent aggression cannot be avoided. Nastiness is nothing but aggression that surfaces.

Here and there pluralistic communities are beginning to appear, small churches which are the image of the real world and in which can be seen the signs of the hope to which the world aspires: the freedom of the person in the truth of his total being. In a structure of this kind, family nuclei live integrated with small religious communities and the contemplative function is assimilated naturally with work. Obedience there is defined not by a superior or by a rule, but by the great human law which obliges anyone who aspires to be a person to be faithful with himself and with the community. Perhaps the moment has come to "lose" the religious community in order that it might live in accordance with the great idea of the Gospel. We can repeat what we discovered in respect to the Eucharist: that inside the church the sign remains and outside the church, the scattered fragments of communion. The religious communities should be the symbol of how the world ought to be organized, the symbol of the direction that should be taken by the process of redemption and liberation which Christ came to place in history. And outside of religious structures there is occurring this search for community which becomes more anguished as the world becomes more threatening. Everything compels our generation to rediscover the image of the primitive Church, as described for us in the Acts of the Apostles.

Every time I read the Acts I see myself again sitting beneath the palm trees of Beni Abbes, where I had come with a group of brothers after twelve days of walking. It had been a purifying and self-emptying experience. There, beneath the palm trees, we reread the Acts in order to discover the community: "And all who believed were together and had all things in common; and they sold their possessions and goods and distributed them to all, as any had need. And day by day, attending the temple together and breaking bread in their homes, they partook of food with glad and generous hearts, praising God and having favor with all the people" *(Acts 2:44-47)*. History does not go backwards, and to rebuild a society is not to create a ghetto. Only people rich in money and culture can allow themselves this. At the conclusion of *Tristes Tropiques* by Claude Lévi-Strauss, I found some ideas, which, although seen from another point of view, may be clarifying: "The self is not only hateful. It has no place between a 'we' and a nothingness. And, finally, I opt for this 'we,' even if it is reduced to an appearance. For, unless I destroy myself— an act which would abolish the precondition of choosing—I have no other possible option between this appearance and nothingness. It is sufficient that I choose, for by this very choice I assume without any reservations my condition as a man. By freeing myself of my intellectual pride, by which I measure futility, I agree at the same time to subordinate its claims to the objective requirements for the liberation of a multitude to which the means for such an option are always denied." The obedience of religious communities, as seen today, has not sufficiently deepened the sense of this "we" that includes all who do not have any possibility of making personal options. In the worst spiritual tradition, humility consists in bowing one's head before a person who is as capable of making mistakes as we are, and at times even more. In a pluralistic community it is the acceptance of one's personal history with its limitations. Today, man feels in a global way and wants to be everything at once. Living seems more an obedience to all the experiences that are presented to us than a fidelity to what one should be. It is an obedience lived on a superficial level. It is indeed an obedience because external conditioning makes man today more obedient and more submissive than the serfs of the soil, even when it costs him less physical effort and gives him a sensation of greater well-being. A community of freedom must have the courage to conquer alienations in the acceptance of everyday existence.

To all priests, religious, and nuns who are asking themselves today what value a consecration to God and a life in a religious community has, I should like to offer these lines of Pierre Restany from *Le livre rouge de la révolution picturale*:

It is time for the artist to stop speculating
on the advantage
small or large
of his anachronistic situation
in order to get ready to confront
the main task that awaits him—
To create joy
the happiness of the greatest number
through the metamorphosis of everyday life.

We cannot discover our religious life, which is a message of freedom, without deeply sharing the determination of those human groups who must achieve global, communitarian, historical freedom. Sharing means accepting all the rules of the game, not being the teachers who know it all, but companions who are finding their way like all the rest. We must never lose sight of the fact that through liberations the new and free man is sought, the man who for us Christians is the one who walks with his God within him, who obeys his interior rhythm and the demands of an external psychological adaptation. I think that to "create joy," the happiness of the greatest number, it is necessary to affirm, not with words but with one's life, the exigency of God as an absolute, and consequently to affirm also an obedience of negation, opposition, organization, receptiveness, and humility.

A Christian is a consecrated person. He is someone who has chosen Christ and not Christianity, because Christianity is not chosen. It is made and created. If we are speculating so much today on our "anachronistic situation," it is because we have chosen Christianity, that is, a culture, and we therefore feel anachronistic. Hence the temptation to modernize ourselves, which gives rise to conflicts, tensions, and dreadful misunderstandings on the cultural level. When thought out on the plane of Christian culture, *aggiornamento* can never give good results. The postconciliar tragedy—if we may call it that—is for me this eagerness for renewal on the level of culture. A culture is not born with cuts and patches, openings and closings, but in the wake of impassioned lives consecrated to an ideal, dedicated to a fidelity, profoundly obedient, free from worrying about what they break or what they create. Culture is the preoccupation of critics, lawyers, and their followers, not of creators. The time of the Church today is a time of creation, and the only people who live it are those who are not concerned with culture. Today it is necessary to have the courage to say, like Mounnier, but with violence and with the rude language typical of youth: *"feu la chrétienté,"* Christendom is dead. Christian culture? It is of no interest to me. The Christian is not somebody with special projects to accomplish in the world. He is somebody seized by Christ as a person.

We have to think out a new *Imitation of Christ*, not like the one of Thomas à Kempis, which in part obeys the demands of a culture. Christ is presented there as someone who condemns nature, life, and creation, because that generation was unsuccessful in reconciling itself with creation. The question, "What would Christ do today? How would he behave? How would he see things?" which has constituted a norm of valid conduct for spiritual generations, must, I think, be considered in another way today. What am I doing to adapt myself psychologically to all the demands created in me by this life rooted and grounded in Christ *(Ephesians 2:20)*? The Gospel can certainly help me to rediscover Christ's attitudes, on the condition that they are separated from the cultural medium in which they were seen and thought out. For example, to make the famous episode of the driving out of the money lenders from the temple into a norm authorizing violence is false. The historical context in which this episode took place is certainly not that of today's industrial and political alienation. But if I belong to Christ, if I am inspired and animated by him, I must feel contempt for injustice, for those who make the house of prayer a den of thieves. If this contempt drives me to guerrilla warfare or to other acts of violence in order to abolish violence, that will be my business. One thing is certain: Today, the whip Christ used would be of little avail against the machine guns and tear gas of the police or against the violence of money wielded through advertising. Biblical exegesis is working in this direction today, helping us to discover Christ separated from the cultural background of his time.

What fascinates me in Christ is that *he submitted to structures while breaking them down.* There is no obedience of his that was not also a rupture. There was the first obedience to his father and mother—"And he went down with them and came to Nazareth, and was obedient to them" *(Luke 2:51)*—which, after his crisis of adolescence, was broken out of fidelity to himself and to his vocation: "How is it that you sought me? Did you not know that I must be in my Father's house?" *(Luke 2:49).* There was his death itself, which was an act of obedience and rebellion, because he could not accept the opinion of the Sanhedrin and Pilate. Christ did not deny Israel as the chosen people, as the holder of the promise, as the people of God, but he discovered the "Israelites" outside. "He also is a son of Abraham" *(Luke 19:9)*, he told Zacchaeus when he decided to love the community and give up his immediate self-interest and thus joined the community of Israel. He did not concern himself with destroying a structure which he recognized to be corrupt and traitorous to the spirit of God. He respected it deeply, by preparing a generation that would overcome it, by transcending the limits of flesh and blood with a vision of faith.

He was deeply a man and had himself called Son of Man. His life was so normal that when he began to speak people asked, "Is not this the carpenter, the son of Mary and the brother of James and Joseph and Jude and Simon, and are not his sisters here with us?" *(Mark 6:3)*. Yet he was not afraid to go away from them to withdraw and pray. It will be enough to cite the text of Luke which shows us that he withdrew at the very moment of great commitment to men: "But so much the more the report went abroad concerning him; and great multitudes gathered to hear and to be healed of their infirmities. But he withdrew to the wilderness and prayed" *(Luke 5:15-16)*. We cannot maintain, at least from the Gospel, that everything is prayer; Christ often withdrew from the community to go out into the desert and meet with God.

Because it must resolve problems that seem to be contradictory, obedience is a difficult virtue. It must be a fidelity to ourselves, to our vocation, to the deep and true self that is continuously rediscovered in the constant return to the roots of Being. At the same time, it must be fidelity to history because a vocation is fulfilled in a history of concrete liberation, of a country, of a time, of certain concrete human groups. It is fidelity to the person also because the Christian must never forget that his commitment to the history of the world must be centered on the acknowledgment of the dignity of each person. It is clear that in the community of tomorrow, the "religious" will not exercise the office of the consecrated religious that is now an anachronism. But the religious will still have the mission to make visible this freedom of the person in his roots, in the right to "act out his vocation." If it is not possible for man to overcome his conditioning, to be himself, to escape everything that waylays and alienates the person, there is no hope for anyone. Small cells within the world must rediscover adoration, which is the opposite of alienation, and reject everything that man uses to alienate man, even when it may be good in itself.

What is being sought is a humanity that is simple, poor, open, without needs, which breaks with the world in the way Jesus did, living a life in the world but not of the world. We need to watch continually over poverty, over the desire to command and to impose oneself. Above all, we must have a watchfulness that is very much open to God. Ours is an apocalyptic time and I believe that we should get used to thinking about it as if it had to start all over again from the beginning, as if all the experiences of the religious life, of the obedience of the past, did not exist. All of us are waiting for something. It seems that in the great caravan marching toward freedom there is a moment of delirium and panic because security about the road to be taken is lacking; this is normal, but the reason for the trip is not very clear either—and this is much more serious. On every side there is arising a supplication and an invitation to trust in the impossible, to harbor grand desires: "Have no fear of generosity nor of the breadth of your vision," said Pierre Restany, and on the walls of Paris we read, "Be realistic. Ask for the impossible." In the encyclical *Populorum progressio* Paul VI speaks of "inventing new techniques." Mistrust of the past is spreading, along with an omen of possible discoveries and an invitation for us to begin to think about man and his incurable situation as if we had just awakened in a world which is as it is and for which our generation has been called upon to be responsible.

I think we must situate obedience within this broad universal framework, beyond all juridical structures. We must have the courage to say that we have erred by making liberating obedience into an obedience of vassals which prevents us from maturing. We must ask God and the community the secret of this new obedience. There is no reason to fear being "men of God," even when this title today is universally discredited. I think that it is the contemporary form of humility. On the other hand, the problem is not new. The paths of illuminism to reach God and to resolve the existential problem of man were known from the first Christian generation. They were called *gnosis,* and Paul strongly fought against this kind of illuminism: "For the word of the cross is folly to those who are perishing, but to us who are being saved it is the power of God. For it is written, 'I will destroy the wisdom of the wise, and the cleverness of the clever I will thwart.' Where is the wise man? Where is the scribe? Where is the debater of this age? Has not God made foolish the wisdom of the world?" *(1 Corinthians 1:18-20).* Paul does not condemn culture or man's eagerness for knowledge. He is fighting against the man who wishes to seek integral human salvation through culture and research. Salvation is found on the cross. The liberator is Christ crucified.

This message is eternal and is the only true and saving message. If salvation is sought outside of this context, mankind will inevitably find itself in a blind alley. How can we speak to man today? In the terms of Paul in which he defines man in this way: "The spiritual man judges all things, but is himself to be judged by no one. 'For who has known the mind of the Lord so as to instruct him?' But we have the mind of Christ" *(1 Corinthians 2:15-16),* which is to say that we are truly identified with the spirit of Christ.

In the poor section of the great city in which I am writing these words, people speak to me about the religious schools and the communities that swarm within, but they are not able to see there the "spiritual man." They see ambitious and prepossessing houses, palaces which the poor are politely but firmly forbidden to enter. From them on Sundays come the messengers of the Gospel, the ministers of good will who come to celebrate the Lord's Supper for the "community" and to "make a community." But they come as strangers who enter an alien house and are more usurpers than friends. Undoubtedly they live an obedience, but it is an obedience that has another rhythm, other leaders, an object distinct from that of those who are obliged to obey from morning till night. There is sadness in the two separate worlds. Inside we find the sadness of a person who feels limited in his capacity for love and self-giving, of one who would like to obey God—not a God of the "supernatural" but a God who is at once creator and redeemer. And there is also sadness outside because the obedience is framed within a timetable; it responds to the rhythm of work; it has a boss; it has become automatism, and therefore the person does not know what to obey. A neighbor of mine says that when he wakes up at dawn with his eyes still closed, before putting a foot out of bed, he puts on the radio and receives orders. He has to give so much money to Coca Cola, so much to Palmolive, so much to the lesser companies of wine, fiber sandals, and overalls. He must obey until night comes, when he is lulled to sleep by the last dunning of the commercials. These are two forms of obediences which, in the long run, connect with God, because in the religious superior and in the structures of the world, even when they are unjust and violent, God is manifested. But these are two obediences that are more mortifying than liberating in love. All of us must obey because to live is to obey. Even the escape from one's own destiny through suicide is in the last analysis basically an obedience. But this obedience makes the world sad and makes man discontented and aggressive. Is there no way to discover an obedience that frees?

In the Exodus, Moses, Israel's great *condottiere,* withdrew periodically to converse with God in order to rediscover the itinerary he had lost. "So Moses returned to the Lord and said, 'Alas, this people have sinned a great sin; they have made for themselves gods of gold. But now, if thou wilt forgive their sin—and if not, blot me, I pray thee, out of thy book which thou hast written' " *(Exodus 32:31-32).* We cannot separate ourselves from the Exodus because outside of it there is neither God, nor mankind, nor history. And a religious cannot claim, by the fact that he is a religious, priest, or bishop, to be the *condottiere* of the Exodus. This is an eternal fact which becomes historical under different juridical and social forms. But the religious does have the responsibility to put hope in the Exodus and to live it not as something chaotic but as a march in time toward Someone. In examining the problem as a man and without preconceptions, Levi-Strauss writes: "Contemplation offers man the only favor which he has known how to earn: to suspend the march, restrain the impulse which obliges him to stop up, one after the other, the crevices that have opened up in the wall of need and to perfect his work while the prison closes. Every society aspires to this favor whatever its beliefs, its political regime, its level of civilization. It is where it passes its time, its pleasure, its repose, its freedom. This is the possibility, vital for life, of disconnecting ourselves. It consists—during the short intervals in which our species tolerates the suspension of its own frenetic work—in taking the essence of what the species was and continues to be beyond thought and beyond society." Out of the destruction of an alienating spirituality arises this kind of contemplative spirituality which does not eliminate man's groping search, his believing and making earthly values; rather it illuminates it and nourishes it with hope.

To see the problem clearly, we can divide the world into two great groups: those who live the obedience of slaves and those who live the obedience of the free. The obedience of the slaves belongs to the person who sells his soul, who lives a life in which he never has the possibility of discovering his true self or his autonomous being. It is a job that is not chosen, but imposed. It is a political structure which is not the result of active participation, but imposed by an oligarchy that makes unappealable decisions. It is organized pleasures directed by advertising with the sole motive of economic utility. It is the Church as the sole zone of freedom, monopolized by people who are monetarily and culturally rich. It is the family deeply dehumanized by the lack of space and time. It is really difficult to imagine a more total and tragic slavery than that lived by men today. In a real sense, the "prisoners" and the "oppressed" spoken of by the Gospel of Luke in chapter 4 are we ourselves. This common slavery includes the poor and the rich, the oppressors and the oppressed. It is not possible that this coercive obedience, without hope, beauty, or poetry, not give rise to a crisis of opposition to authority. All who in one way or another are responsible for these alienating structures, by the sole fact that they represent someone "upstairs," cannot be seen in a good light. I would go further. They can only be deeply hated. In order to survive, there is no other solution left for our society than "to kill the father."

Let us not look superficially at this crisis of authority. It is the other side of the coin from the crisis of freedom. We obey only with a view to liberation. No one identifies the obedience to the jailor who shuts the door after I spend half an hour in the yard with my obedience to a music teacher who is slowly turning me into a musician. Unfortunately, the obedience we live today is more that of a man in jail than that of a person who is becoming free, a person. It is a really blind obedience, without horizons or programs, a fatal and tragic law, a necessity that is identified with man's destiny, an obedience that has no prospect of softening, of gradually withdrawing from the space it occupies. On the contrary, we get the impression that technology offers to one who is on top and holds power the possibility of occupying more space in the person every day.

This slavery presses very heavily on the family, on the man-woman relationships which are becoming increasingly more superficial. Or if there is any attempt to go beyond this, they become tragic. For this reason, morality in sexual relations cannot be faced solely under the aspect of adherence to a law.

There are small communities mixed among the human community who know how to find the interior zones, the contemplative zones, who know how to halt the march, to break this macabre and total obedience to which man is subjected. Contemplation must be liberation from the law, for an encounter with the "thou" of God and therefore with the human "thou," and not an escape from our limitation in "understanding."

I cannot understand everything because I am surrounded in mystery. Faith and prayer have many times become confused with ignorance, because faith has been ingrafted at the point at which research has arrived. Beyond the pillars of Hercules the field of faith began, the field of the unexplored and the mysterious. But faith has nothing to do with this.

"Now faith is the assurance of things hoped for, the conviction of things not seen" *(Hebrews 11:1)*. It is not holding back before what is unknown and saying that we are shrouded in mystery. It is more a tremendous force for believing in things and in their value and therefore for continually overcoming the temptation to devaluation, to fatigue, to sitting down. I see faith rather as an energizing virtue, not a limiting one, because it is nourished by vision and hope. Contemplation that does not mature in wisdom and love is not contemplation. It must, then, mature in the clear discovery of the moment in which we find ourselves and of its meaning. We must thus discover the possibility of total liberation, beginning with the oppressed, because it is among them that the slavery imposed by the powerful becomes substance. There the tumor becomes visible and can be cured or cut out. Contemplation proposes to us again the theme of freedom of time and space, the theme of knowing how to put God, the One, where the many things are.

It is necessary that committed people, and I am referring both to those who believe in God and to those who do not, do the same thing on different levels. This is possible, I know, from the experience I am having in Latin America. Our retreats, which we call encounters, are pluralistic. Some speak quite directly about God, prayer, hope, the eschatological encounter. Others speak of revolution, violence and non-violence, structural changes. They are two levels of the same thing. They are two parts which are complementary, not by dialectical force or the desire for mutual understanding, but by the objective force of things. Unification comes about from the unity of the point of departure and the observations of reality; destitution, injustice, and suffering which truly exist. All destitution, all injustice, all suffering. The encounter is possible in humility, which is the recognition that one cannot be the other and that one is necessary for the other, and in the common conviction that creation cannot come about without breaks and destruction. The word "destruction" is so frightening. Yet it is necessary to accept it existentially in order not to give room for misunderstandings or to fall into the inconclusive moderation of the well-wishing world. This obedience requires a profound and vigilant asceticism, the humility to accept myself when I know that others are more effective, useful, and concrete than I. It requires the control of desires, which is indispensable when there is concentration on and constant search for the One. It requires control in our encounters with others, which must be pluralistic, open and enriching; it requires an attitude of receptiveness and at the same time vigilance. We can easily sell ourselves. Each of us can sell himself, accepting ideas that objectively are good. We must put ourselves in the conditions that prevent us from betraying ourselves, in which we cannot accept ideas against our choice. We must not trust ourselves. An inscription from the May revolution in Paris says, "Let's take the revolution seriously, but let's not take ourselves seriously." This could be transcribed as follows: Let us not trust in ourselves, in our intelligence, in the roots of our convictions, because we can be conditioned by persuasive and perfectly logical arguments. We must trust only in a commitment which obliges us in eyes of others, out of fidelity to the community, not to change, but to follow the awful logic of our option.

As I see it, this is evangelical obedience, the obedience of Christ and the apostles. We cannot deny that there was a hierarchy, a societal structure in the apostolic group and in the primitive Church which required an authority and obedience. But the obedience was a fidelity to the commitment made to go to the utmost, to be faithful to a commitment which has ever new aspects and seizes us ever more deeply, even unto death. This is an obedience to the community more than an obedience understood as an ascetical exercise and a renunciation of oneself: " 'You do not know what you are asking. Are you able to drink the cup that I drink, or to be baptized with the baptism with which I am baptized?' And they said to him, 'We are able' " *(Mark 10:38-39)*. "But when you are old, you will stretch out your hands, and another will gird you and carry you where you do not wish to go" *(John 21:18)*. "But Peter said, 'Ananias, why has Satan filled your heart to lie to the Holy Spirit and to keep back part of the proceeds to the land? . . . You have not lied to men, but to God'" *(Acts 5:3-4)*. To go to the utmost, for obedience to be dynamic, we must be watchful about fidelity to ourselves; we must accept diversity in uniformity, the risk of being less important and less effective.

We must be faithful to those who have the right to be free and cannot be, faithful to their rhythm, faithful in going to the ultimate consequences, even to death. Can you be baptized with the baptism with which I am baptized? No one can trust in himself because no one knows his own capacity for growth and his possibility of relapse. Because of this, we need the support of a community and an authority if we are not to be perpetual minors instead of genuine adults, without wavering, or at least without profound inconsistencies. Thus obedience is a structural obedience, not something totally outside the world, but the great law of the world. Only in this way can Christians recover the total meaning of existence and get back to the essential.

A new world is undoubtedly in the process of being born for which great faith is required. Nothing has been foreseen; we have to imagine it. However, if it is certain that Christ is risen and is with us in this stage, what should we fear? In this age of transition, I discover that we must all deal with obedience. The poor are totally alienated and can do nothing unless there explodes in their world the political revolution and the spiritual revolution, that of the genuine and profound liberation of the person. Intellectuals are alienated by their irresponsibility toward the poor and toward those who have not been and are not able to be persons. Religious are alienated in an obedience which they have made a virtue in itself, a means of killing nature in order to develop supernature; the result is half-men who are walking about and operating on this planet. If all of us could "do likewise" on different levels, could the world really emerge from this crisis? The religious and the intellectuals, those who in the past were called "clerics," ought to have the capacity to feel themselves, according to the leader of the May revolution in Paris, as a "permanent leaven which advances the action without directing it." It is not enough to strike our breasts and to declare ourselves guilty. We have got to give up our places. Can we expect to continue to lead if we have not been capable of giving man the freedom and dignity without which we can give neither faith nor hope?

I am afraid that many people are changing their style of life without leaving the program of clericalism, in which we permanently wear the clothes of those who have to teach and lead. "Let the greatest among you become as the youngest, and the leader as one who serves" *(Luke 22:26)*. We have to be careful with this word "serve." It is even more dangerous than lead." In the present historical context, it seems to me that only as leaven, as salt, as those who "do likewise" on another level, can we animate and encourage others to go forward. The first thing we must invent is obedience, a value that is discovered only in the commitment to do something which is good and true and in the inexorable faith that it has to be accomplished. This is that deep faith that moves mountains, the loyal renunciation of looking good, of gaining something, of making someone happy, of not giving anyone a heart attack. The Gospel is inexorable: "Leave the dead to bury their own dead; but as for you, go and proclaim the kingdom of God" *(Luke 9:60)*. We must decide to give up being the first, being the leaders at any price, the planners, the luminaries. For centuries we have read in Paul: "We have become, and are now, as the refuse of the world, the off-scouring of all things" *(1 Corinthians 4:13)*.

Yet, not only do we not feel ourselves to be the refuse of the world, but we sweep away others and commit ourselves in every way to securing the first places.

This is not a question of serving those who have less dignity than we, as we have always done, but of obeying them, taking on their rhythm, being with them as equals and not in a position of command. When religious who go to live in the slums enter into the process of the liberation of people alienated by money and stop behaving like television personalities, they will discover their proper place. Juridically it is difficult to say what we must do. Up to now, in the dust cloud raised by the postconciliar age, we can still see those who obey religious alienations and those who obey sociopolitical alienations. Positions have not changed substantially. I think that among these two groups who are angrily at odds with one another and fear one another, there can arise groups that have no interest in television performances and no fear of the hunters of juridical definitions. These are *the free*. Those who are quietly within the great liberation movement, who do what everybody does but in that depth in which freedom is achieved and touched.

14

THE CENTER OF FREEDOM

Under this title I shall be referring to what Teilhard calls the "divine milieu." If we accept the Bible, we cannot reject the history of salvation, which begins with a tiny people and branches out and continues in the "Church," the "people of God." I don't want to write a theology of the Church, because there are already two most enlightening works which I totally accept with deep joy: *Lumen gentium* and *Gaudium et spes*. I love the Church with a wounded love, and when people speak to me about her or when I speak of her, my wound bleeds. I must continually revise my position within the Church, asking myself whether my fidelity is sentimental or rational, if I am maintaining it out of fear or if it is authentic, and thus dynamic and creative.

I passed through the "papolatry" of Catholic Action. I feel I was right in leaving that phase behind me; I see the pope and the hierarchy as institutions founded by the will of Christ, but also as leaders who live as they are able, with all the fears, the ambition, the aggressive love, the conditioned intelligence and culture, with everything that I discover in myself and in those around me. To renounce the Church is as impossible for me as changing the blood and the genes I have inherited, even though I am at times irritated when I see appearing the same defects which as an adolescent so annoyed me when I saw them in my parents. The same thing is happening and so I know that I have to accept the insults leveled at my own group.

In spiritual books, being a Christian is described as a grace: I subscribe to this idea, because living makes me happy and for me living is identified with being a Christian. When I was preparing for the priesthood, to be a priest was considered to be a grace "cubed," and I never read a book at the time that did not give a vibrant exaltation of the priesthood. "Vocation" with a capital "V" was commented upon with drums and cymbals. Today, deep within me, I still consider it a grace, and words fail me to ask the Holy Spirit, "How could you have thought of me?" This surprise and this praise have grown over the many years that have passed. In the milieu in which I live, however, the priests who come to visit me are called "sons of bitches," because the wagon drivers who are hauling four or five tons of firewood have to step painfully over to the side of the road in order to let the deluxe car transporting these privileged people to pass. Of course there is nothing wrong in people coming to visit me and confiding their troubles to a friend. But they are able to come and see me any time they want, on any day, and in record time. On the other hand, when a man has a splinter in his eye or a woman is in danger of dying in childbirth, we have no way to send them to the hospital. There is no vehicle, no money, no beds in the hospital. For this reason, one who in dignity is above the angels and according to "edifying" books is a little less than God, from this local point of view is a son of a bitch. And as I too am a priest and do not deny it, I receive this well-earned and painful insult, which is truer than all the poems I have been made to listen to about the beloved pastor who visits his flock or the angel sent from heaven to be enthroned in the parish. Either the Church is of the poor and therefore has to be looked upon from their angle, or it is not.

If the Church is not, then the definition given by the wagon drivers—once the cloud of dust raised by the angel's wings has dissipated— should replace the more pleasant epithet of "son of the heavenly king- dom," "the special envoy of God."

I admit that the first definition is sociological and the second theological. But I do not know whether this distinction serves any purpose except to give an excuse to disregard a problem. I have suffered in the work of the Church, but without the least bitterness, because I feel as if I were in a boxing match in which I too landed some punches. I would not dare to call this suffering "persecution" since it would be unfair to those men of the Church who are not really bad, but are conditioned and made fearful by their "formation." To avoid dramatizing it, I need only face reality. In a political party, a meeting of scientists, technologists, stamp collectors, wherever people come together, there are divergences of opin- ion, more or less democratic clashes, real or presumed persecutions. When I think of the meetings in Paris on Vietnam or of those between the

Russians and Czechs at the border, it seems childish to speak of persecution and to moan the rest of my life because a man of the Church has given me a kick in the pants and another a punch in the nose.

And in this regard, I would say, with all the love I have for the pope, that when the men of the Curia warn that the pope must not be offended or made to suffer, my heart really pains me because the Church is not a kindergarten. I cannot imagine a White House aide telling me, "Don't upset the President." I realize that the pope's life is not lacking in its unpleasant aspects, but what life is? The Church is not a little family or a compact, patriarchal clan in which everything must be done to avoid displeasing the father. The Church was made to the measure of the world. When I heard this kind of reasoning in Rome and observed the pedagogy of Catholic Action, directed toward "pleasing the pope" or "not causing him displeasure," it seemed to me that the Church which I had discovered—strange as it may seem—in the great historico-dialectical fresco of Hegel had been reduced to a confraternity. Of course it would be nice to have a world in which nobody hurt anybody else, in which there was nothing displeasing and everybody was a good neighbor. But the world is not like that. The Americans displeased Ho Chi Minh and he did not hesitate to do likewise to Lyndon Johnson and Richard Nixon, but each thought he was defending freedom and right, or at least hoped he was doing so. It is true that Paul wept for the "enemies of the cross," but he was ready to be cursed and taken away if by doing so his brothers found Christ. In making this review of my life, I confess that I was more scandalized in Rome by this provincialism of the Church, this convent school mentality, than by the palaces of Julius II and the great rooms of the Borgias. In Rome one certainly feels the breath of the universe, but in the Vatican I felt as if I were in a parochial school the day the bishop came for a visit, or in the diminutive patriarchal kingdom that Montenegro must have been.

I believe that this reduction to a domestic and provincial level of something which in its essence is cosmic can have serious consequences. Not only I, but also serious-minded men in whom there is no suspicion of heresy or modernism, have the impression that the problems of the Church, which when lived on the periphery appear very dramatic, in Rome are not Romanized—which would be just what the Church ought to do—but "Montenegrinized." And here lies the difficulty of any dialogue. I defend the highest leaders of the Church from the accusation of being sneaks, deceivers, and "diplomats," because I have discovered that they are quite the opposite. They are "provincials" even if they go to Beirut on Monday, Tokyo on Tuesday, and London on Saturday. Is it a problem of training, of sensibility, or of one-sided experience? Who knows? Many of them, however, see the Church as a turn-of-the-century parish which is getting ready to receive a pastoral visit. I continually wonder whether I am not the one who is overly complicated, whether the Church should not perhaps preserve this childishness amidst universality, this little Montenegro, while the attitude and power of the political blocs are becoming more and more threatening. But I would like to know why the Church, the center of freedom, means nothing to the people, to those with whom I live, although they have all been baptized. Here is where the vocation crisis is. Here is the reason for all the frustrations. Today, heroism is needed more than ever to present oneself as a man of the Church, for more than ever people are crying out—whether they know it or not—for the man of God. I know that I cannot be profoundly a man of God if I am not a man of the Church. For this reason I don't want what I am writing to sound like a negative criticism or a project of reform. It is my way of seeing the Church from here, from my vantage point, and it is my way of living in the Church here.

It is true that the Church contains all the freedom of man for all spaces and all times. "Jesus Christ is the same yesterday and today and for ever" *(Hebrews 13:8).* "For in him all the fullness of God was pleased to dwell, and through him to reconcile to himself all things, whether on earth or in heaven, making peace by the blood of his cross" *(Colossians 1:19-20).* The Church must transmit this force of reconciliation in all times and live it in every culture.

In regard to this transmission, it is perhaps necessary to reexamine a notion that has now become somewhat antiquated. True, the transmission should be conceived actively, responsibly. But we are discovering, I think, that the people of God is an island, a little plot of land where the Word has come down to make it the center of concentration and freedom, like a sum of money entrusted to a financial agent so that it might be administered and multiplied. Both similes are present in the Gospel. But if Mary is the mother of the Church, if the Church is modeled in Mary's image, and if each day this similarity becomes more patent, we must go to the roots. How did Mary receive and transmit the mystery of freedom? How did she receive and transmit the Word? Not, certainly, as something that was her own. She was truly the ground, the island, where the Word became ingrafted in mankind, making this graft the center of the genesis of the universe. The Church today must live this mystery in a cultural context which necessarily modifies it. The context is perhaps no more difficult than others. But it is perhaps more radical, because there is a desire for newness, for a return to the beginning, which may not have been the case in other ages. On the other hand, what do these other times matter? God asks of us the courage and the faithfulness to face up to our own time.

The most evident characteristic of our time is the death of the father. As in the ancient myths, the children have devoured the father. It is a phenomenon that is present in the whole gamut of relationships—from protest against any form of authority to the equalitarian relationship that the youth are discovering today with surprising ease. In a short time the formal second person form of address will disappear from those languages that possess it. And this is not merely a question of words. The vertical attitude of uncritical acceptance of the teacher will disappear. From a tribal state we have made the transition into being a people. If the Church is living in the world, she cannot but feel penetrated by this demand of our culture. No one forbids the Church from living in her own law. But I wonder if the Gospel does not offer more possibility of accepting in the context of the Church what Ortega y Gasset defines as the theme of our time: that of "subordinating reason to vitality . . . transforming relationships and showing that it is culture, reason, art, and ethics that must serve life."

Here and there structures are forming in which authority has not been destroyed, but where it fulfills a function only of stimulus and coordination. Not long ago I saw the presynod meetings of Chile, composed of laymen, priests, and nuns. They seemed to me to be the symbol of the Church, of a generation that had put its father to death and yet still wanted to preserve the principle of hierarchy. A democratic style is not enough. We must create the possibility of a democratic expression. If I ask the laity, "Come on, tell me, do you really believe that the Son is equal to the Father? Do you think that Christ's presence in the Eucharist is permanent or is it limited to the Last Supper?" it is obvious that the democracy spoken of here would not be much different from that of Western societies. But if I stimulate vital interest by asking, "Does it seem to you that in your work the bosses treat you as equals and brothers as Christ wished?" I touch on a problem which deals with facts, and I am inaugurating democracy.

I know this from direct experience. Otherwise I would not speak of it. The Church's authority is no problem; no one thinks of fighting it. On the contrary, we discover that the presence of an authorized hierarchy in the Church is a factor of stimulus and union. The dead father is coming to life again in the now creative community. Did Christ perhaps not make himself food in order to come to life again in an assimilated community reunited in love? To respect this community it is necessary only not to have become committed to anyone or anything. The pastor who had an intimate conversation with the rich landowner has already committed himself to settling the problem of these "rabble rousers" and to suffocating any attempt at democracy. This parricide generation is now free from fear, but it still feels the urgency for coming together and making itself a community and a Church. The vocabulary must change. How happy I should be if "little Montenegro" understood this! Letters to the pope addressed to "Brother Paul" offended and mortified people. They were written, however, by people who still believed that the Church could be accepted by the generation that irrevocably killed its father.

One day, in an argument with a young person, I lost my head and said, "If you don't accept anything from me, it's silly for us to go on talking." "You don't understand!" he answered. "If I had no confidence in you and thought that you couldn't be redeemed, do you think I would still be arguing with you?" Jolif said, "Criticizing the teacher and even getting violently angry with him is to admit that he is a teacher. To refuse to listen to him and to act as if he did not exist is to assert, silently and in a practical demonstration that is more effective than any denial in words, that he is not a teacher" (*Comprendre l'homme,* Paris: Cerf, 1957, p. 53). Above all, we must see this attitude not as a manifestation of ill will but as a cultural phenomenon. In order to understand man in the face of all the universal types of phenomena that appear in time, we must ask, "Underneath all the negations, where is the truth? What is the truth hidden behind all the dust clouds?" The death of the father is something that goes beyond the ambit of the Church, but it has entered the Church and the Church has declared herself very happy to live mixed in with the world. The Church proclaimed this with two words that ring like a clarion: *Gaudium et spes.* No other world but this one, then, can be accepted. Indeed, if our generation has done away with the father in all its expressions, this relationship cannot be restored in the religious sphere. It would be false.

Our culture is seeking to adapt itself to a society which is succeeding the decline of nationalism. We feel that we are on the way toward universality. How? Technology, economics, and science are weaving universal cloth. Universality among the youth is something that can give rise to other universalisms. Speaking with Daniel Cohn-Bendit about the May revolution, Sartre said, "Something has arisen among you which is frightening, disturbing, and denying everything our society has done and is. It is a question of what I would call the expansion of the field of the possible. Don't give this up." The unity of liturgical language, which indeed was a value, has been surpassed, and to good advantage. Today we feel the need to rethink the Gospel in historical contexts that are not national so much as continental. I perceive that a universality of ideas is being formed. And will this not be richer than the juridical universality, than the universality that has been thought out from one center, a universality unavoidably imbued with colonialistic and therefore suspect tradition?

This stage is necessarily characterized by a process of groping, by extravagance, by rebellious pronouncements. But it has to be looked at face on, with prudence and not with fear. Prudence is the virtue of the leaders; fear is a limitation of our person. And we all feel it. These experiments do not touch dogma and truth except by provocation. I used to point out to priests in Latin America that if they began the battle of decolonialization with the liturgy, they would be making a mistake in method; they would be beginning at the end point. When there is a whole area of freedom in which they could move with the laity, why start here? They answered that they felt intimidated by the hierarchy. We frighten one another and perhaps this fear is incited by Satan, the divider. I hope we will know how to exorcise it.

It is clear that ecclesiastical nationalisms have given rise to disorders, but time is changing and history now demands a universality that has a sure and inexorable historical basis. On this basis we can attempt adventures that will never result in nationalistic fragmentation. Something similar happened with the crumbling of the temporal power of the Church, which had been the principle of her universalism. When the free territory of the Church was reduced to the few square meters of Saint Peter's Square, this square was filled with representatives of the peoples of the earth and the Church never felt so universal. Tomorrow we shall see a similar phenomenon: the formation of a universality of ideas, and not chaos, as long as we have the patience to rediscover, beneath the deformations of the spontaneous "internationals," the leaven of the Gospel. A man of faith is convinced, like Ortega, that "in a given age a thousand calamities happen, but the age itself is not a calamity: it possesses a fixed and unerring plot." If the Church actually is the form of the world, the fixed and unerring plot for me is the Church herself. And the calamities flow together to form this fixed and unerring plot even when we often do not clearly see how. These universalisms are vital; others, thought out on paper, are imaginary.

The fear of the Church seems to be something like the fear of a woman in a bad marriage situation..The Church must be continually at the side of the State, at the side of the political society with which she rarely has found a just relationship; she feels that her rights and her freedom are denied; she is therefore mistrustful. Everything coming from society and the world is seen with fear, even though the Holy Spirit has eloquently said that there is nothing to fear. The Church feels insecure and she will always feel this insecurity as long as she looks upon the State as a wife does her husband. Like the wife, the Church raises her voice, and makes a great fuss when she cannot bear it any longer. Then, she accepts her daily life all over again, with its blandishments and its fights, with its ostentatious arm-in-arm strolls—"Look what a fine man I've got for myself!"—and with its reprisals and protests when she catches him in adultery.

But the Church already has her Husband and any other marriage is the adultery of Israel renewing itself in history: "Whom did you dread and fear, so that you lied, and did not remember me, and did not give me a thought? Have I not held my peace, even for a long time, and so you do not fear me?" *(Isaiah 57:11)*. I believe that the basis of the insecurity is in this, and it has been so for centuries. It may perhaps be necessary for this false husband to die, because, even when she is abandoned, she still waits for him, forgives him, and goes back to him. Perhaps this husband is dead now. At least a definable, palpable political structure is dying, with which it was possible to maintain marital relations. And this insecurity of the Church is inevitably transmitted to all of us, just as a mother's insecurity is transmitted to her children. It would seem necessary to break with the mother in order to be free from her. I believe in the liberation of the spirit. But I observe a very widespread phenomenon—at least on this Latin American continent, which I am getting to know more and more: Genuine fidelity to the Gospel, the determination to be seriously faithful to the Gospel, is followed soon afterward by the decision to leave the official Church. I believe that the Church, which the pope calls "experienced with men," with her age-old experience of culture, accustomed to total transfusions, should understand what is behind this phenomenon. For my part, I must confess that I rejoice when I go from Caracas to Santiago, to Lima, to Rio, and meet young people. I see them discussing from different points of reference and at times with differing conclusions, but with a profound unity of vision. A discussion begun in Buenos Aires can be resumed in Caracas, Bogota, Rome, or Paris, with the nuances that indicate diverse degrees of political maturity. I confess that this is the living ecclesiality that makes me enthusiastic: One heart and one soul are found in spaces much larger than the small city of Jerusalem in which the first nucleus of universality was born.

But it is necessary to leave the lover. The State is the tyrannical man, a virile man like the rest, who not only transmits insecurity and therefore aggression to the Church, but who keeps her like tiny Montenegro. It covers her with gold and prestige under the condition that she continue to be a tiny, innocuous state. Therefore, in order to understand the substantial universality, the apolitical but not antihistorical groups which are cropping up today—which could be compared to "barbarian" society being formed during the fall of the Empire—it is necessary to break with the unfaithful husband. The adult generations can see only chaos in what is being formed in the world. Sartre was right. A professor will say, "Do away with examinations? Never! They can be improved, but abolished? Never." Why? Because he has spent half his life taking exams. To understand things that do not enter into political structures is impossible for people who do see only through this prism. And the Church ought to break off this union, which is, if not the sole cause, at least the chief cause of her fear.

The new barbarians have broken the frontiers of the Empire. The Church ought to remember now that those who came down from the North centuries ago and made politicians and philosophers tremble, inspiring lamentations over the fall of immortal Rome, renewed her blood. But these new barbarians cannot be received except by breaking with those powers which as a force are incapable of quelling the wrath that is rising up everywhere, which as a culture cannot give any motivation for tomorrow, and which as a program do not know how to come up with an ideal for a commitment to history now.

The Roman Empire of the little, mediocre Romulus Augustulus! They are trying to repair old cloth with new patches when the Gospel exhorts them not to. At least the Church ought not to trust in these poor menders. Why is this an adultery with the political power? The wife does not commit adultery when she is happily married to her husband. This is the core of the subject: Is the Church the bride of Christ? Yes and no. In regard to chaste love, I confess parenthetically that it has always seemed rhetorical and dangerous that a religious person consider himself or herself a "bride of Christ," even when the notion may have been useful in living seriously and deeply a relationship with him. The Church is the center of salvation, that which exteriorizes and actualizes the work of salvation, that which renders visible, in a community saved and united in love, this work of Christ. This is the function of the Church, and if the function is performed reluctantly or ambiguously, it is the Church's responsibility. If the Word is in mankind, all of mankind is his spouse. All of humanity must beautify herself, get rid of her blotches and wrinkles, and become *formosa.*

The right to belong to Christ is not a decree of citizenship that is extended to all the inhabitants of the Empire out of the kindness of the sovereign. It is the decree of the Incarnation, that mysterious plan hidden in pretime and antitime, which determines universal citizenship. "For in him all the fullness of God was pleased to dwell, and through him to reconcile to himself all things, whether on earth or in heaven, making peace by the blood of his cross" *(Colossians 1:19-20).* Yes, the Church has the right to call herself the bride of Christ because from her flows the blood, the water, and the word. For it is in her that we should find the marks, the signs of that beauty which we all are seeking in our dreams and in our hard and painful commitments. However, when the Church closes herself in, individualizes herself, and separates herself from the world in order to become institutionally the bride of Christ and thus the mother of men, an ontologically false image is created. It is a repetition, on a greater scale, of the relationship of the nun who is the "bride of Christ," who sees mankind outside the walls of her convent, as if she were destined to be a spinster and to grow old, embittered, hysterical to the point of madness, because she lacked love. And thus the Church, spouse of Christ, privileged lady apart, cultivated vineyard ripe with fruit, surrounded by an arid and sterile desert, offers an image that is perhaps the cause of the adulterous loves of the Church.

Churchmen are not men of bad will. We no longer have the popes of the Renaissance characterized by entertaining and enriching their relatives. But if this marriage has gone awry, if it is nonexistent and imaginary, adultery is inevitable. There are automatic reactions that burst out independently from our will. Humanity is the bride of Christ. If following the biblical style, we should wish to sketch out this relationship in a nuptial hymn, we would say that The Church is his center and symbol. Vatican II gave a glimpse of this new relationship. I should say that it gave more than a glimpse, it projected it. And this inevitably gave rise to a movement of psychological adaptation, convulsive and without apparent harmony, of the whole Church. It is obvious that the Pope cannot decide this change all by himself. Therefore, and with due respect, we must understand his pain at the spurts of impatience that are happening in the Church. But fear has to be overcome in every instance. It is an advisory evil, it is an antifaith. In order to overcome it it is necessary to emerge from the state of adultery.

The young are particularly sensitive to fear because in them insecurity and rashness are bound together, two forces which fear certainly does not help. The fear of others disturbs them and makes them tragic and destructive. We must keep repeating this to ourselves, we who are over forty, and not only we churchmen. When Christ made visible in the Church is the bridegroom of the world—and not in the medieval sense of the Church-soul and the world-body—the adultery will be at an end. A normal marriage will have been achieved, a clear and healthy marriage, and not a triangle. And therefore there will be no place for fear. I believe that the question of the Middle Ages is more a phantom than a serious danger. Much water has flowed under the bridges of the Tiber, as Pius XII said. Clashes were not useless nor were polemics wielded in vain. Man now no longer believes in the immovable earth, the center of the universe, and he does not now need a mother. To sum up, when the Church hears the ring of the words of security: "Of what are you afraid? You put on Christ and are identified with him, and you carry him with you"—and I believe that each of us hears these words at moments of difficulty—she should not have to confess, out of loyalty, "I'm afraid that he will see me, that he will find out."

We waste time criticizing people. By doing so we are unjust and Pharisees, because before attacking others, we ought to look at ourselves. All of us, however, should and can think with great love on how the Church should be, because each of us is responsible for her. And perhaps we shall be able to adopt today, without waiting for others, certain existential forms of the Church. It seems to me that this discussion about bishops and cardinals smacks of the sacristy and childishness. If it is certain that we do not need them now except in the strict function God assigned them, just as we no longer need our parents to continue to love, how is it that we speak so much of them? To me this seems tasteless and quite un-Christian. All the Christians who are afraid of the world, and who would like to stage a cinematic battle with cardboard bullets, fight desperately to maintain this image of the mother-Church and the father-bishop. But history is irreversible, and its destiny is to make explicit

Christ's words which "will not pass away." Many who hope in Christ dream of a free Church, one which speaks without fear of provoking a liver attack in the premier of France, giving a heart attack to the president of the United States, or of reducing the number of seats of the Christian Democrats in the Italian Parliament. They dream of a Moses-pope who would go alone up the mountain, would meet with God speaking through the burning bush or in a tempest, and would shatter in his ire the tablets of the law in front of the people who had turned to idolatry. Youth is demanding. It wants to see love and force. I do not think the pope shuns suffering because in the post he occupies he cannot help but have it. "He came to his own home, and his own people received him not." But we should like to see him in the great suffering of the world at large.

It seems to me that this liberation from the fear that afflicts many of us can open the way for the imagination that ought to play a very important role today and in the future. If in *Populorum progressio* peoples and men are invited to invent new techniques and new methods, and if this renewal of the technology of political structures is sought from the bottom up, the problem is posited for us. And the Church has to be inventive because if liberation does not come about, if man seems ever more doomed to new and more serious servitudes and more general alienations and ever less open to the hope of liberation, it means that the Liberator is a prisoner. He cannot work in and through us. And the wrath against us as Christians is more than just, because we have committed ourselves to liberation. For we are the Church, the Mystical Body of Christ who is liberation. We might reread Paul's sentence: "But the word of God is not fettered" *(2 Timothy 2:9)*. We pass from one to another the responsibility for having obscured the word of God. The bishops are asleep, the priests don't understand, the laity are conservative. What am *I* doing?

In the Church as in the construction of a building, there are three stages: the blueprint, the model, and the construction itself. The planners and the theologians have created daring and most beautiful dreams. Many of them have put their whole selves into defending an ideal. Others are retired and—perhaps with the intolerance of an elderly person who thinks his own rights are inalienable—defend designs, which are indeed sumptuous, sketched when it seemed that the Church was in need of restoration. Then came the time for the model, and the Council made it and made it well. We are now in the time of the builders and of the discovery of the paths of God, of the itineraries of freedom in the world. "But the bishops are not allowing it to operate. They're putting obstacles in the way. They don't want imagination. All they want is administration and obedience."

Looking at things as they are, this is true. Many people are despairing and giving up on the structures of the Church. Others are not joining her because they do not trust her. And this is augmenting the aggression, the confusion, the frustration. We must live by faith. Who can chain Christ? He can be made to suffer, be condemned and crucified, but not annihilated. "On the third day, he rises," and moves whatever stone is in the way. We lack faith because triumphalism is not dead. It has only moved its residence. From the palaces of the Renaissance it has moved into the slums, but it has not changed its skin. It wants to win cheaply; it wants applause and the flash of cameras. It wants to be admired. It is necessary that the imagination, which is already at a high pitch and a little inebriated, adapt itself to obscurity, silence, defeat, and disapproval. Christ too had imagination: "Lift up your eyes, and see how the fields are already white for the harvest" *(John 4:35)*. He said this when everything was really going badly, and the adventure gave no promise of any happy outcome. For charismatic people, for those with imagination, life has never been easy in the Church. On the other hand, in what institution is it? The more we are inspired by the fire of the Holy Spirit, the more we burn. I think that our tragedy is not the controversy within the Church nor divisions—which are not schisms but only divergences of opinion and, many times, ignorance and confusion about the role each person must assume. Rather it is the lack of faith. We quarrel among ourselves over Christ's vesture, we roll dice for his tunic, and we forget about him, the Liberator, dying on the cross. If we did see him, we would find that immense blast of freedom which is the wings of the imagination, the irresistible force of creation, that earthly and heavenly energy which at the last breath of Christ crumbled rocks, unleashed storms, and rent forever the veil of the temple. The imagination in the Church is the great force of the Holy Spirit. To respect it and understand it, a total freedom from fear is necessary.

In Latin America there is a phenomenon that is fascinating to me. The Church is so much within its history that the old proverb applies: "They will either hang together or they will surely hang separately." There can be no social change without a profound transformation of the Church. Even those who in other societies would be anticlerical or atheist have to deal here with the problem of the Church.

It is interesting and beautiful to see how without loss of continuity the transformation of society passes over into change in the Church. It is a reality which I think cannot be understood in its full dimensions from outside. The Church and Latin America is a theme which is attracting everybody's attention, Catholics and non-Catholics alike. People see that an important chapter of the world's history is taking place here. I quote a Latin American Catholic who is very familiar with the European philosophical movement and very aware of the social phenomenon happening on his own continent: "It seems to me without doubt that in the measure that pastoral work is nourished by the prophetic-evangelical vision, it should contribute to shaping and fortifying a revolutionary consciousness. Or at least it should contribute to sensitizing those who are lagging behind so that they might at least gather on the threshold of this consciousness. To some extent this is already happening in Latin America. True, it is undeniable that the Church's transition from being a power factor to being Christianity as a strength is coming about slowly. This is creating ambiguous situations for the clergy who are fulfilling the chief roles in the ecclesiastical hierarchy. They thereby participate in the possibility of an influence which is not precisely the one the Council had in mind, but which also cannot disappear overnight, as we have already pointed out. Acts and words of a bishop, even when they arise from a purely pastoral attitude, as a natural consequence customarily pass over into other milieus. It is to be hoped, then, that this influence will be exerted in the prophetic-evangelical direction. . . . Perhaps a more realistic vision is needed in this sense, one which would take account of the transition stage in which we are living. In any case, only those bishops who maintain or assume the line laid down by the Council will in the long run be the ones who will have any effectiveness in favor of or against what is happening" (C. Eggers Lan, *Cristianismo y nueva ideología,* Buenos Aires: Alvarez, 1968, pp. 212-13).

In my opinion, the Church's fear enters a great deal into this anxious and feverish search which is so characteristic of the self-appointed apostolic-pastoral structures, the structures of conquest. It is the fear of being a small number, of not making a mark in the world, of lacking effectiveness. And it ought not be confused with the commitment and thirst for proclaiming the Good News to every creature. The suffering that arises from gradually becoming marginal people and from discovering that the world and the youth can get along very well without us is very similar to the suffering that the world gives us when we realize that God is not known. Yet it has unmistakable characteristics. It is something like a healthy affection and a neurotic one which in the long run are discovered to be what they are and are defined. The hysteria of the conquistador and the proselytizer has done great harm to the Church and still does. We do not have to be many or few; we have to be *true* and authentic. The aggression that calls itself apostolic does harm to the evangelical mandate, which is pure and authentic. In the Church it has favored the element of "doing" and atrophied the element of "being." If a political party had the number of propagandists, the economic power, the organization, the structures for meetings, that the Church has, it would have the nations of the world under its control. Making the proper differentiation of the content of the message, I am convinced that to a great extent the Church is frustrating her imposing and well-meant efforts. Only in rare instances is community present in the Church, community in which freedom and love are manifest and in which Christ appears as freedom and love. The conviction that men are no longer fascinated by power, if they ever were, must be a profound, dogmatic, and indisputable conviction with us. Strength, yes, but not power. When we say that we have passed from vertical to horizontal authority, this has special repercussions because the power of doing and of execution is giving way to the strength of being. The Church should be very satisfied with this, because it is her own direction. But fear constantly sidetracks her and leads her in the direction of "doing," and therefore in the direction of power and in trusting in power.

All of us must "prostrate ourselves to the ground," as Catherine of Siena wrote to Urban VI, and recognize that we are not so authentically Christian as to be able to discover in ourselves the strength to speak with the pope and the bishops and truly help the Church. In the Council there appeared a demand for a Church that is poor and that serves. Perhaps this may be interpreted in an extrinsic and partial manner: Poverty and service are not methods or tactics since in such a case they would be false. They must become *being,* as in Christ. Being, that is, emptiness. They must be the capacity to receive a new form of barbarism which is being born.

Anyone who has seen a movie like *2001: A Space Odyssey* realizes the extent that linear culture is no longer of any avail. Before that world, which is not merely a prediction since it is already partly with us, we feel admiration and terror and a genuine and profound poverty. Christ is truly the great person for whom we have been waiting, the absent one, the one on whom we call. When I think of this world, I understand a word which has always seemed abstruse to me. "Paraclete" means "the one who is invoked." Invocation, in my opinion, is appearing everywhere and in all shades. When I observed the men in the film, obeying a law different from that of gravity, move in this different rhythm, I saw the image of the immense disproportion between our culture and the historical reality in which we live. The last power which we must give up is that of our culture, *exinanivit,* the self-abnegation which must be as total as was Christ's. The Church's "form of a servant" can be nothing other than this. A receptive Church is certainly not a Church which accepts everything and finds everything good, but a Church which receives everything and in everything seeks the good. "Test everything; hold fast what is good" *(1 Thessalonians 5:21).* The Church alone can and must perform the miracle of assimilating this new Barbarism, a term I use not in the pejorative sense but in the historical sense, for this is a new culture and a new force with regard to our humanistic and rationalistic culture.

Freedom from fear continues to be the basic hypothesis because it can produce that inner receptivity, that clear vision that is capable of seeing the signs of the times and the timeliness of acting, a gift which the Church does not always have. I recently read in a French text a phrase that is very much to the point: *Les pas rapides remplacent les sauts brusques,* "Quick strides are replacing abrupt leaps." If we do not want convulsions and abrupt breaks, we must not wait but work quickly in response to a world that is very demanding. There is no organization or structure on earth capable of integrating this new barbarian culture except the Church, because in her view every culture is nothing more than the permanent blossoming of the seed of the Gospel. Many fear man's adventure. If the Church is frightened as well, we are in a sorry state indeed. Has Christ abandoned us? Has Christ abandoned the world? Our world is afraid, very afraid, and the Church must manifest the tranquility on Christ's face on the night he quieted the storm. If the world becomes free of fear, all will be well.

To be freed from doctrinal fears, it is enough to realize that our culture is dangerous precisely because it does not have a doctrine in the classic sense of the word. Technology communicates enthusiasm, expectation, and fear. Everything but security. Against whom today could an inquisitional tribunal be set up? The Holy Office has been shut down because heresy does not exist. Today researchers are right in irately defending themselves against those who accuse the world of "technocracy," because even if we can speak of a monopoly of technology in culture, no "government by technologists" exists. Technology produces and will continue to produce. It must penetrate the cosmos. It is the great drill that continues to dig ever deeper, uncovering, producing, and enriching. Who can slow it down? And then, why slow it down when "possess the earth" is a mandate from God? There is no milieu that can shield the earth, protecting it, giving it security, and freeing it from anguish. It is like a new avalanche of barbarians who are young and powerful, have broken down frontiers and inundated the lands of the empire, our empire. Only the riverbed of the Church can receive this violent overflow, this ruinous tide. But to do this she must make herself a channel, emptiness, poverty, service! We do not know what kind of culture will result just as we did not know with the hordes of Attila and Odoacer followed by their youthful multitudes, hungry for land and sun, a violent and anarchical current, with its demands, its structures, and its definitions which suddenly made the proudly established Roman juridical tradition obsolete. The Church no longer has an Arius or a Luther to fight against, nor even a Galileo, consumed by his research and fearful of God. We must understand that against the Church's frontiers are pressing barbarian forces which do not want to be integrated into an institutional Church. Rather they want to win the right of citizenship which all societies and all human groups deny them.

The "wrath of the poor" is pressing forcefully against the wall with which the Church has defended herself. The supreme tribunal of the Holy Office is now called the "Congregation for the Doctrine of the Faith." The intriguing name of "Congregation for Research and Investigation" might suit it better. The name would startle more than one person, but what is the use of a new name if it hides an attitude that does not change? It should be a Congregation of Research because the men of global culture, the new "idea men," are in their own way searching for the faith. When in a Church context people speak of a dangerous culture or a dangerous world, this way of speaking is understandable and correct because man today truly feels that he is living in something provisional, tragic, and unknown. The conquest of space has unexpectedly cast him out from the womb of mother earth into a qualitative and spatio-temporal infinity without limits. This can offer him a moment of inebriation, but brings insecurity and fear once his reason awakens and returns. A person who has seen *2001: A Space Odyssey* will never forget those child's eyes through the transparent visor, which went from wonder to surprise, insecurity, terror, and madness. But the culture of this man who has leapt out of the earth's atmosphere is outside of our zone, just as it is outside the zone of faith, or of a faith conceived within earthly limits. Therefore, to speak of heresy or danger to the faith is like telling a man who is flying off in a space capsule what precautions he should take for a train ride. The world is now in another space and another time which, true, is filled with Christ but in which "Christian culture" has no longer any right to citizenship. Therefore, to speak of neomodernism, of the heresy of renewalism, causes the same effect as speaking of Nestorius or Arius. But it sounds even more anachronistic because Nestorius and Arius are still within our orbit, while modernism and the modernists and everything that can be expressed in our apologetical theological phraseology is outside the world's orbit. Today more than ever this phrase rings true: "Let the dead bury their dead."

The Church has a song of the planets: *terra, pontus, astra, mundus, quo lavantur flumine.* The earth, the sea, the stars, the cosmic spaces, the universe are all washed in the blood of Christ. Therefore I accept without fear the generation that comes back from space, fascinated and terrified, proud and insecure, which looks at earth from outside and which therefore sees it as a little town with petty interests and petty quarrels among neighbors. Ours is a deprovincialized generation. We must not forget this. But it is not deprovincialized in the way one would replace a medieval village with the city of the year 2000, but rather in the way a person leaves solid ground for the void. We must find the courage of security and daring, of the clear and the undefined which is the language of faith: "And in the fourth watch of the night he [Jesus] came to them, walking on the sea. But when the disciples saw him walking on the sea, they were terrified, saying, 'It is a ghost!' And they cried out for fear. But immediately he spoke to them, saying, 'Take heart, it is I; have no fear.' And Peter answered him, 'Lord, if it is you, bid me come to you on the water.' He said, 'Come.' So Peter got out of the boat and walked on the water and came to Jesus" *(Matthew 14:25-29).* I shall not make any comment on this passage or I would spoil it. I thought of it when in the movie I saw the man in the space suit floating about slowly in space. But Jesus did not stay on the shore with his feet on solid ground. "When they saw him walking on the sea." And perhaps this is what the "barbarians" are asking for: that the Church venture out into space. "Take heart, it is I; have no fear." The only ones who will stay on land are the fearful and the "diplomats," or in other words, the dead.

15

THE FREE WOMAN

Mary shares the destiny of woman: Either she is left in the shadows, considered a detail of creation and liberation, or she is placed on too high a pedestal. In both cases she is outside. This alienation of Mary is perhaps due to the fact that the interpretation of her virginity dwelled too much on the physical aspect and therefore on her solitude. Mary is presented more as the virgin-mother than as the wife of Joseph, more as an ideal of a disintegrated state than an integrated one. Perhaps this is the reason why the love professed for Mary by certain persons, mature perhaps in years but not in spirit, inspires a certain mistrust in me. There is something immature about them, not integral and therefore inauthentic. They are half-persons, unfulfilled, and they project on Mary the lack of integrity, this nonfulfillment that characterizes all their choices. It is difficult to know whether a spirit is like a child because of fullness or immaturity, because of a victory of the spirit or a defect of the psyche. Furthermore, who is normal? This question inhibits me when I feel tempted to make a judgment.

But on the theme of Mary—as on the theme of the Church—I have to think carefully and reflect every day, because the love I feel for her is fierce and a little wounded. I do not believe that childhood left me with a negative image of the mother; the image which I now reject was presented to me later, when I ran into people who offer flowers to statues and pictures and keep and care for them with fetishistic concern. The remembrance of one's mother is natural and constitutes a value in a person's life; but there is a nostalgia for the mother which is pathological. For this reason I am trying to rediscover the person of Mary through the trauma of the projections of celibates, those who are continually compensating—by a memory or an ideal—for what they did not accomplish. And for this very reason I must find Mary again in the simple and normal framework of the Gospel.

The Gospel shows her as an ordinary girl of her time who one day received an extraordinary message. The angel greeted her as "full of grace," and said "the Lord is with you." Mary lived with that full integrity to which every person aspires, knowingly or not. With her finally begins that generation which is "not of flesh and blood" but "of God," which means, not the old flesh that carries with it ancestral specters, fears, desires, and anxieties that lead it to other alienations, but new flesh that has been reborn integrally sound. Mary is the model to which all mankind tends. Mary is like the personification of our hope.

In Mary, integrity is this profound and total adhesion to vocation. She is truly her whole vocation, which is that of giving the Son of Man to the world and of putting, through him, a force of salvation and freedom in the world. She is the soldering point, the entrance, the receptive ground, the nature which envelops mankind totally sheltered in her, receiving from her the principle of salvation. In Mary, freedom becomes her. It is not an extrinsic process because the spirit that overshadows her came down on her, carrying her to the pure heart of being, to that extremity of being in which no one enters because it is prior to existence—which is already a choice and therefore an alienation. Mary was chosen totally, without the possibility of choosing something else, because the Holy Spirit demands entire receptiveness in being. It did not require her to do something. Mary is not the prophet who was set aside to go and "root up and plant," to announce peace and defeat. She was chosen to *be* the mother of the Son of Man. The supreme liberation of the person, his true freedom, is in this concentration in which he can give all his being before it is divided and fragmented into various choices.

Beneath the characteristically modern refusal to make concrete choices, there are outlines of a profound truth, because it is true that the various choices that man must make do limit his freedom. In fact, however, historically man's freedom does not come about except through choices which at once liberate and limit. Throughout his existence, man seeks his being, that is, a profound identity with himself—the truth which "will make him free." Who am I? What function am I performing in the history of the world and what are the forces that continually make me be something different? In her total receptivity, in making herself a hand-maiden, Mary reached the supreme liberation. She is the mother of the Savior; she enters into the essential function of the person which is to be a liberating energy in the community and in creation. We have nothing more than work and sex by which to choose, share, know, and possess. But these two functions, while they fulfill being, draw it out of itself and alienate it. Mary chose Man, although "she did not know man." At that moment she entered history with a function that was totally love and liberation because her choice was made not in flesh and blood but in the spirit of God. Through a generating process which introduced a liberating force into mankind and creation, Mary entered into communion with mankind and with the whole of creation. By deeply and fully following her vocation, which was her integral giving of herself to the Being that filled her totally, Mary did what she had to do. In other words she virtually liberated all mankind and all creation.

I knew a woman who was unhappily married. I asked her, a little ingenuously, how it happened. She answered: "First I saw being and then nonbeing, the falling back, the impossibility of fulfillment." She had married with the confidence that she would be collaborating in the liberation of the world, and he had given her every guarantee. Then came his profession, money, and success, and she was incapable of saving him. At times the opposite happens. In any case the problem is that when love is separated from the vocation with which the person is identified, love ends. It is as if love had become increasingly displaced from being and had become reduced to functions, episodes, and symbols which are outside of being, the meaning of the profound vocation. As a consequence, the process does not go toward freedom but toward an alienation which advances inexorably like an illness. Mary achieved total integrity because her function, love, and vocation coincided with being, which is God. Hers was not an extrahuman path; each person must discover more or less clearly this coincidence. The discovery of the meaning of life is like the discovery of being, which becomes increasingly more clear in consistency with and fidelity to this meaning and which is clearly and indirectly a discovery of God or an act of faith in God. When a person does not attain this fidelity or does not know how to or want to attain it, it is necessary that the role player diminish in order to achieve identification with the true being. Perhaps this is the sense of pain, of illness, of growing old, with its whole series of disillusionments and the death of chimeras—the reduction to being. Mary's integrity became evident from the first moment because the Son of Man came to the world as "our peace" *(Ephesians 2:14)*. In her the person achieved that profound identity which is peace.

The essential and permanent integrity of Mary was manifested and became a sign in all the episodes of the Gospel in which she figures. The first is her betrothal to Joseph, with whom she forms the image of God on earth. Joseph is not just the "chaste guardian" of the Virgin—and therefore not the eunuch we hear about in stories of dissolute kings and imprisoned concubines. Joseph is the *husband:* "Do not fear to take Mary your wife. . . . When Joseph woke from sleep . . . he took his wife" *(Matthew 1:20, 24)*. Integrity was incarnate in both of them through a profound and faithful love which reproduces the image of the Trinity on earth. Joseph is not a "representative" of the Holy Spirit. He achieved with Mary the profound unity which happens only in the finding of the true self, discovered and freed from all alienations, in the acceptance of a common vocation in truth. It is a discovery that is not outside of sex, but more deeply within than sex itself. And why is it not outside of sex? Because if the essential fulfillment of the person is the image of God and if the world is in peace and freedom to the extent that it is a projection of the true, fulfilled image of the person and in the person, then the image of God is the man-woman person, which is formed in a progressive love defended from caprice, arbitrariness, and relapse. It is more deeply within than sex because the achievement of this image—which is peace brought about in the person in order that it may be brought about in things and in history—is not ontologically and essentially bound up with the function of sex, which in itself is ambiguous and provisional. "For in the resurrection they neither marry nor are given in marriage, but are like angels in heaven" *(Matthew 22:30)*. The Holy Spirit is symbolically the husband of Mary insofar as he who was conceived in her was not conceived by flesh and blood but by spirit. But Mary is Joseph's true wife; he loved her, received her, and shared his life with her.

Mary's integrity is much more profound than physical virginity or the absence of sin. It is the substantial reconstruction of being in freedom. It is substantial identity with her own vocation. It is being and existence uniting integrally and fully for the total freedom from the forces of alienation which are outside and within us. Since we do not have any other terms of reference, this liberation is represented from without as an obedience; therefore Mary seems less alive, less human than those who make their choices with the hesitations, doubts, and errors of the living being. Her perfection seems something that is less human, which deeply estranges us from her. I overcome this image if I see Mary's function as "service to being," as a way of making me participate in that integrity to which I aspire with all my strength because it is my truth which is made hope for me. For this reason, I feel that Mary is deeply rooted in my life. Like Christ, Mary has deeply participated in mankind's struggle for freedom in a way that—because it is freer—is more intense and dramatic.

Integrity forms the person as a center of attraction for liberations. As the person becomes aware that freedom must be brought about in what is around him, the more that he discovers that freedom is achieved within him, so much the more will he sense the suffering of freedom. So much the more will he sacrifice himself for the urgent attainment of all those freedoms to which his own freedom is inevitably bound. This happens in a man who sees and loves freedom as an attribute of being. In Mary—in whom all being is freedom—suffering and the co-participation in liberation are much deeper than in any other person. Sexual polarization has made us see in Mary a rather icy perfection, remote from man and his struggles and vital interests, even when this same man draws near to her out of a kind of sentimentalism that is quite alien to his true life. The freedom that came about in her is a freedom with and for men and consequently is an extremely painful freedom. What do these words from the Gospel mean: "Behold, this child is set for the fall and rising of many in Israel, and for a sign that is spoken against (and a sword will pierce through your own soul also), that thoughts out of many hearts may be revealed" *(Luke 2:34-35)*? In this context I believe that freedom in the person consists in being in truth, and this anchoring of Mary in the truth and in integrity will be for her the reason for great interior suffering. It will oblige men to define themselves in the face of the truth. It is impossible for me to see Mary as a queen, dressed in white, standing high on an inaccessible iceberg. I see the woman who weeps. She is one of us, involved in our struggles. In a land of slavery, what good is it to know freedom and to be free? How many times has each one of us looked at the world through loopholes of our consciousness and felt that all this look did was to show us how wretched we are?

Another very enlightening insight into the mystery of Mary is the episode of Jesus' being lost, narrated in Luke's Gospel: "And when he was twelve years old, they went up according to custom; and when the feast was ended, as they were returning, the boy Jesus stayed behind in Jerusalem. His parents did not know it . . ." *(Luke 2:42-43)*. More than a child, Jesus is a young man at the age—especially among the Eastern peoples, who mature early—proper for leaving his family and beginning to live his own life and his own vocation. Mary is a perfectly balanced mother. She loves her son without possessiveness, as is proved by the fact that she could have spent a whole day without seeing him. She thinks he is perhaps with their travelling companions. This normalcy in maternal love is due to the fact that Mary feels herself loved and lives her life as a wife in fullness. Without a dialogue between the two who form the couple, without a profound co-participation in life by both, there is almost inevitably an affective imbalance which turns the woman excessively to motherhood. The "maternalistic" mother is the woman who has "not been taken," who "has no husband," even when she is living with a man. More than by rational principles, children are brought up by this climate of normalcy which the husband and wife ought to create through a love which is a reciprocal giving of self and the total community of living. And this community must be not only in one's affective life, but also in one's active life, the life of work and of presence in the world. It is well known that the father and mother who exercise their functions in a parallel way instead of doing so in communion ruin their children. The children recognize, more or less consciously, a love that oppresses rather than frees.

When I was speaking of this to a group of women, one of them had this objection: "What about widows?" During this brief period of her marriage a widow may have experienced this liberating function of love which she should continue to live even though it is painful. Either she was married and in a certain sense is always married, or else she was never married because the man with whom she lived was not really her husband. In this case, her affectivity is as imbalanced as that of the woman who is joined only physically to a man. In this Gospel episode all of Mary's anxiety shines through, all of her concern as a mother, and at the same time that freedom which allowed her son to "be about his father's business." Mary is a mother who does not solve her son's problems, who does not do everything herself. Each of us must live his own deep obedience to God, which is personal and identified with the person.

Popular devotion has projected on Mary the phantasm of an overly protective mother, one who solves everything, who thinks of everything, who takes upon herself all the struggles, hardships, and annoyances, so that her child can be comfortable, sleep on two pillows, and live in a perennial childhood. This is not the picture of Mary given to us by the Gospel: a discrete, quiet woman, immersed in a life that is magnificent but also commonplace and without anything extraordinary about it. It is the life of every man, without respite from work and without any special exemption from daily difficulties. The period of Jesus' public life shows her to be alone. It is very likely that her husband died in one of those epidemics that in those times decimated mankind. He died, even though the Son of Man who raised Lazarus was there. But he did not perform a miracle. Joseph died like everybody else. To transfer to Mary our need for magic, the residue of our unsatisfied childhood, the void left in us by unfulfilled love, thus avoiding the effort of reaching human maturity—which is ultimately spiritual maturity—is to denature her real image. It is miraculous that God lives with us and that this co-habitation has a focus, a *phylum* as Teilhard would say, which is Mary. But this co-habitation of God does not change life as it is historically. It changes it substantially only for the one who knows how to discover this imponderable *quid,* indispensable for life, which we call hope.

The sign of a wise mother is the maturity of the son, the mature affection that he continues to have for her, which is not marked by childishness or false nostalgia. I would say that the sign of having lived in the context of a healthy maternal relationship is above all detachment. We are scandalized by Christ's words: "Who are my mother and my brothers?" *(Mark 3:33).* Yet I think that these words are the best possible praise of Mary. Christ's detachment is not, as we shall see, a lack of love, but a pencil stroke wonderfully sketching his mother's face. Mary's motherhood is balanced and responsible; it creates a responsible man, not an eternal baby.

I am not shocked by expressions of tenderness toward Mary, provided that one's whole attitude and life are marked by a maturity that means facing up to events and our responsibility—without trusting to extraneous and imaginary powers the decisions which only we can make. However, when I see men praying the rosary who wash their hands magnificently of the problem of the world's liberation—abandoning this to the forces imminent in history, as if they were like the forces which produce the ear of corn from the seed—then this Marian piety annoys me. It is either childishness or, worse, hypocrisy. Mary truly sums up in herself all of man's ideals. But for this very reason, she can be transformed, if we are not careful, into a pathological projection. She can be the breast for one who has been poorly weaned, the ideal wife for one who has not become integrated with the woman he has chosen, the imaginary and available eternal feminine for a man who has not wanted to commit himself to a woman, the impregnable and icy rock for one who makes chastity a privilege and a means of breaking with the world. She can be the fairy with the magic wand who solves problems by exempting us from the intellectual difficulty of confronting them and from the practical difficulty of giving one's life to solve them. She can also be the ultimate escape of one who sees death coming and, afraid to look at it straight on, prefers to take the step with his eyes covered by a scapular of Our Lady of Mount Carmel. Who is Mary for Christ? She is the point of his being rooted in the earth, the point of his insertion in time, in mankind, and in history. And for this to be a center of freedom, it was necessary that there be in it all freedom as a center of gravity for the new history.

The biblical analogy of Eve-Mary and Adam-Christ is fascinating and is an area that is still unexplored. Eve represents the point of our being rooted in the ambiguous world in which we lose ourselves in our search for freedom. Mary is our being rooted in another genealogy which is equally earthly but is spiritual at the same time: "those born in the flesh" and "those reborn in the spirit." Both genealogies are of the earth and of history. But one is the genealogy of perdition and death, the other that of freedom and life. It was not possible for Mary not to have been wife and mother at the same time. As a mother, the woman is Eve who was joined to the earth, in its richness and ambiguity. From the mother there comes to us all the fullness of being a person and all the ancestral ambiguity, the beauty and the slavery of flesh and blood. It is an involvement that we must accept and from which we must at the same time free ourselves. The Oedipus complex is that mysterious synthesis of attraction and rejection, a tendency to remain and a tendency to leave. Only the woman who is a wife can contribute to liberation through her being rooted affectively, dynamically, and progressively, a stopping point which must continually be transcended. Mary is the symbol of the Church-Spouse rather than that of the Church-Mother, of the center of liberation more than of a static radication. "A man shall leave his father and mother and be joined to his wife" *(Matthew 19:5)*. The first bond must in some way be given up, overcome, or transformed. The second bond, which is dynamic rather than static, must be transcended continually; but at the same time it is the permanent bond, the one which should last a lifetime.

Even in errors we can see truth emerging. I remember a woman whose religious attitudes bordered on bigotry. She spoke to me about her rebellious husband who would not listen to her advice. "After all, if he's unwilling, I can't do anything. . . . He's not of my blood." She was alluding to flesh and blood relationship, which automatically gives the right to inheritance in a legal and static way; but there is another relationship, the "kinship" of the spirit, which one enters freely by a conscious acceptance in faith. To accentuate the aspect of Mary's motherhood is like accentuating the aspect of the Church-Mother. They are real aspects which are synthesized in the woman. But a mother is not only the mother of her children, but also something of their wife—and the pathological aspect of the Oedipal situation alludes to this. Insofar as the woman is profoundly the wife of her husband, and is thus liberated, she initiates the children into the quest for freedom.

If we lay too much stress on the aspect of motherhood, there is the inevitable consequence of introducing the presence of the "carnal"—in the pejorative sense—into the "spiritual" and of giving rise to that legalistic and carnal frame of mind against which Paul rebelled. Mary is called "mother and bride of Christ" because her relationship with him is not based on flesh and blood but on the spirit. The new Eve bore in her womb the earthly, cosmic root of the Son of Man, gave birth to him in the time of the community and history. But since she herself was liberated, he was free and the liberator. She shared in Christ's flesh and blood and is truly the mother of God because she is the mother of the historical person Christ. But she did not give birth to him for herself but for others, for others and for the Father, that is, with faithfulness to the vocation which is the will of the Father, God's design for her life: "Whoever does the will of God is my brother, and sister, and mother" *(Mark 3:35)*.

Mary sums up in herself permanence and transcendence, the acceptance of the carnal and earthly in order to transcend them, not with the intention of abandoning them but in a process of liberation and transfiguration. I often have occasion to rediscover this experience in the ambiguity of human relationships. The woman represents stability, the root, and many times the fear of newness, but she also represents courage, initiative, the decision to put aside "human respect" and "what the neighbors will say." Just last evening—and I cannot keep from smiling when I discover in these encounters the "style" of Providence—I was speaking with a couple who are friends of mine. The man said to his wife with somewhat exaggerated vehemence, "Now you ought to tell our friend that you quote him when it suits you, when you do not want me to go hunting or fishing, so I'll stay home and talk to you or so we can go out together. But when it is a question of sharing the land with the workers or giving them part of our property, then you don't agree with him. You say that the property belongs to us and to our children and that we don't have the right to deprive them of something which ultimately belongs to them." The wife accepted her part of the responsibility. It was true; that is what she had said. It was a flesh-and-blood cry, but not a deep one; it came out of her unliberated self. I wanted to make the husband understand that both responsibilities were intertwined and interrelated. It is hard to know where to begin, but it is clear that the root of this cry of defense, this staticness, is not eliminated if the woman is not liberated with "water and the word." This means sacrificing herself and commitment to dialogue. For this reason, I should say that the source of liberation in Mary is the Holy Spirit, the author of her unique and unrepeatable integrity. And the sign of this is her function as wife, in which the aspect of liberation, transcendence, and exodus are apparent. "My mother and my brothers are all who do the will of the Father." Mary could not be better represented than in this symbol of free and liberating love.

It seems significant that the only time Mary appears in what Christ "does" is at the wedding at Cana, which the Gospel of John narrates for us in the second chapter. I am not being an exegete; I am merely reading the Gospel as the man in the street. The symbols in this narrative assail us, but man's whole life, his history, is a reality and a symbol. If we live in the faith, everything is *real and at the same time a symbol* of something hidden. Jesus and Mary are present at this wedding where at a particular moment the wine, the symbol of joy, has run out. It is a banquet which began well, but threatens to end in sadness. They have run out of that which gives joy and continuity to the celebration—the wine. With a woman's intuition Mary gives the alarm: "They have no wine." They lack that joy of a feast which is found solely in the vital energy communicated to man by wine. It is a common, almost trivial story, the story of one of those wedding feasts which begin with much joy but then lose their momentum and run the risk of losing from within the courage and the interest to go on. "They have no more wine." And Christ answers with some harshness: "O woman, what have you to do with me? My hour has not yet come" *(John 2:4)*. But Mary intuits that this is not a negative answer.

In this episode I see the union of man's power of initiative with the faith, the hope, the intuitive daring of the woman. Only the woman contains within herself the two elements of the *law* and the *life* in history: First there is the assimilation of the past, of being rooted in reality, in tradition, in the true ground. This is a dangerous but indispensable moment. How beautiful if we could remain at this point! But then comes the moment of "Come on, let's go!" It is not important to know where; the horizon need not be clear. Let's move! "My hour has not yet come." "Do what he tells you." At the wedding there were six jars of water for the customary Jewish purifications. I think it is important that this water did not come down from the sky, but had been prepared by men for their ablutions prescribed by law. This seems to imply that all the Jewish prescriptions and all the legalism were not going to be able to save the wedding from gloom.

Here, where I am writing, the men of the forest constantly are showing me plants which grow to enormous size but give no fruit. "These are defective," they say, or "They grow badly." They attribute this to planting at the time of a bad moon. I am reminded of this when I see marriages and persons who "grow badly," like the marriage of Cana which threatened to go badly for lack of wine. They have not discovered that the juridical bond can be accepted only if it is the symbol of an affective bond which really exists. And the affective bond must be transcended continually in order for it to subsist: If it is not nourished and is not continuously transcended, it becomes water and "goes bad." This transcending comes about in concrete deeds, which can also be polemical and seem continually to challenge the sentimental bond. But it is a rediscovery of this bond in order to transcend it and enrich it with value and content. The joy of the wedding seems to depend on such an accidental and trivial factor as the lack of wine, and yet that was the case. The strength and fragility of love oblige man to be tirelessly vigilant, because he intuits that if he fails in this point he fails as a person and therefore dries up life at its root. An analogy spontaneously comes to mind. Mary notices the sadness that is beginning to appear like an asp hidden somewhere at this joyful banquet. They have no wine. In the *Song of Solomon* the bridegroom who has come into the garden and tasted its delights, invites his friends to drink a toast: "Eat, O friends, and drink: drink deeply, O lovers!" *(5:1)*.

A boy asked me why Jesus performed a "superfluous" miracle at the marriage feast of Cana where people had already eaten and drunk, and yet he did not change stones into bread so that all the hungry of Israel might eat. There are many answers, but the most appropriate is that this joy is nothing superfluous. It is the equivalent of the motivation for living, without which there is no movement toward freedom. If we take the fact as it sounds and appears, obviously the lack of wine would have produced one less drunkard and therefore a greater tranquillity. But in the mystery of marriage, which is the constructive and liberating encounter of the person, his ontological repacification in the recomposition of his original unity, the wine appears as a symbol of the joy of living, which is nothing else than the rediscovery of interpersonal communion: "Eat, O friends, and drink: drink deeply."

Man has everything and he can do everything. He must only be identified and motivated, which are the same thing.

Mary was present at the moment when the water of purification contained in the six stone jars was changed into wine. It was her boldness and courage that determined the time. Mary broke the ambiguity of time and changed it by her fearlessness into the time of salvation. The time of humiliation, of water, is changed into the time of salvation, into the "beginning of the ages." The time of the law ends and the time of the spirit begins, the time of those who are "drunk" with the spirit of God. The marriage between a man and a woman, the marriage of the person with nature and things, are eternally threatened by the temptation to staticness. Everything is decaying and the gnawing worm is appearing: "To what avail is all this?" It is useless to break one's back filling up six jars of water. Either the bold faith of Mary changes the water into wine or the water goes bad and purifies no one or nothing. We priests always dream of calm and moderate weddings with wine in right measure, and our couples are sad. Mary is well married and deeply happy in being identified with her vocation. She understands the gloominess of a marriage without wine and hastens the time: "They have no wine!" I see Mary more as the bride of the *Song of Solomon* than as the solicitous and protective mother: "Drink, and drink deeply, friends." "Do what he tells you." She is sure that he will produce wine and thereby joy and inebriation at this wedding feast. Here Jesus manifested his glory, which is that of situating himself within mankind as the leaven of liberation which moves it. Pharisaical purification is changed into this inebriating wine, which has the taste of freedom.

Among the "many women" who had come from Galilee to follow him to Jerusalem was naturally Mary. "And when Jesus saw his mother and the disciple whom he loved standing near, he said to his mother, 'Woman, behold your son!' Then he said to the disciple, 'Behold, your mother!' And from that hour the disciple took her to his own home" *(John 19:26-27)*. The tradition of the Church has seen in this moment the investiture of Mary as the mother of all men. Mary's motherhood is manifest and almost concentrated in her gift of her Son to mankind for man's liberation. Calvary has been reproduced in tragic paintings and sculptures that are pompous and at times horribly decadent. They distill a cheap sentimentalism and move us more to compassion than to comprehension. I believe we shall have to go back and revise the meaning of a form of piety which has been very widespread in Christian spirituality: I am speaking of reparation. The *Pietà,* and especially the ugly plaster representations of the *Pietà* which we see in well-lighted niches in our churches, provoke an immediate feeling that is very like what someone feels on a visit of condolence: "Don't cry, take heart. We are at your side. We want what is best for you. Your son [or husband] was such a good person, so well thought of. What scoundrels they were who killed him!" Our reparations are more or less artistic and profound variants of the conventional dialogues that go on in the house of a dead man. Mary is the mother who has lost a son and we have come to tell her how deeply sorry we are.

I confess that I have never been moved by the lamentations I have heard or read; despite the fact that Saint Bernard thought that anyone who was not moved had a heart of stone, I have never been able to weep for the sorrow of a mother who lost a son two thousand years ago. But I have discovered Christ as the profound reason for all the painful, tragic, and absurd movements toward the freedom of man. Its liturgical expressions, like the mass or meditation on the cross, need to be nourished by a continual discovery of their relevance to the daily effort to advance toward personalization. How costly it is to be a person! How many tragic "yesses" and "nos" we have to utter at every step, and with what pain do we pay for the demolition of a dike which then is built up again! I see the "Sorrowful Mother" every day in women like the mother of thirteen children who came to see me this morning to ask me for money to buy a sewing machine so she could work at night. The suffering Christ is the woodcutter with whom we spoke yesterday at length on the possibility of one of his nine children being able to attend night school in order to improve their situation. In the terrible human sorrow in which there glimmers this longing for freedom, this desire to be more a person, I see Christ and his seed of freedom. I see reparation carrying on the effort, not letting one's program falter, accepting our share of the work and also of the unpopularity, the insult, and the contempt of Pilate's tribunal and the Sanhedrin. It is true that Christ suffers and is in agony for our sins. But I do not make any reparation by sighing or weeping, but by accepting the struggle for justice against everything antihuman and depersonalizing in the world.

Reparation often consists in spending an hour in church, in making the effort to shed a tear, to light a candle or carry some flowers to the Widow who also lost her Son and is alone in the world: "Here I am, a good child, to keep you company." But this is of no avail with her, since she gave up her "good boy" for salvation, which has its historical part called freedom, dignity, acknowledgment of the essential value of the person beyond racial, economic, and social judgments. Mary is a mother and not maternalistic. She has a son, not to keep him at her side but to give him. From the Jerusalem of the first pilgrimage of his childhood, to the Jerusalem of his last day, her motherhood is extremely consistent and has a centrifugal rhythm. One phrase from the Gospel, which seems contradictory, expresses this motherhood, which is both something still and something in motion. "I appointed you that you should go and bear fruit" *(John 15:16)*. This "appointing" gives the idea of the static, of keeping one's feet on the ground, and would seem opposed to the idea of "go": "I appointed you that you should go." This being rooted in being is in order to make us go, to move with security. Mary's motherhood is a being, an integrity, an adhesion to existence which consists in engendering the Savior. And this integrity is actualized in a marriage which is the reproduction of the image of God and in a motherhood which is pure giving. It would not be integral if it limited, even if only in the will, the integrity of Christ, by which he is the Savior, the liberator, and, I would say, freedom itself. Mary can weep because freedom is not joyful, but she cannot dissent and cease to participate voluntarily in the movement of liberation of Christ, which coincides with his death on the cross.

Even if we say fourteen hundred ejaculations of reparation a day, we can be more on the side of Pilate and Caiaphas than on Jesus and Mary's. Words do not make reparation for anything. I was thinking of this in my community where a short while ago a small businessman was killed—one of those little people who did not make much money because he did not rob. And the murderer, or at least one of the chief instigators, was at the wake with those who were strongly condemning the crime. This time the police were not fooled by the ruse. I do not say that the accomplices of Herod, Pilate, and the high priests ought to be sought in the first rank of those who make reparation by words. But certainly there must be some there.

After his first Greek style *Pietà*, Michelangelo sculpted others from living rock, such as the Medici or Randanini. They seem to me like the Christ emerging from Creation, an image so dear to Teilhard, the Christ emerging with sorrow and weariness. It seems that the artist passed from Apollonian contemplation to the painful search for *Man in history*. And

Mary, who is free, gives birth to this liberator enveloped in a world of stone. To those who believe that the transformation of the Church has been sought and imposed by a small group of enthusiasts, I would like to say that it is the whole of history and time that have radically changed concepts which we had accepted superficially. We have discovered Mary among the poor women, consumed by privation and the effort to live and to emerge, like those whom I met in the slums of Valparaiso, joined in a common effort to take a step forward at any price. It will be difficult for us Christians to present our condolences to the noble Widow decked out in her finery in a grandiose temple of marble as cold as she, beside the people who are moved at having put her Son on the cross, and who look with indifference at the crucified Christ in the poor, the humiliated, the marginal people of the earth.

For me, Mary is the person who all of us are trying to be. She is our secret ideal, the cause of our uneasiness and our suffering; she is the integrity and the identification which become a self-giving in love, a total and consistent fulfillment of existence in love. Mary's consistency has a secret. At least this is what we can deduce from what the Gospel shows us: "And his mother kept all these things in her heart" *(Luke 2:51)*. Mary tried never to lose her person or her motive from sight. She was attentive to the events going on about her and tried to understand them from within, pondering them in her heart. Mary is a woman who lived a very normal life like every other woman, but with the dimension of depth and truth. Every event is an offering of freedom or slavery, of progress or retrogression. No event is absolutely good or absolutely bad. At the moment of the Lord's Supper the Church teaches us to pray that "the eating of your body and the drinking of your blood, Lord, may not become occasions of sin for me but a motive of salvation."

A friend of mine had a remarkable encounter with God which began with a conversation with a prostitute. At times God is within events which seem empty and obscure, and we are not successful in finding him in those appointments which we set with him. Mary was attentive to what was happening and pondered it in her heart, that is, she translated everything into that fidelity to being which was her reason for being. Her interior look has that center of the person where God is. It is not narcissism because its substance is the events which are organized and unified in this center. One phrase from the Gospel contains all the best that can be said about contemplation—which is nothing more than this deep look at events in order to discover their meaning, their unity which is constructive of the person, and thus save them from their diabolical power of alienation. Luke says this in the same chapter: "And they did not understand the saying which he spoke to them." Then further on, "His mother kept all these things in her heart" *(Luke 2:50-51)*. This antithesis is difficult for those who see things from the outside, but it is clear within the contemplative context. The contemplative look is not the magic eye through which things are immediately seen in themselves. It is the groping search, sharpened by the desire to see, for the true meaning of events, the personalizing meaning through which the event is the word of God.

I do not look upon Mary as the good fairy dispensing favors and rewards from her throne, but rather both as a model and as the creative virtue of the person. I know people who call themselves "Marianists" because they talk about her all the time and wear medals and often hand out very commercial pamphlets. And I know other Marianists who have achieved that peace, that simplicity and that acute sense of events, that constant trust in what is essential in life, which is so characteristic of Mary. I believe in Mary's mission in the Church today. It is to remake the Church more in her image, a poor, humble, integral Church, in love with the Bridegroom and in the service of mankind. This Church will be made by the contemplatives who are made in Mary's image. They do not run away; they are not deserters. They live in Nazareth, in the small or large city of man, discovering the hidden meaning of things which seem small and common, and yet are the message of God. I think that this is Mary's special mission, because we have not yet succeeded in unifying the world we have cut in two, into the sacred and the secular.

Our words betray us as we speak. I noted this in a meeting with some Latin American students. I felt that Manicheanism was overflowing everywhere. Prayer is seen as a desertion, involvement in the world as clericalism. The very word "Christian" causes an allergy because for many centuries it has been superimposed on the concept of man. Just tonight here in the forest, they told me, "Today the horses and the Christians both suffered from the heat." They did not know that they were making an identification that we could not make in a university or a European *banlieue.* No one could unite what we have separated with violence and polemics. I am reflecting a great deal on the mystery of Mary, who united in one vital synthesis the divine and the human. God was made flesh in her while allowing her to be a woman. The Middle Ages said that the Incarnation *integritatem non minuit,* i.e., it does not diminish Mary's integrity. It is true that in the Middle Ages people were thinking only of the seal of the flesh and a certain kind of affective solitude. We are discovering fuller dimensions to this integrity. Truly God has not destroyed her magnificent balance as wife, mother, and woman living in Nazareth among relatives and friends, who left with her in the caravan when Jesus was in danger of falling into the hands of the authorities. But she has one special aspect that is not seen: an integrity that is unattainable for man, kept intact by this profound gaze of the contemplative viewing history as the chain of events of liberation that extends and interconnects from generation to generation.

16

THE SPIRIT OF FREEDOM

Revelation begins with these words: "In the beginning God created the heavens and the earth. The earth was without form and void, and darkness was upon the face of the deep; and the Spirit of God was moving over the face of the waters" *(Genesis 1:1-2)*. And revelation closes with Christ's promise to send the Holy Spirit, which will help him achieve his mission in the world: "And behold, I send the promise of my Father upon you" *(Luke 24:49)*.

The creation of the world out of chaos into cosmos, the liberation of man, from the first efforts at contact—continually frustrated by the hostility of man against man—to the ultimate dialogue in love and the integration in the unity of the mystical body, these are oriented from within by the Spirit of the Lord. "The spirit of the Lord fills the world" *(Wisdom 1:7)*. When I think that from formless chaos through the spirit there slowly emerge life, its organization, and its unity—possible only if a principle of love unifies differences—I do not despair now either of the Church, of the world, or of man's becoming. When I see with my own eyes this law of love and freedom at work in the world, hope is reborn in me. Perhaps it is my illusion, but if we look at the world as something completely made from the beginning it seems like man is degenerating and that consequently history is a great process of dissolution. It would be like a decadent fifteenth-century palace, in which the descendents of the Sforzas or of Charles V are slowly and inexorably crumbling away both economically and humanly. The people are symbolized by the great house whose frescos are being gradually worn away by saltpeter and whose walls are crumbling into a powder covering the worm-eaten furniture. If we think of a static world that was created perfect with its privileged inhabitants—who often seem more destructive than creative—it all might seem like a slow decay. We might wish that a drastic decision would put an end to the sluggish process of dissolution. But if we consider that out of the original chaos there rose up the person, and with him, music, poetry, painting, the projects of the organization and humanization of the world, thus the unknown God is made visible to us, this hidden spirit that moves the universe.

In the Gospel we see that Christ's mission is to free man from the law and from death, that is, from fear, in order that he be reborn in the Spirit. It is to free man from physical and spiritual fear, both of which negatively tell us something about the essence of the person as a cosmic being and as the center of individuality and freedom. At the Last Supper, Jesus developed the following theme: The moment is about to come in which he will entrust men to the Spirit of God. Obviously, this is not a question of chronological but of qualitative stages. Man must free himself from the law and death in order to be reborn in the Spirit. The Spirit is freedom. The wind blows where it wills and we hear its voice without knowing whence it comes or whither it goes. This is what happens with everything that is born of the Spirit *(cf. John 3:8)*. The Gospel puts us on the road to recognizing the unknown God in the actions of man. The Holy Spirit is the interior strength, the intellectual clarity, of the person: "And when they bring you before the synagogues and the rulers and the authorities, do not be anxious how or what you are to answer or what you are to say; for the Holy Spirit will teach you in that very hour what you ought to say" *(Luke 12:11-12)*. The person is a person insofar as he has internalized an idea, a vision of life in which his own special vocation has been integrated. This leads him to successive choices which are either creative or destructive of the person. The law is only an external and general rule; it is not creative. Personalized choices are guided by a kind of instinct which is reinforced and refined insofar as we are faithful to it. The choices themselves give it clarity and deepen it. Or they make it futile and scattered. We are pursued by the need for the Incarnation. I have thought that Paul's phrase, "Woe to me if I do not preach the Gospel!" is within this basic choice which determined his history as a person. Woe to me, because I am destined to this. If it is the Spirit of the Lord who orients us, we must see the coincidence of the *personal* with the *universal*. The individualist and separatist instinct is not spiritual because the Spirit is the soul of the Church. The Spirit fills the universe and can inspire man, limited in time and in space, to choices that have a cosmic value.

These choices cannot be understood from the outside except in retrospect. And not always, for the world is run by laws, traditions, and what appears to be certain and solid. But the Spirit is creation, a looking ahead, projection, and of necessity a dialectical relationship is established between the two forms of life; therefore persecution is unavoidable. The Holy Spirit inspires in us what we must answer before the synagogues and tribunals. The strong and patient calm that disarms more powerful forces is the characteristic of those who are guided by the Spirit. The mature man is one who is ever more faithful to a rhythm which is interior and personal, but which is at the same time universal. Many generous, ardent people lack strength at a given moment and do not reach the fulfillment of "laying down their lives for their friends," because their revolutionary commitment comes from the outside and not from this concentration point of the person. The great history of a world, of an age, is concentrated in the history of a person. Thus, since man is the cosmos and in him are all the reflections, echoes, sounds, and power of the cosmos, the person himself is history. This time and this space must be concentrated in the person and must become personal history. This supposes a concrete knowledge of the world and a grasp of the world that must be almost intuitive. When someone asks what he must do—whether or not to take part in the revolution, whether or not to give up a lucrative position in order to better serve the poor, whether to reject a system or to accept it with the intention of changing it from within—he is still not mature. The choices of this type are subjective even when they correspond to schemas, the objective historical situations which confer on them a kind of general foundation. Despite this, I say they are personal. And they will be profound, stable, and universal according to the level on which they were thought out.

In general, the purity of this choice is authenticated by a sense of modesty, by uncertainty, by fear. We know that the person who speaks a great deal about revolutions, conspiracies, and giving his life is not a revolutionary. He sees life as a gesture and not as an inexorable fidelity to vocation. Jesus intentionally provoked this fear, this mistrust of the self, this doubt: "Foxes have holes, and birds of the air have nests; but the Son of Man has nowhere to lay his head" *(Matthew 8:20).* "Are you able to drink the cup that I drink, or to be baptized with the baptism with which I am baptized?" *(Mark 10:38).* "Truly I say to you, one of you will betray me, one who is eating with me" *(Mark 14:18).* "Watch and pray that you may not enter into temptation" *(Mark 14:38).* He invites us to go deep within ourselves, to find within ourselves the root of courage, to go beyond the fear of the flesh to the courage of the spirit, which is achieved deep inside of us.

A testimony of the Holy Spirit is the prudence which arises from discovering and living the place of one's own responsibility in the human community and in history. Prudence is not synonymous with fear but with the capacity of choosing what is continuity with one's personal history; it is making choices that are enriching and personalizing. Thus the Spirit does indeed blow where he wills because his presence and his action are not always visible in the people who believe themselves to be guided by the Holy Spirit. I believe that there are hidden here some possibilities of error: The Holy Spirit gives to each Christian an ecclesial function for the building up of the Mystical Body of Christ, which is mankind becoming Church.

It is very easy to see oneself as a function and to forget that each of us is a person. I have discovered that we have fallen into this error in the methods of Catholic Action, in which we created functions that were unconnected with the meaning and history of the person. Christian peda-gogy, if it intends to be meaningful, must result in this liberation of the person in fidelity to his own spirit. This fidelity can be reduced to three aspects: *ontological* fidelity or fidelity to one's own state; *existential* fidelity, which I would identify with the profession, which should make explicit the profound demands and possibilities of the person; *political* fidelity, the fidelity to the concrete and historical forms of serving man-kind, by announcing the Good News to the poor, caring for the contrite of heart, freeing prisoners . . . *(cf. Isaiah 61:1; Luke 4:18).* Prudence is mani-fested in the choices that make these three aspects of the person increas-ingly visible and profound. And it is manifested in the energy with which we reject everything that deters us from them. Everything that is extrinsic, that is not consistent with these three points, does not come from the Holy Spirit. A Christain is no different from any other person since the structural lines of his life are identical. But he knows the origin of his fidelity and therefore lives the human condition with joy, stability, and continuity. If this has not happened up to now, it is because we have not sufficiently thought through religion as a component of the human condi-tion, but have considered it rather as a kind of superimposed, troublesome task. We must educate the person in fidelity to himself, but this fidelity must be looked at from the viewpoint of the community and history; we must therefore prepare the person for loneliness, for persecution, and for being unafraid to make decisions which are courageous and instinctive, in the deepest sense of the word. Christ promised mankind courageous persons, with this most human kind of courage.

With the coming of the Holy Spirit, the duality of the dependent man, the child being led by the hand, is overcome. The Spirit is identified with force: "... He who believes in me, as the scripture has said, 'Out of his heart shall flow rivers of living water' " *(John 7:38).* We have the first fruits of the Spirit *(Romans 8:33).* It is time to pay our IOU to man today by giving this witness to the Holy Spirit. This new man is awaited by all, whether they know it or not. The deterioration of structures is always a prelude to the time of the Holy Spirit. What must we do to hasten this time of the Spirit?

The first decision is to be extremely loyal and authentic: "A holy and disciplined spirit will flee from deceit" *(Wisdom 1:5),* that is, from what is artificial, accessory, from the artificial personality, in a word, from the role player. The Holy Spirit requires a profound loyalty to our self. We must continually review the structural lines of our person and be faithful to them to the utmost. To do this we must be constantly vigilant that the center of the person, his ontological structure, be not invaded by intrusive values which gradually deflect his attention. The Holy Spirit is purifying and transforming. We must convince ourselves that the root of lies is not in the intellect or in the will, that is, in our consciousness. It is much more deep-seated; it is in the ontological structure of the person, in which is found the center of unity and love.

The Holy Spirit is the spirit of truth which "the world cannot receive." The immense step forward that man has made and is making in history is in the psychic line, as Paul would say, more than in the pneumatic one. This means that man's capacity for understanding things is growing, but his capacity to know the person and his relationships is not growing proportionately, nor, consequently, is his capacity for organizing himself into a community. But the force of the Spirit is successively breaking down the structures we form and is inspiring the formation of new structures of freedom. Whoever is on the side of the Spirit of truth favors this breaking down because the Spirit is renewal. The lesser evil, new patches on old cloth, new wine in old wineskins, is the ideal of politicians. The ideal of the Holy Spirit is to look at things as they are, to see them in their reality, even when this is bleak, and to call them by their right name.

This is one more reason for the Church to rid herself of any compromise with the structures of society, which must be continually renewed. Preserving them inevitably implies resorting to simulation and calling things by their wrong name. Once their turn is over, certain programs for structuring society become outdated and for this very reason false. We must not love anything because of some preconception or to defend our own privileges or positions, those of others, or anything which is not the truth. I think that the hour of the Holy Spirit has arrived and that this hour is expressed as a desire for authenticity, as a courage to destroy in order to rebuild. Here again the criteria for distinguishing a constructive destruction from one that is purely destructive are the individual and the communitarian dimensions. If one destroys by destroying oneself, out of desperation, this is obviously outside of the realm of the Spirit. But if we destroy in order to build a more modern and human world, this cannot be called destruction or violence, but love.

At times—we see this in Latin America—there is no greater violence than conserving, the prudence of leaving things as they are, the fear of something worse. When the majority of the family to which we belong cannot fear anything worse because things cannot get any worse, then fear of something worse becomes an accomplice of the evil which man does to man. The Spirit does not love vacillation, calculation, and fear; he wants us to bear witness to the truth, to do it, to live it deeply. Why are the publicans and prostitutes preceding us? Because it never occurs to them to think of themselves as upright persons, and when someone treats them as such, they think the person has made a mistake. And this mistake moves them so deeply that they give up their possessions in order to achieve this fascinating state which, ultimately, is that of being a person. All of us are threatened by the spirit of deceit because we all have compromised with evil. Only the Spirit of truth can free us.

This liberation in truth does not happen by a miracle, by means of a solitary inspiration of the Holy Spirit. It happens through dialogues, encounters, reading, vital experiences. The truth does not come to us only from those who think like us. Indeed, seeing the truth from but one side, enclosing it within a ghetto, within a small club, is extremely dangerous and falls easily into error. If we have not shut ourselves off from dialogue, I believe that all of us, in our dealing with people whom we consider to be "of the other side," have discovered in ourselves abysses of hypocrisy and the falseness of certain attitudes that seemed pure and right to us. The Gospel is a proclamation intended for all men. It is salvation for all and consequently can be discovered in depth and in truth only in an open field, in a pluralistic context. One phrase from Vatican II opens up this panorama: "In a wonderful manner conscience reveals that law which is fulfilled by love of God and neighbor. In fidelity to conscience, Christians are joined with the rest of men in the search for the truth, and for the genuine solution to the numerous problems which arise in the life of individuals and from social relationships" (*Gaudium et spes,* no. 16). I have heard many Christians say, "We have the truth. Why do we have to go and look for it among atheists, Muslims, or Marxists?" The objection arises from an extrinsicist and intellectualistic view of truth. No one asks a Christian, Marxist, or a Muslim to cut off a piece of every theory and make a Harlequin suit with the cuttings. Despite the fact that Gandhi was deeply moved by the Gospel and received the central inspiration of his life from it, he still did not become a Christian. Marxism has given us a better understanding of certain aspects of the Gospel, the deep significance of certain words which would have continued to be incomprehensible or would have seemed more superficial. This is something of no little importance.

We cannot say, "A Marxist loves more than a Christian," or, "A Christian loves more than a Marxist." We certainly all have met a Christian who loves more than a Marxist and a Marxist who loves more than a Christian. The great discovery, which for me coincides with faith, is that "in the beginning was the Word," "The Spirit of God moved over the waters," and all history, all time and space, are an explication, a revelation of the Word and of the Spirit, of what I would call the "spiritual meaning of the word." "No one can say, 'Jesus is Lord,' except by the Holy Spirit" *(1 Corinthians 12:3).*

A Spanish psychiatrist who is well aware of the problems of social psychology wrote me, "If I had been born in the third century, I would be a Christian. Since I am born in this century, I am a Marxist." It is true that this dichotomy is justified historically, but objectively it is unjust. If a person is a Christian, he must be disposed to having the ground beneath his feet disappear, to having other perspectives opened up to him, to becoming more and more profound, to having a new and disquieting understanding of the truth. "Foxes have holes . . . the Son of Man has nowhere to lay his head." The phrase does not refer solely to Christ's earthly life. It is his history and it is ours. At the risk of scandal I would emend my Spanish friend's words to say, "I am a Marxist because I am a Christian." By the fact that I am a Christian, I am participating in man's advancement and I am vitally interested in all the discoveries and acquisitions of culture so that I might understand what God requires of me, what is the historical way for me to give myself totally. This is the only way to be religious and to love God. Therefore, in this context, to say that we possess the truth and that we do not have to ask anyone else to lend it to us is simply ridiculous. The Holy Spirit penetrates the whole universe and is more universal than we can imagine. Without untiring attention, without a receptiveness to the Spirit who blows where and when he wills, we who follow the One who said he was the way run the risk of losing the meaning of life. I was very impressed by a definition given to me by a Peruvian friend who was showing me the fantastic ruins of Cuzco: "Peru is a ragamuffin sitting on top of a mountain of gold." And I thought that a Christian is often like that. He sits on top of a mountain of gold, but he is poor, precisely because he is sitting and the mountain has not been discovered. The Holy Spirit preserves the Church by jolting her from within with the wind of prophecy; she will always give the impression of something dying and something being born.

Paul, who was a messenger of the Holy Spirit because he felt called to evangelize beyond the frontiers of the Church, said, "Do not grieve the Holy Spirit of God" *(Ephesians 4:30),* and he said this in a context in which it appeared that human relationships were being compromised by a lack of sincerity, openness, and receptiveness. "Let all bitterness and wrath and anger and clamor and slander be put away from you, with all malice" *(ibid., v. 31).* To grieve the Holy Spirit is to grieve love, Paul is saying. The snare of love is deceit. "Leave off lying." Today we know much more about the possibilities of lying in man, about how each one of us believes he is and is saying one thing when he actually is and is saying something else. We have no other way of purifying ourselves and of making ourselves truer than by love—understood as a going out of ourselves, going out to meet the other with receptiveness, feeling the other's need, loving him in his true being with profound respect for the structure of his being. The famous phrase, "I am Plato's friend, but I am more the friend of truth," has been taken many times as a defensive weapon by fanatic and dehumanized "right thinkers." For a Christian, truth has become incarnate and we cannot separate it from its incarnation. Only in the real human situation can it progress in man, become actualized, present, possible, and concrete. This must not be taken superficially, because truth in the human situation is beyond and deep within, not above or outside. But to the extent that we commit ourselves to man and suffer with him, we discover the truth that lies beneath the surface, his real need, which is beyond the episodic.

We cannot know without love and we cannot love without a concrete commitment. To grieve man is to grieve the Holy Spirit. It is to treat him not as a person but as an object. It is to subdue in ourselves and in him this mystical presence which should be manifested as freedom in truth and in love. The new generations are becoming increasingly liberated from the need to win others to their ideology, and therefore they no longer look upon human encounters from this point of view. They are thus discovering liberation in love with less pain and with greater speed than we did. And they will run less of a risk than we did of grieving the Holy Spirit with "diplomacy," cunning, and hidden intentions. They no longer go to the movies "for the apostolate," nor to a football game in order to make themselves congenial to a group of friends and win them for Christianity. Today we are discovering that this militant attitude was not so deeply evangelical as it seemed to us. All of us need to be liberated from the spirit of evil, from the old man, and be reborn in the spirit of truth. All of us need to be loyal, authentic, truly available to others. And we can give ourselves liberation only mutually.

The only conceivable proselytism today is what the hippies are able to catch a glimpse of as hope and as possibility in their eccentric search. I have great trust that the Holy Spirit is blowing among the youth, freeing them, not from ideologies, which are historical and therefore necessary schematizations of human values, but from the absolutisms of ideologies. I am discovering that when I touch on the theme of Marxism, revolution, or change, young people grasp very easily the meaning of my words. They do not rend their garments as if they were faced with inconsistency, because they have thrown off the cloak of absolutism. People of my generation, on the other hand, receive ideas only with an absolutist mentality. We have passed from one culture, which was mythical and therefore absolutizing, to a global culture, which instinctively orders values and ideas with a capacity of synthesis and receptiveness toward history which we do not have. In this connection I see the young generation as more essentially "spiritual," and I see the responsibility of teachers who are trying to make their "absolutes" survive by transferring them to the youth. This is a deep lack of respect for the person, for youth, and for their truth, and it can produce nothing but outrage. When we try to hand down our political ideologies, our integralisms, whether fascist or Tridentine, to the youth, I have the painful impression that we are sending the young people as hostages to defend the little life we have left; this is our sad decline. The young must go forward, be the defensive line, and therefore be sacrificed. To ask heroism from them appears legitimate to me, but not in defense of what is old and dead.

Jesus' answer to the boy is exceptionally youthful. "Lord, let me first go and bury my father," the boy said. And Jesus answered, "Leave the dead to bury their own dead" *(Luke 9:59-60)*. Not to grieve the Holy Spirit means especially, I would say, knowing how to die at the right moment. It means not continuing to contaminate the air, not holding back the path of the Spirit by imposing with power and arbitrary authority a culture, a way of looking at life, a "truth" that deprives the young generation of their role and makes it old by making it dependent on the history of our generation. It is impossible to know how to die if we have not prepared ourselves for it our whole life. And man today needs no skull on the table to remind him that he must die and that he ought not to become too enamored of the futility of the world. He has to know how to die in the profound respect for man, in the giving up of his own absolutisms, in other words, by being genuinely humble. When I see young people separated from history, obliged not to think for themselves, with a practical commitment which is apparently dynamic, youthful, and heroic, but is substantially old and therefore not creative, I feel as if I am attending a spectacle as obscene and sad as the rape of an adolescent girl. It is true that the Spirit is strength and conquers all. Paul knew this better than we and believed it with more conviction, but—despite this faith—he manfully exhorts us not to grieve the Holy Spirit of the Lord.

"Do not quench the Spirit" *(1 Thessalonians 5:19)*. This is Paul's second admonition, and he transmits it in a context of knowledge: "Do not despise prophesying, but test everything; hold fast what is good, abstain from every form of evil" *(ibid., vv. 20-21)*. The Spirit blows where he wills and his law is freedom. "The spiritual man" must keep watch, be attentive, and take what is good; he must take what the Spirit reveals to him through all events and all persons. Today it is incumbent upon young people to form this *prophetic and ecumenical* Church, the Church of search and union. Young people can do it because their culture does not constitute an obstacle. What is important is to orient their search with trust, by making them feel that we have a real need of their discovery and their example of knowing how to live together. Often we have quenched the Holy Spirit by not having respected him. We have lived a religion without newness, without hopes, closed in and defined, petrified in itself. The imagination had no room within those walls and inside them we continued to become stiff, and static, finding only what had already been done, what had already been determined; this was antiinventiveness.

Today the religious attitude has changed substantially. We sense it as a search, a hope, a creation. The age of the Holy Spirit, as Joachim da Fiore thought of it, is a utopia, because all ages are ages of staticness and movement, of conservation and rupture, of law and spirit. The "Age of the Holy Spirit" is an illusion, because in history there is an alternation between the moments of security and sufficiency and those of insecurity and insufficiency. And our age is more an age of doubt and insecurity. In a few words, it is a critical age, pregnant with newness and creativity. In this sense I believe it can be called an age of the Holy Spirit. Many are hoping for the birth of new structures to replace the old and for new ideologies, Thomistic syntheses, which will probably not appear. The age of the great doctrinal disputes has come to an end. Man is groping and one of the forms of courage that attracts him most is patience with the uncertain and the provisional. Thus, there will certainly not arise in our time protective structures and doctrinal systems that offer security. We are hoping today for new Christians, that is, Christians who are free and renewed, with eyes capable of seeing and judging where God is and what his concrete epiphanies in the world are. "Test everything; hold fast what is good." The Holy Spirit blows where he will and in any direction. But in order to know what the Holy Spirit is and how to allow ourselves to be consciously guided by him, great spiritual maturity is required.

Do we have to know that the Holy Spirit is the guide and the deep source of inspiration? The answer comes easily if we consider that all of man's great and painful ascent is toward consciousness. All the sufferings of men find their significance in this widening of the horizon of visibility of the consciousness. And what is most hidden in consciousness—the consciousness of consciousnesses, the heart of hearts—is the Holy Spirit. The revelation of the Holy Spirit is like the discovery of the most mature point of human consciousness. It is its ultimate exaltation, capable of knowing a particular thing with a richness of meaning which the human glance, left to itself, is incapable of achieving. It is capable of seeing the small lapse of history which belongs to each generation and each person and intuiting its significance is part of the great history of the world.

To live constantly in the breadth of the Holy Spirit is very difficult. Not everyone has the courage of freedom. The Galatians whom Paul had liberated lapsed back into the most secure and most visible elements of the law. Paul confronts them with the choice between the law and the spirit: "If you receive circumcision, Christ will be of no advantage to you" *(Galatians 5:2)*; and ". . . every man who receives circumcision . . . is bound to keep the whole law. . . . For through the Spirit, by faith, we wait for the hope of righteousness" *(Galatians 5:3, 5)*. The Christian today must be able to take steps toward this "superconcentration of consciousness," to show practically how this life, which is full, supremely interesting, and launched toward incalculable quantitative conquests, has a profound and real spiritual dimension. And this cannot happen if he does not leap decisively and permanently from the individual consciousness, which spontaneously looks for certitudes, to that superconsciousness, reborn in the Holy Spirit, which is total boldness. I know that I am running the risk of not making myself understood, but I cannot refuse to give this witness of the Holy Spirit. The Christian is not mature until he changes from being an individual into a man of the Church, from being a person who has his individuality, his history, his rights, and his demands into a function of the community. This cannot be done from the outside, but through the internal, harmonizing, and unifying action of the Holy Spirit. In this respect, chapter 12 of the First Letter to the Corinthians is very enlightening: "Now there are varieties of gifts, but the same Spirit; and there are varieties of service, but the same Lord; and there are varieties of working, but it is the same God who inspires them all in every one. To each is given the manifestation of the Spirit for the common good" *(1 Corinthians 12:4-7)*. Yet in order to become fully a function of the common good, it is necessary to have the personal experience of "surrendering one's own soul," of entrusting oneself entirely to the Holy Spirit, without fearing loneliness and persecution—a price necessarily paid for prophecy. And if this position is risky on the one hand, on the other it is deeply human and constitutes a source of interior joy.

When it speaks to us of the Holy Spirit, the Gospel does not speak of some redoubtable and dangerous personage. On the contrary, it presents him to us as the consoler, the defender, the one who speaks in our name, who is our light and internal strength. Paul mentions the fruits of the Spirit, which are "charity, joy and peace," or the opposite of harshness, intolerance, and restlessness. If this maturity comes to the Christian from the Holy Spirit, there cannot be a definitive contradiction between the Christian and the institutional Church, which is also guided by the Holy Spirit. There can be *incomprehension,* but not *incompatibility.* The Holy Spirit does not succeed in obtaining a total and permanent docility from men. What is "our own," as individuals, always resists him, more or less; and it constitutes that opaque margin, that point of contrast, which can be most painful between two parties even when both are guided by the Holy Spirit.

The sign of the Holy Spirit will always in every age be patience, deep peace, and charity. It will be patience because there can be truth in intuition and error in time, that is, the intuition can be pure, but the time can be determined by us, anticipated in impatience and therefore not in correspondence with the time of the Spirit.

It will be peace, which is the fruit of faith, because when we are convinced that an intuition comes from God, we know that there is no force on earth or in heaven capable of definitively obstructing it. God always conquers, but not in the way we think; the triumphs we decree for him are always false, because they are based on seeming victories. But God conquers anyway.

The Holy Spirit is also revealed in the maturity of love. To what point can we—out of fidelity to an ideal—make others suffer? The problem of whether it is just or unjust to "hate" one's father and mother cannot be resolved from outside. In this case, the law does not help. Judgment is intuitive and interior; it is a subjective responsibility. When a person plays a game to the fullest, he risks everything for everything; living in the Holy Spirit therefore requires uncommon courage. The more we discover our own consciousness, which is the consciousness of a mission, of being in the Church and in the community as one charged with fulfilling a function, the more profound and serious is the hour of sacrifice, the step toward death. We can be reformers only if we are within the society, within the institution which we have been called to reform. But we must not be menders, people who sew new patches onto old cloth, which is antievangelical. We must bear within ourselves such a powerful spiritual blast that we are able to make things crumble and break and change completely. People who see no other alternative than rejecting or accepting a bad situation without intending to change it, see reform very materialistically. A reform of the Holy Spirit is not brought about by mending, but by the infusion of a new spirit.

After Christ's death, the Twelve had the idea of preaching the kingdom, the Good News. But where, when, and how to begin? After the great crisis they came together like survivors of a shipwreck or a war, and little by little they began to regain hope. The appearances of the Risen Christ infused hope, but not without dark shadows of doubt and crisis of dismay and depression. "Afterward, he appeared to the eleven themselves as they sat at table; and he upbraided them for their unbelief and hardness of heart" *(Mark 16:14)*. Finally the Holy Spirit came and transformed their fears and doubts into a kind of intoxication. In their message they proposed neither a reform of the synagogue or the temple nor a violent break. They continued to go to the temple to pray, but filled the ritual formalism with another spirit. They were arrested by the leaders of the synagogue; they accepted authority although they questioned its exercise. "We must obey God rather than men" *(Acts 5:29)*. With the force of the Holy Spirit they transformed the synagogue into the Church. Something new arose of its own strength, something which was both a break and a continuity, a profound renewal and a fidelity to the "stubborn will of salvation of God," which was handed down from generation to generation. The apostles were animated by the Holy Spirit, who is the force of the whole body of the Church and of the whole community. There is no reform from outside, because the Spirit dwells within the institution and tries to jolt it and continually renew it from within. But this requires persons who are capable of grasping the Spirit, docile and mature persons, in order that the Spirit may have the necessary strength to break down, from within, the old structures with new creations.

Will the Church as an institution, as a structure, disappear? And consequently will all the structures that have been ingrafted upon her like branches on a trunk disappear as well? I think not, because it is evident that Christ wished and planned for a center of unification and liberation of man that would make visible the hidden force of the Spirit that leads the world—along diverse and strange paths—toward salvation, a center that would become a symbol and an efficacious hope of this salvation. But the institution is called continually to modifications and changes, not so much by persons, but by the Holy Spirit dwelling in her, jolting and disturbing her complacency. The presence and the action of the Holy Spirit are manifested in the history of the world by orienting in a visible way all men toward love and freedom. "God is love, and he who abides in love abides in God, and God abides in him" *(1 John 4:16)*. "Where the Spirit of the Lord is, there is freedom" *(2 Corinthians 3:17)*. Therefore, beneath all the movements of true love and of a search for freedom, that is, beneath all the lines of man's confirmations of this mysterious action which leads the world out of the primitive chaos toward the concentration of consciousness, which is the consciousness of making with others a world that is more human, more adapted to the person. Every liberation, under whatever sign, is an epiphany of the Holy Spirit mixed with elements that seem foreign and contrary to the action of God in the world.

Vatican Council II centered the reality of the vocation of all men in salvation. "All men are called to belong to the new People of God.

Wherefore this People, while remaining one and unique, is to be spread throughout the whole world and must exist in all ages, so that the purpose of God's will may be fulfilled. In the beginning God made human nature one. After his children were scattered, he decreed that they should at length be united again *(cf. Jn. 11:52)*. It was for this reason that God sent his Son, whom he appointed heir of all things *(cf. Heb. 1:2)*, that he might be Teacher, King, and Priest of all, the Head of the new and universal people of the sons of God" *(Lumen gentium,* no. 13). The Holy Spirit gives to those who are aware of being in the Church the knowledge and savor of this plan of God which is being accomplished in history with the gift of the Holy Spirit. And man through faith succeeds in contemplating and savoring the divine plan (cf. *Gaudium et spes,* no. 10). The Holy Spirit permanently forms the community of the Church in order that it might be salt and leaven in history. "The Church, at once a visible assembly and a spiritual community, goes forward together with humanity and experiences the same earthly lot that the world does. She serves as a leaven and as a kind of soul for human society as it is to be renewed in Christ and transformed into God's family. That the earthly and the heavenly city penetrate each other is a fact accessible to faith alone. It remains a mystery of human history, which sin will keep in great disarray until the splendor of God's sons is fully revealed" *(Gaudium et spes,* no. 40).

The Holy Spirit is universal, penetrates everything, and guides all men and the whole of history. Those who know and see this and witness to this history of salvation which is coming about in the world perceive the mysterious action which is within history. They therefore become witnesses of hope and keep alive in the world the reason to go on. Teilhard said that it costs too much energy and too much grief to make the earth move continually. If this impulse were not the external expression of a movement which is within history itself and which inexorably leads man toward the interior personalization which he is groping for, all this energy and suffering would be wasted. We agree when people say that the Gospel infuses something more than an earthly hope, that Christian hope transcends earthly hope. But it is something "more," not something "outside of." And here, in Latin America, earthly hope is called "change." It is a front-line transformation with means which the will of God will show through history and events. Discussions will seem sterile as long as the time for action is not ripe. Then the decisions that each of us has made in personal choices will become mass decisions. But can we speak of love to man, of the defense of his dignity and his freedom, without challenging the structures that concretely stand in the way of this dignity and freedom?

The Church as an institution enters into this problematical sphere. But she capitulates too easily before the expressions of good will on the part of government leaders who know the techniques of religious language. Deceit is possible because the Church is accustomed to seek a balance of power among other powers. On the level of the people and the apostolate, she sees man and his needs, the injustices that are committed against him; on the political level she sees the prince with whom she must deal and compromise. On the pastoral level, she carries Christ's mission and mandate forward, and when this is done under the inspiration of the Holy Spirit, we can hope for rich intuitions, a paschal movement; on the political plane, she becomes immobilized in a cultural reality and the demands of another time, and therefore she is not on the wavelength of the Holy Spirit. Although she is sensitive to man on this level too, she does not seem to be sensitive toward political and economic techniques which change and which in practice determine man's destitution or dignity. The pope has spoken of the need to invent new techniques, and he even said in other words what the French students had written on the walls: To be realists we have to ask for the impossible. But, in practice, the Church accepts and inspires men who have not the least intention of seeking new techniques, but rather are disposed to risking everything to maintain the *status quo.* And this is the more serious as this political attitude inspires parallel and conservative religious structures; they seem to aid one another reciprocally and be two sides of the same coin: the religious and the political.

The present configuration of Christians in Latin America can be characterized by four distinct tendencies. One is that of the conservative or integralist Christians, who are increasingly hiding behind the old tactic of formal obedience to the Church, the bishop, and Rome. They are the most fearful enemies of the Church because they anesthetize her. They use a language of obedience and fidelity—exactly like the son in the Gospel parable who announces that he is going off to work but then does not do so. They create structures and activities that are seemingly fruitful, but they are outside of history and thus isolate the Church from the historical process. If it is true that the "Church . . . goes forward together with humanity," her cultural and apostolic creations cannot be outside of history, nor can they be directed toward an abstract man without a particular time and place. This group unfortunately is quite numerous, because quantity will always be proportionate to comfort and ease in all times and in all institutions. But this group will end up by converting the Church into something foreign, because the process of change in Latin America means being freed from a culture and a civilization which have no roots in its history. Something is happening here, with more serious consequences, analogous to what occurred among those Catholics who fought for Austria's dominance in Lombardo-Venetia or for the Bourbons in southern Italy. The consequences are more serious because the liberation process today involves the whole man and because it is much richer in elements of justice than the simple passage from one government to another. I do not know how much force these Christians have, but if they are considered to be representatives of the Church, it seems to me that they will be handing down an image of a completely separated Church.

Another group is the revolutionaries. Impatient and lacking depth, they separate themselves from the Church in the name of fidelity to the Gospel; out of fidelity to man and history they lose their Christian message. They lack training and depth and do not know how to live in the Church as the apostles lived in the Hebrew community, suffering persecution, remaining always on the inside and being continuously pursued. I should like to say to these companions of mine in the faith that it is necessary to persevere and to discover in the Gospel—thought out afresh in the Holy Spirit—the meaning of persecution, the consolation in loneliness, and the beatitude of tears. I feel that these people will not only fulfill an important stage in the liberation of man, but that they will discover the new Church for which people are searching. To them has been entrusted the task of nourishing man's hope with hope, of serving as a ground and a motivation for liberation.

There is a third category. To this belong the illuminists, those who see the hopes of Christianity in a cultural change and await the purification of Christianity through a process of theological clarification. These people are midway between the integralists and the revolutionaries. Open to what is new, the illuminists seem prepared to collaborate in the building of a Church which penetrates and is penetrated by the earthly city (cf. *Gaudium et spes,* no. 40). But they seem to accept the historico-political content of a liberation more to succeed with their own ecclesial renewal than out of a personal conviction that the Gospel is concentrated on liberation, that liberation is the flesh, the reality of the Gospel message today in Latin America.

Finally, there is the great mass of Christians, believers who have not been evangelized. They have been made Christian through the sacramental symbol, but they do not have a Christian vision of life. They wear a Christian symbol over diverse religious contents. This great mass of people is waiting for a liberation. In general they have a great horror of communism because of bad experiences, propaganda against it, or an instinctive allergy to it. These people are neither in the Church nor outside of her. They have a Christian soul, because it is deeply human; their practices and their beliefs are Christian. In order for this mass to make history, the new society, and the new Church, it must be understood and interpreted. But this group cannot be interpreted and thereby made more aware, stronger, and more efficacious, except by people who enter into its history, into its search, into its true contemporary demands.

Today, in this land of expectation, I await the Holy Spirit. I do not know whether I am naïve, but I am convinced that here a new hope is being reborn which the West in its decline has lost. I am hoping for a miraculous palingenesis, which is not in the style of the Holy Spirit. The Spirit inspires man and works through man and in him, in a human way. The miracle of Pentecost is enclosed within the formation of a little, ardent group, prepared for death, which slowly constructed the Church in a process of opposition, of obduracy of every kind, like any political group. I am hoping for the revelation of the Holy Spirit in the little groups that pilot history, shedding light on the theme of justice and love and dreaming, bravely dreaming, of accomplishing it in our day and on our earth. In these groups the theme of liberation can and must be integral. It can be because the Latin American is by instinct and culture deeply humanistic and no superimposed culture has obfuscated or diminished this attitude. It can be because technical progress arrives here in waves, as an import, and here the person is still profoundly involved in basically human problems: justice, living together, racial integration. The conditions of receptivity and poverty, of true ontological need, are here, so that the Holy Spirit can come down upon us and here can begin the Church that is being born.

17

THE OUTRAGE OF YOUTH

The youth revolution characteristic of our time is the sign that liberation is near and that it is already underway in the world. Young people today either take drugs or protest: They reject the present moment. What is the meaning of this protest? We have to ask this of young people, who do not accept dialogue with us insofar as we represent another generation. They do not accept a solution to the crisis from us. When we look at the last three centuries, we can say that the eighteenth century represents a break from vertical dependence. "The divine right of kings" was then violently challenged, and as the people became aware they discovered that they were the depositaries and arbiters of authority. In the nineteenth century the relationship between man and things was questioned: The person felt capable of organizing the world of goods and production, of controlling them so that they would cease to be an alienating factor. Our century is the age of the great questioning of the identity of the person: Who are we? What are we doing?

We want to know whether this difficult step called "life" is worth it. The inscriptions on the walls of Paris are the most sincere testimony of this revolution. They say, "We don't want a world where the guarantee of not dying of hunger is achieved only with the guarantee of dying of boredom." All revolutions are basically episodes in the great Christian revolution. Only inertia and stagnation in the *status quo* are anti-Christian. Where there is movement, man's aspiration to be more, there is Christ. We think now that Christians ought to have questioned the French Revolution to seek Christ in it; so too we must discover that presence in today's revolution. Our task seems easier because the center of this revolution is the person. We must seek the outrage of youth in their *graffiti* rather than in conversations with them. In a conversation, if we ask them what they want, they answer, "Nothing," because they do not know. And do we know? They want a new order in which people do not die from hunger or boredom, an order in which salvation from dying of hunger is understood within the context of the salvation of the integral person. The demand goes down deep into the core of being and is not on the level of one's particular need or function. To continue with the analogy, it could be said that the revolution of the bourgeoisie in 1789 is the revolution of the death of the monarch. The industrial revolution is the revolution of the mother's breast which ties us to things. And ours is the death of the father.

A revolution destroys one order so that from this destruction a new order might arise. "It's not a revolution, it's a mutation," it said on the Paris walls. The reason behind the revolution of our time seems to me to be the death of the father; this is its true dynamic and the source of its unity throughout the world. A revolution grows and gains strength because all the necessary changes have not been brought about historically, or else they have been only half done, imperfectly done. It is to be expected that this revolution should become powerful because of the cries of the Third World and the unjust relations existing in the world of the worker. This complicated tangle, this confluence of distinct demands, these differences which are present in the various historical stages through which countries and entire continents are living, can easily confuse the way we read this protest of youth.

Why are we not also willing to see in this revolution the anger of the woman which has been handed on to her children? This anger is becoming consciousness and protest through them against a society that denies the right and the possibility of being a person. The young people's anger is borne in the mother's womb, nurtured by the family, and explodes before being lost in the chain of adult alienations, that is, the deformations of the power of the father. It has been nurtured in the family because the person is denied in the failure of the first relationship—that of the couple. The image of God which enters into Creation divided in two, man-woman, separated in a dialectical relationship rendered tragic by man's sin, must be restored to unity. It is restored through a dialogue inspired and nourished by love, a movement of one person toward another. The relationship, the dialectic, must become a dialogue and must proceed from hostility to love. This presupposes the acknowledgment of an essential equality, an equality discovered within the structure of the person. It presupposes the autonomy which signifies a right to be "one's own" and not a function of another; and it presupposes the responsibility which is the result of three elements: vocation; creativity; presence in the world, in the community, and in history.

But neither autonomy nor responsibility have been acknowledged in woman. Profiting from her being structured by motherhood and therefore necessarily dependent, man has fully denied her any right to independence. Without a true vocation other than that of reproducing and preserving being, the woman finds herself in the realm of nature rather than of the person. In our time, in which her presence in the working world has become a technological and economic necessity, most of the time she performs functions that pay less and are thus rejected by men. By giving her activity for a lesser price, she represents a greater economic benefit. On a lower social level, there is appearing a feminine proletariat oppressed from every side because most of the time the woman is able to rest and to distract herself from her work outside the home only by her work at home, which is not considered work because it is unpaid. On the level of those who "run things," she is always an appendage to her husband's vocation and profession. Her function is to collaborate, not at the creative moment, but in his success, when he steps out into the public eye.

It is very true that a husband's worldly success depends in great part on his wife's *savoir faire*. But this public relations function is the perishable, ephemeral, and unjust part of human creativity. We are living in a world in which intellectual or real production must be imposed by propaganda. Men or things have no strength in themselves resulting from their own value or being. The woman who has leisure time, who does not have a "vocation" of her own, has an "attraction" which acts as a protagonist in the process of public relations, that is in the structures of alienation of things and persons. Many women seem to accept this role gladly and enjoy it, but deep inside them rage is piling up. Their subconscious cannot be truly liberated by a tiring, absorbing activity that is totally within the realm of alienation. Jesus said, "Not what goes into the mouth defiles a man, but what comes out of the mouth, this defiles a man" *(Matthew 15:11)*. This is to say that what is impure is so first in intention. This participation of a woman in "advertising" her husband rather than in his creativity is defiled from the very beginning. I understood this when in speaking to a group of middle class women I said, "You who belong to the ruling class," and they objected with a most strenuous "no." They do not belong to the ruling class because they have no part in the decisions made in the business of which their husband, brother, or father is a director, foreman, or supervisor of some kind. The hiring and firing, the technological changes, the classification of products, all these are decided by men. The women are involved only in the publicity aspect or in the enjoyment of the profits, that is, in the centers of alienation of work in which man depersonalizes himself and depersonalizes the woman.

If they are not rescued on this level, the two persons, the man and woman, cannot become one because they have lost their profound identity, their true being. The mother's anger, which is expressed in open revolt or in frustration, joins the suffering or the grumbling of the proletariat or, in the women of the middle and upper classes, becomes a neurosis. In every way it poisons the family and is the vision which provides the background for the evolution of the children from infancy through adolescence and young adulthood. The father no longer has enslaved concubines, it is true, but he does have in his power a more or less well preserved and cared-for tool which is useful for him. So as not to be completely pessimistic, I think that love is not totally absent. Its strength is such that it succeeds in saving itself beneath the ruins; it stands erect, like a climbing plant amid the rubble, entwining it among its leaves. But anger is stored up in the house; it passes to the children, and explodes into rebellion against the father.

Many women will certainly be opposed to this view. They feel they are accepting their role out of love, when often they are accepting it out of passivity, lack of depth, or simply out of convenience. It is more comfortable not to see or to refuse to recognize what is beneath the small surface of knowledge sufficient to live. And now in their search for reasons for living young people are breaking our comfort to pieces; our tiny basis is no longer enough for them. And the outrage piles up in the subconscious of this person who has been rejected in her essential structure. She has been rejected by the man who has tried to preserve her by speculating with her gifts and leading her into all sorts of anger and disorders. And this rage has become conscious in this generation which has barely left home, impatient for this essential vindication.

The hour has sounded for rebellion against the father, for rebellion against the constituted order. These new hordes, the young people, have discovered that there is a much deeper revolution to be made than the economic one. It includes the economic revolution as something less within something more, but it is necessary to go all the way and discover where the true alienation of the person is. It is rising today up to the level of consciousness at a moment of great historical maturity, like the one which the first barbarian hordes brought about in the dark ages. But perhaps the murder of the father out of love for the mother will occur on a more symbolic plane, which we must know how to interpret. The mother is *life* because the woman is the generator of life and *in the name of this life young people are challenging the status quo,* the established order which is disorder. They are rejecting what is dogmatic and fixed to open the way for the imagination. If we look at things in depth, we are greatly struck by the analogy of this youth revolution with the revolution woman must bring about in order to get out of her marginal condition. But if this youth movement represents her, it is very important to understand it, because this revolution, although temporarily checked, has not arrived at its end. To understand it means hastening its outcome and sparing blood and victims. The reaction of the bourgeoisie and respectable persons is a reaction of deep offense and protest, since they think that it is better to perpetuate internal, invisible wounds than to run the risk of shedding blood. They facilely judge the authors of open violence, but without asking themselves whether it was not they who for centuries have been creating hidden violence.

The most obvious and immediate result of the youth revolution is the blow dealt not so much to constituted authority but to the authority of the teacher and the father. Youth challenges it in a very simple way, coming back with the same question they are asked: What do you want? What do you think you are doing? You tear things down but what do you want to put in their place?

When these questions are directed to our generation, we realize that our answers were lacking in clarity, continuity, and that logic which up to now we have raised as the banner against all revolutions. All of us agree that the order we are defending is disorder, because we have not yet succeeded, despite our progress, in giving food to all men and in guaranteeing every man the possibility of responding to his own vocation; nor have we succeeded in eliminating war and in historically incarnating the basic equality of men. We trust in time, as the farmer of the past, ploughing and sowing, trusted in the balance of the rain and the sun. But when we look inside our civilization, can we honestly say that we can see indications of these human liberations—which are all the more urgent the more there is an increase in our economic and technical potential and the samples of well being which are appearing here and there in the world? I think not. Therefore, if the young are seething with impatience and rummaging through our files and our plans without finding in them any hope, any program for which they could be patient and hope, with what force and what fortitude do we exhort them to patience? The death of the father can be tragic or melancholy for a person who does not have the courage of rejuvenation.

I love the Gospel episode of Nicodemus. He was "learned," a "father of Israel," who found himself living in Jerusalem during a May revolution (did it not also happen in springtime?). Sensing the way the wind was blowing, he had the courage to question himself. Instead of walling himself up within the indisputable Sanhedrin, he crossed the barricades and tried to search into the meaning of this revolt against the "Fathers," against the *status quo,* a revolt that was growing day by day. Christ treated him with a certain sarcasm, like the impudent student who turned the question back on the teacher: "Are you a teacher of Israel, and yet you do not understand this?" *(John 3:10).* And he advised him that if he wished to understand the times he must be "reborn"; he must turn within and no longer be guided by logic; he must completely change his way of facing life, of judging and acting.

A person who does not want to die must give up being a father and teacher and leave behind the category being attacked by the youth rebellion. In the question posed by the generation of fathers to youth today, there is, as always, the search for facile solutions and agreements; but the youth are confronting us with a radical modification which implies a profound conversion in man. They want a world, as Marcuse says, in which competition, struggle between individuals, deceit, cruelty, and massacre have no reason for being. They want a mode of human life which truly puts the aggressive instincts at the service of the life instinct and trains the younger generations with goals of life and not of death. To acquire this vision, dialogue alone can be of help, the transformation of the vertical relationship into a horizontal one, the transformation of the function of power, the will for domination, and arbitrary dogmatism into dialogue.

Dialogue presupposes poverty and humility. That means discovering and acknowledging that we cannot make it alone. It is a readiness to leave behind everything that is not essential provided that a new order of life is affirmed. In other words, it means knowing how to sacrifice our dogmatisms for the rights of the coming generation. We find ourselves faced with a society that can be saved only by imagination and invention, because up to now it has been constructed and defended only by masculine logic.

Young people are afraid of being enclosed within an established order and of finding themselves tomorrow—after their university studies are completed—subordinated to the system, with a permanent loss of the sense of revolution and the taste for questioning. The university students are discovering that it is the whole system that has to change. They see that upon leaving the university tomorrow, the graduates and prize-winners, without any regard to class, will find themselves having to live in the very way that they are challenging today.

The first thing they feel must be changed is the arbitrary division of social groups. "In the present system," asserts Cohn-Bendit, one of the protagonists of the youth revolution, "people say that there are those who work and those who study, and all labor remains divided, even if reasonably. But it is possible to imagine another system in which everyone shares in the duties of production, reduced to a minimum thanks to progress in technology, and in which everyone also has the possibility of pursuing continued study. It is the system of productive technological work and concomitant study." Parallel with technical progress and automation are the lines of demarcation between students and workers, manual laborers and mental laborers. But it is necessary that man adapt himself psychologically to this new world, because up to now the progress in technology and economy has not had decisive influence on the transformation of the person.

Involved in this transformation is the radical change that must be brought about by the woman of our day. Her destiny is curiously bound up with that of the proletariat. Capitalist society has continually permitted a greater number of women to have access to culture and to different professions, *but not to decisions,* nor creations, nor to the social structuralizations, which have always been decided by man alone, separated from woman. In Marxist society, there does not seem to have been a substantial improvement of woman's condition. It is true that in Marxist society there has been a step forward. Yet this same society acknowledges that a change in the condition of women does not come about automatically with a change in structures. According to Garaudy, "It has been said by all the leaders of the Marxist parties that the prejudices, and particularly the prejudices about the inferiority of women, would remain for a certain time." It is not only a problem of the transformation of structures; it is a problem of interior conversion. It is necessary that a man become small and be capable of accepting the voice of the future.

It is clear that the "death of the father" represents a break with the past, with what is static, predetermined, with what can be foreseen by logic. It is an opening toward the unknown, the new, *toward what is to come.* Youth can "liberate" the mother and therefore the woman enclosed within the system by breaking down the system and conceiving the idea of a new creation, a continual creation—but being watchful that the new order not become closed in and crystallized. To avoid this crystallization, it is necessary to think about a permanent search that keeps man's imaginaton fresh and creative. As a woman, the woman cannot and does not know how to break down the order preventing her from acting as a person, but inside her that rage is accumulating which she then transmits to the community.

Are there signs of the Gospel in this youth revolution? It seems that the Gospel shines forth on every side. The profound motivation of the revolution is essentially evangelical, because more than a vindication of particulars, it is the comprehensive defense of the person, denied by the machinations of present-day society, and with no hope for tomorrow. At every step the Paris inscriptions resound with evangelical themes: "The new society must be founded on the absence of selfishness and every kind of ego-worship. Our way shall be a long march of brotherhood"; "To build a revolution is to break all internal chains." Thus we see in these inscriptions the anger of the mothers, because the point where one either becomes or does not become a person is the first fundamental relationship, which in God's plan is in accord with the trinitarian image in the world.

With the liberation of the woman from her role as an appendage to man, as a person without a specific vocation and therefore not a person, the *coup de grâce* will be given to capitalism. The day when every person, and therefore also the woman as a person, takes a real part in the commitment to produce and to organize and thus to share in the continual creation of the world, capitalism as a structure of preservation will no longer have any reason for being. On the level of the person, capitalism's projections include all the parasitical forms of life: the woman with a public relations function, people who live off their income without working, the masses who obey the suggestions of advertising and who therefore have no space of autonomy for themselves. It is these parasitical forms that permit the establishment of a system which does not acknowledge the primacy of the person; in practice it denies his basic right to exist. If theoretically all men could be given the right to evolve in accord with their vocation and this right were denied to woman—by characterizing her and orienting her by a sexual and not a vocational criterion—then the revolution would not be a profound mutation, but only a superficial change of class positions. "Change washes whiter then revolution or reform": This profound mutation can come about only by reaching the very center of life itself.

The permanent Christian revolution has its center, its base of operations, in these depths, and it jolts the world so that there might occur a mutation that ultimately transforms the person. Christ spoke to a woman *(John 4:7-26)*, and his message is like the synthesis of the revolution he brings to the world: to make the man who is a slave of the law, order, and structure into a man free in spirit—not an anarchist, but a man liberated in the Spirit, who is the Spirit of truth and love. And truth and love are in the rediscovery and acceptance of the basic structures of the person and a respect for them. Only the person is the perfect and fulfilled image of God, and therefore God is more completely and entirely in the person than anywhere else. To the woman to whom he entrusted his message, Christ said. "Go, call your husband." He entrusted her with the mandate to transform a man into a husband! Alienated man, the cause and principle of alienation in things, in creation, is called to be a husband, that is, to be integrated with a person and through that person with mankind. He is no longer merely a producer and a reproducer, but a husband. He is integrated. Christ came to bring to the world this reintegration, which does not destroy the order of creation but deepens and purifies it.

Sex is the force of the integration of mankind, the force which comes from our origins in the night of time. And it continues to be the common axis of copulation, in the present phase in which man is endowed with the divine gift of the Word. Sex is the force of copulation, but it does not necessarily create a couple. On the contrary, it can happen that sex unites and divides at the same time. It is a function which orients one person to another, through an appetite of attraction, but it also permits all alienations: "Your desire shall be for your husband and he shall rule over you" *(Genesis 3:16)*. The invitation to the Samaritan woman is a symbol of the grace which Christ came to bring men: "Go, call your husband," that is, not only through the attraction of sex but through the Word. Call your husband! The woman, who knew men but was not a wife or a companion, intuits that in Christ's language there is a *new order*. She is to call not the male but the husband. This is a proposal of a new relationship which she does not know. And she confesses simply, "I have no husband." None of the five men whom she had is her husband.

Christ presents himself as the common axis of the couple insofar as he is the Word. Through "water and the word," through the profound regeneration in Christ, the copulation is converted into a couple. This means two people integrated in love, two people forming the one image of God. Christ spoke of eunuchs for the kingdom of heaven, persons who transcend the function of sex by reflecting the eschatological image to which mankind tends, the image of God integrated in love. Joseph and Mary reproduce in chastity the perfect model of integration which must come about in the world. In place of copulation, there is the couple; in place of momentary union on the level of the flesh, there is permanent integration. Paul speaks of being married in Christ, alluding to the integration in the couple that can come about only in the Word.

Love always and everywhere is expressed in poetry and song. All animals sing in love because song and poetry are the expression of being which is in harmony, of being which is not alienated or falsified, but rediscovered, identified, restored to its true essence. And being aspires with every fiber to integration, to coming together. Copulation is a form of integration. The song of true integration, where love is discovered as a force which integrates and reconstructs persons, is called *The Canticle of Canticles.* A song and a canticle are two variations of the same reality: One is singing on the level of the flesh, the other singing in its deeper and more human dimension. I do not call it spiritual for fear of stressing an image that we must erase: the spirit against the flesh. We must rebuild the biblical image of the spirit as the fullness, depth, and truth of the flesh. In the Word sex becomes a function creative of the person; here it achieves its deepest truth. And Christ entrusted the woman with the function of calling her husband, calling him by name, making him a husband by means of this call. The Adam who came from the hands of the Father, still half asleep, discovers the woman at his side, the complementary "thou," and it is he who calls her, greets her, and gives her a name: "This at last is bone of my bones and flesh of my flesh; she shall be called *Ishshah* [woman], because she was taken out of *Ish* [man]" *(Genesis 2:23).* Man discovers her as an appendix of himself, without a name, and gives her an extension of his own name, thereby almost denying her an identity. Changed through sin, which is pride and egoism, an offense against truth and love, he tries to dominate her by every means, with the force of his person and with that of structures—which are the incarnation of his malice.

From that point on there has been a painful history of reciprocal aggressions, which are passed on to the children and the children's children, expanding like a river, forming that "deposit of rage" which explodes at certain moments of history. And our moment is one of these. The Word sends a woman to call her husband by name, to recall him from the dispersion of sex and promiscuity back to unity and integration: "Go, call your husband." Woman has not fulfilled this function or at least has not fulfilled it to the extent necessary to make the world operate well. The system in which she has lived has practically prevented her from protesting. Or it has alienated her in the pleasure of a life of permanent adolescence, without true freedom but with the impression that she is operating completely on her own, without true power over creation but with the false image of being a queen with absolute power. Without a true preparation oriented toward the knowledge of things and action upon them, there is the illusion of possessing a culture capable of having influence. When man has been able to do so, he has enslaved woman in heavy chores with no time off, with duties that take from her all freedom of initiative. When he has not been able to do this, he has deceived her with false images, so that she could not participate in creative activity, so that he alone could build the world and its order—against which the young people are protesting today.

"Their [i.e., youth's] only offense," read the Paris walls, "is to reject an authoritarian and hierarchical system which silences any radical opposition. It is to refuse to be slaves of this system." The change vehemently demanded by the protesting youth is a change in the person, in attitude, and cannot come about unless it starts out from this center of the person. Thus we must reflect: It is easier to raise salaries, reduce the rate of unemployment, increase the number of university classrooms, accept administrative boards, than it is to change man. It seems to me that through the youth protest, Christ's words to Nicodemus—the learned one, the adult, who still asks what he must do—are quite contemporary: *Be born again.* It is not a question of advancing objectives, of following rules. It is necessary to be reborn, to make oneself a new man. "Young people are asking for a completely different form of life," said one inscription, and theirs "is not only an intellectual demand but also an instinctive one," that is, it resides in the profound root of being itself. If women cannot form a political force nor protest for want of an adequate framework, their protest against the violence inflicted on the person has a voice and a force in the youth rebellion. Woman preserves and incarnates this outrage which culture and the social structure inflict on the person, and she transmits it to her children, thus putting this ferment of change into history. She who is preservation and who in the conscious sphere expresses herself better with traditional attitudes guards within herself this revolutionary impetus which urges man on to cast his lot in the defense of the person.

We have often spoken of this age as the age of the death of the father. But does not this demand of our culture appear to be clearly antievangelical? Where are the traces of the Gospel in this polemical and revolutionary rupture? Christ came to reveal the Father, and this revelation is so marked in the Gospel that in the past the Gospel could be identified with the revelation of the fatherhood of God. "And call no man your father on earth, for you have one Father, who is in heaven" *(Matthew 23:9)*.

But if we look closer at this revelation of the father, we discover, as always, how *new* it is. The fatherhood of God is a situation into which man is born, but it is also a conquest. Man is called upon to break with one fatherhood, to reject one fatherhood in order to win another. There is a fatherhood of dependence which keeps us children and minors, and there is a free fatherhood: "And do not presume to say to yourselves, 'We have Abraham as our father'; for I tell you, God is able from these stones to raise up children to Abraham" *(Matthew 3:9)*. The preaching of John the Baptist is directed with much harshness to the Hebrews of the established order, sure of an inalienable possession, protected by a fatherhood which envelops them like a matrix and shelters them in life and death. We must not trust in this fatherhood which comes to us by birth, by belonging to a particular race, because God can raise up sons however and wherever he wishes.

In the hypocritical world in which the death of the spirit is justified by formalistic obedience to the Father, Jesus came to tear up the cobblestones from the street like today's students: "For I have come to set a man against his father, and a daughter against her mother . . ." *(Matthew 10:35)*. And for Christ the liberator and for the Gospel, a man must be ready to "abandon his father and his mother" *(Mark 10:7)*. Not only must we break with the father and mother in the flesh, but we must do this "for me and for the Gospel," that is, for a liberation and to proclaim the Good News to the world. And we also must break with tradition, with the established order, with that umbilical cord which binds the person to his race and his tradition, thus giving him security at a cheap price—as if salvation and liberation were an I O U given to whoever belongs to a particular race.

Chapter 5 of Matthew is an energetic break with the past, which the

Messiah has overcome with a more profound and essential vision. "It was said to men of old . . . but I say to you." This is not an anarchical break which says to man, "Do whatever you wish." Rather it is a powerful hatchet blow against the *status quo,* against the crystallized order, against a security that comes from an original fatherhood. It was not born from Abraham because "God is able from these stones to raise up children to Abraham," . . . one becomes a child of Abraham! In the Gospel the fatherhood of God is seen more as a conquest than as a possession to be preserved, more as a value that is still ahead of man, a goal, rather than as a value that is behind and prior to man. And to win this fatherhood we must break with the other one, that of flesh and blood, the fatherhood of security, tranquillity, and immobility. The Gospel does not counsel an ordinary disobedience but rather a conscious one that is a conquest. One of the inscriptions of the Paris youth revolt says, "Obedience begins with consciousness and consciousness with disobedience."

To clarify the idea that the fatherhood of God is a conquest, an arrival point, an eschatological value that emerges in the encounter with man's history and represents its fulfillment, it is enough to quote a passage from the Letter to the Romans: "We know that the whole creation has been groaning in travail together until now; and not only the creation but we ourselves, who have the first fruits of the Spirit, groan inwardly as we wait for adoption as sons, the redemption of our bodies. For in this hope we were saved. Now hope that is seen is not hope. For who hopes for what he sees?" *(Romans 8:22-24).* We have received the first fruits of the spirit, the seed which must germinate in us, the seed of this new man made in the image of Christ, the Son of the Father. And we groan for this fullness as our goal, whether we know it or not. To keep ourselves straining toward this arrival point, we must break continually with an order that threatens us, a comfortable and ancestral dependence which attracts us by its facility. "But now that you have come to know God, or rather to be known by God, how can you turn back again to the weak and beggarly elemental spirits, whose slaves you want to be once more?" *(Galatians 4:9).*

Adoption is an inheritance but at the same time a conquest. I am fascinated by the very concept of adoption, which is the name of the new relationship of the person with God that has been revealed to us in the New Testament. The revelation of God the Creator leads us to conclude that we are dependent on creation, one among so many creatures, who— even if we are the most important and are endowed with greater power—

depend totally on the Creator. Christ comes, in a certain sense, to break our creaturely dependence in order to establish this new relationship which must be sought, that of the adopted son. On first sight it would seem that we are going from something more to something less, but, upon reflection, we can glimpse the transition from the order of necessity to the order of freedom. This relationship is given to me, but at the same time I must choose and want it. It is a conquest which is made in freedom more than an acknowledgment of a dependence. "Now we, brethren, like Isaac are children of promise" *(Galatians 4:28)*. "Now Hagar is Mount Sinai in Arabia; she corresponds to the present Jerusalem, for she is in slavery for her children. But the Jerusalem above is free. . . . " *(ibid., 4:25-26)*. More than a radication in the earth, this adoption as sons is a hope from on high toward which we must tend. Therefore the fatherhood which the Gospel reveals is at the core of life and is the result of our growth in freedom. We must, then, continually break with the fatherhood of the flesh, which threatens to sufficate us with its protection and its ordered structures.

To support the break with this "fatherhood of origins," Christ stirred up tradition and lifted the veil from what was beneath formalistic obedience. "But you say, 'If a man tells his father or his mother, What you would have gained from me is Corban' (that is, given to God)—then you no longer permit him to do anything for his father or mother, thus making void the word of God through your tradition which you hand on" *(Mark 7:11-13)*. This seems like a denunciation of the world today. In the name of a tradition, of an obedience to our fathers, the person is violated, justice and love are continually denied, and this is often disguised as an offering to the temple.

The adoptive sonship, to which each of us must tend and which is a landing point rather than a stem to which our life is attached, is amply commented upon in chapter 25 of Matthew: "I was hungry and you gave me to eat; I was thirsty and you gave me to drink." This is the page of brotherhood and identification: "Truly I say to you, as you did it to one of the least of these my brethren, you did it to me." It is the dynamic, creative page of the Gospel. Man will be judged not on the basis of obedience to a static, formalistic order but by obedience to man's ever new historical needs and by his opposition to whatever over the course of the centuries threatens his integrity as a person. Man must see, discover, and get inside the history of his freedom as a son of God. "Freedom is the awareness of need": This student inscription could be a heading to the twenty-fifth chapter of Matthew. Man is identified with Christ, becomes like him—that is, free, the Son and the Father—as he becomes aware of the need of the world and of needy men, not looking down from on high or from outside, but in the very action of eliminating this need.

The surprise on man's part is a remarkable commentary: "When did we see you?" Or, "When did we not see you?" Because this new man in Christ, this reborn person, comes about in the hard and rough cement of a history which seemingly has nothing religious about it. It seems alien to the concept of religion, which for us is something polished, ordered, beyond the fray. "When did we see you?" "If what you see doesn't surprise you, it's fake," one of the graffiti says. The believer does not see because he is not used to this perspective, and the nonbeliever does not see because he is looking for man and not for God. But identification comes about in this way. "They put me in prison and you came to visit me." It goes without saying that this creativity, this precondition for salvation, the sole means of identifying with the Son, is achieved by challenging a culture and an order, and also by challenging those who are responsible for the hunger and thirst, the prisons, the lack of dwellings and clothing to shelter our brothers from the cold. To give food and drink and visit the prisoners is to shatter chains, to tear down barriers, to oppose an established order. It means the death of the father, the break with those who are responsible for the order which leaves people hungry, naked, and without shelter.

To make the fatherhood and sonship which Christ proclaimed as his essential message into a static stratification, a despotic authoritarianism, a discipline more than a creation, is to betray the Gospel. The Gospel is an invitation "to attain to . . . mature manhood, to the measure of the stature of the fullness of Christ" *(Ephesians 4:13)*. It is a rebirth which comes about only in relationship with others; it is a growth which is achieved only in the comprehensive understanding of the situations of men who suffer hunger, thirst, cold, and imprisonment. Man is born a son of flesh and blood, with all the burden of the heritage of his race, tradition, and history. He becomes a son of the Spirit of God through the seed of grace which must develop and grow in time. The fatherhood of God is at the end. In this youth rebellion we see also this symbol of the Gospel: the awakening of a person before it is too late and before the present order completely suffocates him, thus denying him the air and room to which he has a right. It is the awakening of a proletariat that is much broader than that formed by industrial society: "A proletarian is one who has no control over the use of his own life and knows it," says the walls of Paris. And these are not only the workers. They are the young person, the

woman, the person marginated from a society born out of the multiplica-
tion of money and centered on this ideal. If we are against this society,
when our ideal protest takes shape and becomes revolution we must
understand it and help it. If not, where is our consistency? The Gospel
becomes history, that complicated and ambiguous history, a play of light
and shadow that is the only history of man.

Young people today are calling us to a clarity and consistency which
we shall not find without the impulse of this criticism. That there is
exaggeration in their challenge is obvious; but they would never be listened
to if they did not exaggerate. We have little time left to protest against a
society in which "people wash ten times a day, and at the same time kill
and burn Vietnam in all purity," as they wrote in May. It is only the youth
that can do this because we are already enclosed in the system. We must
sense that the young people are our liberators. From them I await the
message of renewal which the Holy Spirit wishes to give to the world of
today. We are made in such a way that we have precise ideas about what is
and what is not. But the young people dream and use their imagination;
they are open to what is new and imaginative. We have the right to oppose
their protest only if we can acknowledge that our society is good and that
we have acceptable prospects for the future, if we truly are preparing for
the time of the spirit and the time of the person. If we cannot affirm this,
we must be honest and give way freely to new projects and new ideals. I
do not know what the outcome of this youth revolution will be, but it is
certainly a step toward personalization. The liberation of woman, the
death of the father, will certainly not be definitive, because history is not
coming to an end. But the young people must want this with all their
might, as if it were their job to bring history to its fulfillment. Christ
allowed his generation continually to touch the arrival point of history and
to live this tension as if history were already ended. "They [the Twelve]
supposed that the Kingdom of God was just about to appear" *(Luke
19:11)*. The cowards, those who see nothing more in the youth rebellion
than chaos, without anything positive, ought to read the Gospel carefully:
"Whole countries will be in despair . . . . Men will faint from fear as they
wait for what is coming over the whole earth . . . . When you see these
things happening, you will know that the kingdom of God is about to
come" *(Luke 21:25-26, 31)*.

Before doing so with words, Christ clarified his position in an
episode of his childhood. His manifestation among men was at the age of
twelve when he remained behind in the temple during the yearly pilgrim-

age to Jerusalem. The two fatherhoods appear clearly: that of the starting point and that of the arrival; that which for us is the fatherhood of flesh and blood—order, the past, discipline—and that which we must choose and which is chosen in the vocation, in the concrete discovery of the will of the Father: " 'Son, why have you treated us so? Behold, your father and I have been looking for you anxiously.' And he said to them, 'How is it that you sought me? Did you not know that I must be in my Father's house?' " *(Luke 2:48-49)*. This is not disobedience. It is a declaration of independence, of freedom, in the name of a vocation. It is a break with a fatherhood which is given, which is prior to the person, which is previous to his becoming aware. And the break is made in order to respond to a fatherhood which calls for coming out of ourselves—a call coinciding with the vocation inscribed in the structure of the person which the person must discover and do in history. In a certain sense, Mary's mission as mother ends here, and this end could not be decided by her. It is never the parents who decide when their function is over; it is the children. The son who wrote these words in the Sorbonne may appear insolent. "You don't beg the right to live, you take it." But this is the great law of life.

The renewals of history, changes, never come about as the munificence of the groups responsible for the existing state of affairs. They are the work of those who suffer, who feel the structure as a burden and are aware of it. And to a certain extent this always seems to be a usurpation. Christ's words can sound harsh, but they are realistic. They are the translation into words of an existential truth. The mission of the Son of Man is to break with the world of the law and to establish the world of the spirit by freeing man from structures—not with revolt but with a new creation. Therefore, with this essentially youthful act there begins the breaking of the first tie, that of dependence on one's parents, the tie of the past. He is not the son of Abraham, Isaac, and Jacob. He is the son of God. He does not deny his past, the bond that links him to the race and makes him a son of Israel; but he is the son of the new Israel, the Israel of the spirit, a son of the people who is the heir to God's promises. They are no longer an indolent, sleeping, passive heir, but one who must win by faith and active, committed, creative love the promises which God has deposited in this people. Their mission is in the line of prophecy, that which extends the right of sonship to all men of good will—both inside and outside the bounds of race, flesh, and blood.

His action is not a disobedience, a revolution. It is truly a mutation. And it begins—as the Gospel says—among the learned ones of Israel. He listens to them and asks them questions. It is a remarkable picture. "Action must not be a reaction, but a creation," say the youth today. "If somebody asks you a question, answer with a question." And Christ asked questions of the learned ones of Israel. It is very sad to think that in the dust raised by the youth rebellion no one was aware how there was a repetition of the gestures of the Man who is the model for all generations. Few of those who wrote on the Paris walls—perhaps none—thought they had a precursor in the One who challenged the past by introducing into it a creative unrest. And this unrest resembles imagination more than the cold rationalism of the person who thinks that everything has already been done and all that is left is to become integrated into the established order, into the rigidly structured systems of laws.

Someone who has the obedience-disobedience alternative in mind and does not see the creativeness of this break—which is a profound change of order and perspective—is annoyed by the youthful attitude of Christ. Joseph and Mary's position, on the other hand, is most normal: "But they did not understand the answer he gave them." It is the normal amazement at a child who has suddenly grown up, the painful break which parents never wish to see. "Everybody," says one of the Paris inscriptions, "wants to breathe and nobody can. A lot of people say they'll breathe later. Most of them don't die because they're already dead." During the public ministry, Jesus said to those who told him that his mother and his brothers were waiting outside: " 'Who are my mother and my brothers?' . . . 'Here are my mother and my brothers. Whoever does the will of God is my brother, and sister and mother.' " *(Mark 3:33-35).* In a most excellent way Mary belongs to this group. Those who discover life as creation and do the will of God and obey the profound and personal law of their presence, which is unique and characteristic for each one of us, they are his brother, mother, and sisters. After observing that "they [Joseph and Mary] did not understand," the Gospel adds that "his mother carefully kept all these things in her heart." The woman's mission, even when she does not understand it, is to guard and keep in her heart the matters of family, this life in which is reflected the great history of the world. Joseph and Mary say nothing to the painful answer of their son. Mary keeps these things in her heart. She does not understand, but she keeps them and meditates on them.

Man is concerned with building and doing; he continues on his way, tending to efficiency and the works which grow and are accomplished. Often he upsets the values of personalization, without noticing that he is becoming emprisoned in the one-dimensional society which robs him of the power of negation and rejection. But the woman keeps within herself all the human residue, rejected or denied, the "fragment of the soul" which man's march has left beside the road, on the fringes of action. This preservation is what started the protest. From this deep place hidden in the womb of the woman rises the force accumulated by the new generation, oppressed by the indifference and violence of man. It has become rebellion and creation, the need to dream of a new reality, to believe in the impossible. We can clearly see the motivation which sustains the violent, painful clash between the generations: the spirit against the law, freedom against law and order. No compromise can hold back this barbarian force and only a radical, profound change in society can channel it. Instead of denying or repressing it, we must understand it and integrate it. To understand it we must be ready to lose. Only with the readiness to lose our own world view will we be able to find poverty and receptivity, the preconditions for dialogue.

We all agree on the level of ideas, but existentially we give the lie to what we have in theory accepted. Many men of the Church are revolutionaries until the revolution comes; at this point they hold back and recede. Rather than a precursor of the attitude of youth, Christ appears responsible for a deadening discipline and a historical situation which we feel must somehow be broken with before the new person can be born. We are not discovering the relationship which exists between what is happening today and the young man who two thousand years ago broke up an order out of obedience to the future, to the new creation. Without knowing it, the youth are liberating themselves from the prison in which we have shut them up. Doesn't the twenty-fourth chapter of Luke come to mind? "But on the first day of the week, at early dawn, they [the women who had been at the crucifixion] went to the tomb. . . . And they found the stone rolled away from the tomb. . . . While they were perplexed about this, behold, two men stood by them in dazzling apparel; and as they were frightened and bowed their faces to the ground, the men said to them, 'Why do you seek the living among the dead?' " *(24:1-5)*. All who yearn for the New Man—no longer in the gloomy garb of fear which makes him "diplomatic," miserly, and aggressive, a wolf or a fox but not a person, but rather now in the dazzling apparel of the transparency of a person in communion—let them move aside the rock behind which we always try to hide the risen Christ.

18

FREEDOM IN PEACE

The voice of youth does not come to us solely from the barricades of Rome or Paris, Madrid or Warsaw. It also comes to us from the young continents, from those who have not yet even won the right to be persons. Their anger constitutes the great reserve and the great hope of the international outrage of youth. "The forest preceded man. The desert follows him," said a Sorbonne inscription. Here in Latin America—a continent which is supposed to be Christian—there is still the air of the forest. I breathe it in in my contacts with the young people of the forest where I have my roots. They are the grandchildren of Indian women raped by the barbarians who came from Europe at the time of the conquest. They are an explosive mixture. In them is the violence of the conquistadors and the rage of those who were the victims of violence. This explains the hatred and love for Europe growing on this continent. In proportion to the growth in awareness, the quotient of love and admiration is lessening and the rage quotient is on the rise.

I have just received a letter from a Latin American studying in Paris. He writes me from his tiny room on the fifth floor of a hotel in the Latin Quarter: "Inside we are all right, but we cannot say the same thing about outside. The Parisians are ultra-individualists, almost xenophobes and racists. They are not easy to get along with. They seem like a people who don't love themselves and who drag around this lack of love with bitterness and meanness. Could they be so old?" Still with his roots in the forest, despite the fact that his body is in the Latin Quarter, my friend sees the desert. But between the forest and the desert I hope that man, the person, will be born.

The Europeanizing Latin American Church, modeled after the Spanish Church of Charles V and Isabel the Catholic, had a prophetic moment in 1968 at the Medellín Conference after the triumphal Eucharistic Congress in Bogota. But because I do not think that the Church as such takes the initiative in the transformation, I do not share either the enthusiasm or the disillusionment of those who are expecting change to come from the Church. I believe in the prophetic Church and know that her orientations do not go wrong; she moves in the direction that history is going and in the direction of the exodus. Christ admonished those who know and do nothing: "The scribes and the Pharisees sit on Moses' seat; so practice and observe whatever they tell you, but not what they do; for they preach, but do not practice" *(Matthew 23:2-3)*. On the other hand is not the torpor of the Church as such historically understandable? It is not the Church of the fathers and the doctors, of those who command, that can change society, for the change would go against themselves. A Latin American magazine writes opportunely: "A politics of God? Let us say immediately that we do not want to resurrect Christendom. We do not want the Church as such to be at the head of the political life of the peoples of Latin America, nor to consecrate new secular institutions, nor to integrate them into her structures, nor to make them an object of her power. In accordance with the directives of Medellín, we do want the Church to accomplish her mission within the agenda of men, to be in a fellowship of hope with the peoples whom she serves, to contribute her part in molding the world as the kingdom of God, this world of which she forms a part and to which she was sent in order to make the face of Jesus Christ the Savior shine forth. The hour is very grave. It goes without saying that this mission cannot be only in words nor too varied in accordance with the multiplicity of choices and the action of each person. The people of God must come together and give themselves collectively to the politics of God, to his politics of the liberation of men" *(Vispera* 2, no. 7).

Here peace no longer is seen as the tranquillity of a static order, a result obtained by putting out all the fires of rebellion, or a benevolent concession from those in authority—with whom we make a deal so that a little more bread, instruction, and entertainment will keep the people quiet. No, peace is seen as the result of a long, hard commitment to eliminate "white" violence, that is, hidden violence. Today we are realizing that we have been drugged by those who are concerned with preserving this peace. All those who don't agree with this kind of peace are called sowers of hate and bloodshed, who dismember the people of God and transform the Gospel of love and brotherhood into a doctrine of hatred and division. But a hand guided by the Word of truth wrote on the walls, "One unrevolutionary weekend is infinitely more bloody than a month of permanent revolution." We have discovered the white violence of the conservatives who make the poor pay for their expensive vacations in Miami, Copacabana, or Long Beach, and we have awakened from our narcosis. Only by somehow placing ourselves within the outrage of the poor can we become men of peace.

Peace is the result of an order sought through liberation. It is not achieved by corrections and modifications of the existent order, but through a movement of liberation. The peoples of the Third World are slaves because they depend on a "center of economic power" around which they gravitate. "For this reason, our nations frequently do not have control over their goods or the economic decisions affecting them. It is obvious that this will not fail to have political consequences, given the interdependence of the two spheres" (*Medellín,* "Peace," no. 8). From this relationship are derived the unjust structures that threaten the rights of persons. First of all, since in the capitalist world fierce competition requires a strict control of prices, this situation results: "The countries which produce raw materials—especially if they are dependent on one major export—always remain poor, while the industrialized countries get constantly richer. This injustice, clearly denounced by *Populorum progressio,* nullifies the eventual positive effect of foreign aid; furthermore, it constitutes a permanent threat to peace, because our countries perceive that what is given to them with one hand is taken away with the other" (*ibid.,* no. 9). Thus we see the hypocrisy of aid abundantly paid for by those who receive it.

There can be no peace without destroying the capitalist system, which situates economic profit in the central place that the person should occupy. Man's study and intellectual training are not directed toward the growth and liberation of the person, but toward increasing his economic power. This is so much the case that there is a parallel flow of capital and technicians from the poor countries to the rich countries in order to increase the economic return of the capital. In this way, the countries of the Third World are stripped of capital and technicians. In Buenos Aires there is a little group called the *Centro de Investigación Filosófica.* It was formed by a small number of dedicated young people of different philosophical convictions and today is in the process of repatriating little by little the young intellectuals who abandoned their countries first in search of specialization and then attracted by higher salaries. They call them back to serve their country and to work in teams in the name of friendship that can give strength and courage to isolated voices. It is a great boost to the hope of the poor.

In the capitalist system, *Medellin* says, it is possible to "evade the established tax system by subterfuge" and to send "profits and dividends abroad, without contributing adequate reinvestments to the progressive development of our countries. . . . In the system of international credits, the true needs and capacities of our countries are not taken into account. We thus run the risk of encumbering ourselves with debts whose payment absorbs the major part of our income. . . . We wish to underline that the chief culprits of the economic dependence of our countries are those forces which, inspired by unbridled profit, lead to economic dictatorship and the international imperialism of money, condemned by Pius XI in *Quadragesimo anno* and by Paul VI in *Populorum progressio.*" Consequently, "We hereby denounce imperialism of whatever ideological stripe which is exercised in Latin America indirectly and even through direct interventions" (*ibid.,* nos. 9-10). The document says very clearly that peace is not a result of psychological, affective, or religious good will. It can happen only by overcoming the center of economic power, which functions with specific mechanisms of banditry and aggression, analyzed in the document. Political oppression is carried out no longer under a flag, but rather under the economic sign of man's greed for profit and for the possibility of increasing profits on the basis of an already established economic power. This *must be denounced*; we cannot remain silent. But why then do we rend our garments when we read the following in a Paris manifesto?: "These struggles are looking not only for an improvement of the conditions of the workers within the capitalist system; they imply the destruction of this system. They are political in the true sense of the word: Don't fight to get a new Prime Minister, but so that the boss has no more power either in the factory or in society. Your form of struggle offers us students the example of truly socialist action: the appropriation of the means of production and the power of decision-making by the workers." If we do not know how to rediscover in practical application the ideas we have set forth and defended, it means that we are not free and that we have bound our own interests to the system.

This unjust international order, which perpetuates the simultaneous existence of poor and rich countries, is nothing more than the projection of an internal order that is deeply deranged and off-balance. Peace begins at home; it is reflected in the first community—which is that of national administration—and extends to the international order. *Medellín* points out the different forms of marginality, "socio-economic, political, cultural, racial, and religious, in both urban and rural areas" ("Peace," no. 2). The woman is marginated in the family, even if she is queen of her household and her husband grants her total freedom in domestic matters—provided that she doesn't intrude into his creative sphere where history is made. Woman must make a common cause with the other marginal people.

With a vision that has its roots in adolescence, man is used to seeing the theater of his action in a world emptied of persons. Into his vision enter technical, economic, public relations (and today we add psychological) calculations, aimed at an instrumentalization of the person, and from all of these calculations the person is excluded. The calculations are successful if they keep persons marginal, if they do not deal with their basic needs; these needs are excluded from one's mental horizon from the earliest age of preparation.

This situation is due to the economic inequality between the classes. Wealth in Latin America is in the hands of the few; while economic development "has favored those who helped establish it in the beginning, it has neglected the masses of the native population, which are almost always left at a subsistence level." Such an imbalance provokes a state of "growing frustration," proportionate to the growth in awareness of those who are its victims. The dominant oligarchies are insensitive to this outcry of the poor (*ibid.,* nos. 3-5). "The walls have ears," said a Paris wall, "and your ears have walls." And people think that they can erect a dike against this force of desperation with "legal" violence, accusing everybody who raises his voice in defense of the poor. "It is not unusual to find that these groups or sectors, with the exception of a few minorities, characterize as subversive activities all attempts to change a social system that favors the perdurance of their privileges. . . . Some members of the dominant sectors at times resort to the use of force to repress drastically any attempt at opposition. . . . It is easy for them to find apparent ideological justifications (anticommunism) or practical ones (the preservation of 'order') to give an honorable appearance to this action" (*ibid.,* nos. 5-6). Finally we have a clear attempt to unmask words and to see what there is behind them. To achieve this clarity it is necessary to crush the defenses of the oligarchical groups, which avail themselves of every means to weaken the protest movement aimed at the establishment of peace.

The same thing has happened in the student rebellion. The press campaigns have attempted to isolate and discredit these movements. If the student revolts make the front page, this is not due to a particular sympathy on the part of newspaper men. Quite the contrary. They are trying to organize a hate campaign against the potential danger threatening the social order. We must get our eyes used to seeing where peace is and where it is not, because too frequently it has been confused with apparent order and with all those movements involved with violence and war. But for Christ, the "rumors of war" are the prelude to peace: "Raise your heads, because your redemption is drawing near" *(Luke 21:28)*.

The Medellín document vigorously and clearly denounces the attempts at defense by those people who feel harassed by the force of truth and by the powerful pressure exerted by those who have suffered injustice. "The reality described constitutes a negation of peace, as understood by Christian tradition. . . . The oppression exerted by power groups can give the impression of keeping peace and order, but in reality it is nothing but the continual and inevitable seed of rebellions and wars" ("Peace," no. 14). Thus, where this social peace does not exist, where there are unjust inequities—social, political, economical, cultural—there therefore is a rejection of the peace of the Lord. Even more, there is a rejection of the Lord himself *(cf. Matthew 25:31-46)*. If the Christian believes in the productivity of peace in order to achieve justice, he also believes that justice is an inescapable condition for peace.

It is impossible not to see that in many areas Latin America finds itself in a situation that demands transformations that are global, daring, urgent, and profoundly renewing. Nor should it seem strange to us that the "temptations to violence" spoken of in *Populorum progressio* (no. 30) is being felt in Latin America. "We should not abuse the patience of a people that for years has borne a situation that would not be acceptable to anyone with any degree of awareness of human rights. . . . The privileged often join together and with all the means at their disposal pressure those who govern, thus obstructing necessary changes. In some instances, this resistance takes on drastic proportions which result in the destruction of life and property ("Peace," nos. 16-17). The document strongly indicts the violence which is present and perdures under the appearances of peace and tranquillity. It indicts the rejection of God, even when he is accepted on paper and in words. It indicts the nonexistence of peace, due to the terrible social inequities. The document certainly is not an invitation to violence or guerrilla warfare as a means to achieve peace. On the contrary, it hopes that change can come about without violence. But it acknowledges that institutionalized violence, which is increasing daily—because of a growth in people's consciousness, because of an increase in population and marginal areas, and because of the growing insensitivity of the privileged classes—can cause violent reactions.

If that should happen, what should the Christian do? I think no one can offer an absolute answer. The Christian is a man of peace but not of a prefabricated peace. His peace is sought after, suffered for, yearned for, fought for, and defended. It is a peace which goes to the roots of being, which presupposes brothers living together in peace and that the conditions for this be present. Therefore, it is his duty to discover everything, from whatever source, that stands in the way of this living together in peace and to denounce it loudly, without fearing persecutions and calumnies. He must struggle with all his might so that the necessary, substantial social changes come about effectively, quickly, and, if possible, with nonviolent means. But when the situation is explosive and to defend himself against violence there seems to be no alternative but violence, what should he do?

This is a situation of "manifest, long-standing tyranny," spoken of by the pope in *Populorum progressio* (no. 31), which makes recourse to violence lawful and necessary. No Christian's conscience was disturbed during the last world war by participating in the Resistance which was certainly violent, because this was the only way to get rid of an obviously unjust violence. Now the Latin American bishops have discovered a state of unjust violence on their continent. The Medellín document stresses the responsibility of those who have power in the spheres of culture, politics, and money for provoking the explosive revolution of desperation. It stresses the "noble impulses of justice and solidarity" ("Peace," no. 19) which are often discovered in those who put their hope in violence. The bishops are living the Latin American reality and are discovering from the inside what the conditions of peace are. In accordance with the directives of Vatican Council II, the episcopate is making a prophetic balance sheet of the Latin American situation and is discovering everything which is not peace and everything that should be peace. If we are to be consistent we must not fall back and we must not be scandalized by the great rejection on the part of the youth who are repudiating a society which has been so solemnly and unanimously condemned.

There is a certain inhibition in the Conclusions of Medellín. Here and there they suffer from the Church's traditional fear. While on the one hand they very energetically attack neocolonialism, on the other they suggest a solution of reform of the social structures, "which would be gradual, absolutely assimilable, and would come about contemporaneously and unanimously." The limitation of Medellín was the absence in the assembly of real workers and laymen actively present in the process of liberation. The Latin American situation was examined in a broad and unprejudiced spirit, but by men of the Church, by men who were operatively dissociated from reality. They do not make history; they judge it. And to judge history without making it is very dangerous. Thus they see the possibility of bringing about justice through peaceful dialogue. As men of the Church they cannot leave their hierarchical structure outside the meeting rooms; and this may be a deformation. They cannot for an instant succeed in forgetting those who stand in power. They insult them with the hope of jolting them, of making them think. Zacchaeus was no common man, Reverend Fathers. How many of his type have you met along the way?

It might be possible to multiply the number of Zacchaeuses, if we knew how to create around them the atmosphere that surrounded the publicans. Since today's Zacchaeuses have marginalized the masses, it is necessary that they in turn feel marginalized and despised. If these rich men felt that they were publicans, perhaps they could be converted. Perhaps the look in the eyes of young people, of their children, will be able to make them blush with shame on discovering that they have loved money more than their wives and children. Will this succeed?

But even if they are converted, we cannot ask them to make concessions. We can never say, "The social and economic transformation of Latin America basically depends on them." We cannot even dream of it! They might be able to understand and accelerate the process. But changes are never made from above; they are always made from below. The purest, holiest change in history, that of Christ's relationship with his parents which figures in the Gospel as an exemplary model, came from below. It was not Mary and Joseph who emancipated their adolescent son. It is the adolescent son who emancipated himself. And his parents, like all parents, did not understand. It cannot be said that Jesus came down from on high, because he behaved like the Son of Man and not like the God who miraculously solves problems. At the marriage of Cana it is Mary who sounds the hour of the miracle. It is the woman who moves things, not with authority nor as mother, but as a companion. I do not want to venture too far into the realm of exegesis, but as a man in the street I am powerfully drawn to the fact that on this occasion Jesus calls his mother "woman."

The young people are beyond, way beyond this modest project of reform of Medellín, even if it is considered "radical." The French students are saying this: "Why are we students, the children of the bourgeoisie, criticizing capitalist society? For the son of a worker to become a student means leaving his class. For the son of a bourgeois it is perhaps the opportunity for him to know the true nature of his class, to ask questions about the social function to which he is destined, about the organization of society, about the role you are developing for him. We refuse to be the elite, cut off from social reality. We refuse to be used for the profit of the ruling class. We want to abolish the separation between the work of execution and the work of the intellect and organization. We want to build a classless society. The meaning of your struggle is the same."

The duty of the Church is to uncover sores, to denounce injustice with the force of the prophets, to unmask unmercifully those acts in which God is rejected, even if he is received triumphantly in the liturgy—which we, unfaithful as we are, have allowed to be profaned. Doctrinal solutions do not come from on high, just as practical ones do not. The Church can continue in the process only by taking into account the symbols of hope and the veins of justice which can be glimpsed in the tangle of history: "the noble impulses of justice and solidarity." Latin America will not be liberated from injustices, from the tremendous obstacles to peace which were denounced very clearly and courageously by the bishops, by putting into practice a reform worked out by the bishops and executed by political bosses or leaders. The document maintains that "the vocation for development implies today, in every Latin American Christian, a concrete commitment against the socioeconomic situations of the continent and the demand for a real and radical change." But the men who write this out of a prophetic impulse are the "sensible" people, those who stand with the professors, the industrialists, and the politicians. They are the "old men" who ask youth, "What do you want?" They will never succeed in understanding that what they want are transformations that are "urgent," "inevitable," "radical," accepted, signed, and promulgated.

Medellín speaks of "the muffled cry that is coming from millions of men who are asking their pastors for a liberation that does not come" ("Poverty of the Church," no. 2). What is this? A kindergarten cheer? This kind of naïveté leads to simplistic and antihistorical proposals which would emasculate the protest. To those who have been invited to conversion, those who are threatened, it offers arguments that the whole thing is not really serious after all. The prophetic value of a denunciation vanishes completely when deals are made with those in power and cheap solutions are suggested. To maintain the force of the prophetic admonition it is necessary to make no compromise with those in power. One must be detached from them. Let them not say to us, "Begin to do something about it yourselves!"

The document on justice is weakened by these concessions or by an abrupt change in viewpoint. It looks at the world from the viewpoint of the poor and the marginated, and then suddenly, without any explanation, it changes over to the viewpoint of the rich and the powerful. But the document on peace is very forceful, because it discards any solution of evolutionary politics and speaks of a struggle against national oligarchies and imperialism. Peace will be achieved only if we face up courageously to this struggle. It is important that the Latin American bishops saw neocolonialism as a grave danger to peace. But they believe that this monster can be conquered by reforms decided willingly by the ones responsible for this neoimperialism. This is part of a professional deformation equivalent to panic in the face of a fight or the ultraoptimistic attitude proper to those who do not have to sweat and break their backs to live. There are also involved the interests that inevitably bind to the force of power and money. The laity living in the world probably do not share this optimism; nor can they expect so much, because for them it is a problem of life or death.

Medellín invites these laymen to become responsibly involved in political life: "The lack of a political consciousness in our countries makes the Church's educational activity absolutely essential, for the purpose of bringing Christians to consider their participation in the political life of the nation as a duty of conscience and as the practice of charity in its most noble and efficacious sense for the life of the community" (*Medellín*, "Justice," no. 16). Implicitly they acknowledge that not all "Christian education" has been political, since the result is that political consciousness is lacking. Only a few years ago, to denounce the fact that the religious schools—through which passed 90 percent of cultivated Latin American youth—had educated splendid individualists was a crime. The bishops are now drawing up a balance sheet of this "Christian" education and observe that a political consciousness is lacking. The Latin American laity, and that of the rest of the world, can welcome this prophetic cry which comes from a land which is especially and obviously afflicted by the neocolonialism that is invading the whole world. Their autonomy, responsibility, and creativity will help them to discover the means to cut off the root of the evil. "Action ought not to be a reaction but a creation." Here ends the competence of the bishops who are not creators, especially of social structures and the profound changes that foster the new man.

What is the new man, the real builder of peace in the world? The Latin American bishops at Medellín gave a surprising outline of the three types of Christians in the world today: the conservative, the developmentalist, and the revolutionary. With whom do the sympathies of the pastors of souls lie? I think that in practice they lie decidedly with the conservatives. The bishops meet with them at Rotary and Lions club luncheons. These pastors are pleasant, smiling, cultivated, generous. They are revolutionaries with a tie; and above all their fingernails are manicured so that they can hurt no one. This keeps the Church in a permanent state of ambiguity; thus anyone who wants to be faithful to the words of the Gospel must steer clear of her.

The description given of the conservative group is negative, almost vicious; it is where "the dichotomy between faith and social responsibility is most frequently encountered" ("Pastoral Concern for the Elites," no. 10), that is, they prolong in the world the separation between Church and life, religion and history, clearly wiped away by Vatican II. "The faith appears to be merely an adhesion to a creed and to moral principles. Membership in the Church seems a matter of tradition and at times self-interest" (*ibid.*). This is an exact photograph of the traditional Christian; according to the lens of the Medellín bishops this picture is none too pleasant. But this is "the Christian people" who go to mass. This is the faithful group allied to the bishop, those who say that the bishop's word is absolute, that it is necessary to listen to it with complete devotion, since they are confident that the bishop will continue to be the mouthpiece of the members of the group. And when the bishop raises his voice, he always has an escape clause for them, a phrase, an oversight which saves them. For us ordinary people this is a problem that deeply disturbs us.

Already in the time of Pius XII the nobility were told that "history had definitively turned a page," that "the pope is poor and has nothing to give." One would need tremendous patience and humility to continue to frequent the doors of a palace where it is said, "I am poor and have nothing for you." A truly poor person would not be seen there any more. But the nobles continue to make their visits and to order people around in the corridors and salons where it has been clearly stated that they have nothing to do. The Roman Curia was informed in a delicate and interrogative manner, but clearly and forcefully, that career making held sway. But we do not know whether since that day career making was really sent packing. Will the Medellín document put those who "belong to the Church out of self-interest" in their place? It is too early to tell, but at the moment there are no precursory signs. I would say that these Christians rather than others are multiplying in Latin America.

To send them packing does not mean dooming them to hell; it means truly loving them. But the relationship of the bishops with them is one of convenience and not of love. It is a real marriage of convenience on both sides. How many bishops will tell the *estancieros* of Argentina, the *petroleros* of Venezuela, or the *fazendeiros* of Brazil, since Medellín, what Paul said: "For even if I made you sorry with my letter, I do not regret it (though I did regret it), for I see that that letter grieved you, though only for a while. As it is, I rejoice, not because you were grieved, but because you were grieved into repenting . . ." *(2 Corinthians 7:8-9)*? The bishops are not asked to renew the probably anachronistic Pauline anathema: "You are to deliver this man to Satan for the destruction of the flesh, that his spirit may be saved in the day of the Lord Jesus" *(1 Corinthians 5:5)*. We, the men of the street, simply ask the bishops not to wink their eye over cocktails, consoling the rich and making them think that what they said in the document is for show and not really serious. We ask nothing more than an example of love, of true and evangelical love for those who have little or no social conscience, who are "concerned with maintaining their privileges which they identify with the established order." As long as they have not been told, they can say they do not know. But now they do know.

The developmentalists, less antipathetic to the bishops, are not Christians according to the Gospel, because they put more stress on economic progress than on the social advancement of the people, which implies the participation of all in the decisions of the economic and political order. One often notices in them "a tendency that expresses itself in religious indifferentism or in a humanistic view that excludes religion, due especially to their preoccupation with social problems" ("Pastoral Concern for the Elites," no. 11). This group of persons lacks the sense of the Gospel and does not know the thought of Christ, because they seek economic progress before the person. They are mitigated capitalists. They broaden the participation in the system, but they do not strive to give the death blow to the heart of capitalism, which is above everything else economic profit. "We want structures in the service of men and not men in the service of structures; we want to have the pleasure of living and not the pain of living," say the young people. And we agree with them. But in practice we must not forget that it is not working for peace when we collaborate in the progress of people if our collaboration is not part of the struggle against capitalism. If our work reenforces capitalism, obviously it is counterproductive. We are destroying with the left hand what we are building with the right. Not everything that directly and immediately helps a person, a poor person, is part of true liberation. I recall one of the inscriptions of Paris: "Life is beyond." It is very beautiful. At times we lack depth and a certain patience. Those who dedicate themselves to human progress can fool men of good faith, and indeed they are of good faith themselves. Money is always ready to make deals and seek allies wherever it can. And we can very easily become these allies. We would avoid falling into the net if we were free persons, attentive only to what truly is consistent with the person, without trying to impose what seems good to us, but only what history, the great movement of mankind, discovers to be in line with genuine and profound human progress.

The group the Latin American bishops regard with obvious sympathy are the revolutionaries who "challenge the socioeconomic structure. They desire its radical change, both in goals and implementation" ("Pastoral Concern for the Elites," no. 8). For this group, the people are or ought to be the subject of change; thus they should participate in the decisions necessary for the ordering of the entire social process. It is the revolutionaries who enter most clearly into the Christian perspective. The parable of the prodigal son leaves no doubt about Christ's sympathies. The insolent and rebellious younger son is closer to his father's heart. His attitudes are substantially more human and generous than those of his conservative brother who did not leave home. This group of revolutionaries is the most congenial, because it wants the people not only to have a little more bread and work and a better house, but also to "participate in the decisions." They don't want the people to be eternal children obedient to the decisions made in their name. It is true that among those groups there occur with greater frequency real crises of faith; "regarding the Church, they criticize certain historical forms and some manifestations of the official representatives of the Church in their attitude toward the social order and in their concrete manner of living within this same order" ("Pastoral Concern for the Elites," no. 12).

When I read this document and these notes, I am optimistic; once a person of normal intelligence, virtue, and will has seen such a flagrant inconsistency, it is impossible that he could continue to accept it. The bishops have picked up the tomatoes and rotten eggs that have been thrown at them from the sidewalks, and they say, "You are right. We deserve it." This is a definitive and irreversible step. When criticism is faced and accepted, a decision has already been made. The profound crises of faith arise with regard to the attitude of certain representatives of the Church in the social sphere. The moment seems to have arrived in which the believer must adopt Christ's advice: "So practice and observe whatever they tell you, but not what they do; for they preach, but do not practice" *(Matthew 23:3)*.

It seems that to follow the Church we must be against the Church. "Do not accept the conservatives because they do what they do out of self-interest, because they empty the message of faith of its content. Mistrust the developmentalists because they do not wield decisive blows against profit—which we solemnly execrate and condemn. Be revolutionaries, because they do not accept the *status quo* and want real, authentic progress for the people." Do you speak this way to Christians? Then you must be ready to go with them to the end. The fathers know this and point out that "this assembly Medellín was invited to make decisions and establish programs only under the condition that we are ready to carry them out as our personal commitment, even at the cost of sacrifice ("Introduction," no. 3).

We are moving toward another kind of Christian, better related to reality, more present in history, more incarnate. The Church prophetically senses this and salutes this new man from afar as the prophets saluted the promised land. They aspired to a land different from that which was beneath their feet, but they had to content themselves with hailing it from afar. "These all died in faith, not having received what was promised, but having seen it and greeted it from afar, and having acknowledged that they were strangers and exiles on the earth" *(Hebrews 11:13)*. This sentence from the Letter to the Hebrews calls to mind a profusion of images and ideas. The fathers of Medellín greet the promised land from afar. They are only asked to feel as "strangers and exiles on the earth." The total balance sheet is positive, despite naïve programs of social structuralization and concordats with those responsible for neocolonialism. The language is prophetic and felicitous, it delineates the real situation in Latin America, and it will certainly wake up those Christians who have fallen asleep.

CONCLUSION

We have come to the end of a long and complicated conversation, Michael. I could have told you all this in two words, but I have dragged it out over a period of months. It was delightful having this conversation with you, nearby or far away, during all this time. I wanted to rediscover with you that the Christian is not dead but alive. If your observation had not deeply impressed me, I should not have set out on this search. It impressed me because death is continually snapping at our heels and I feel it up against and within our being. In the Church structures there are too many pale faces, too many imaginary pains, too many badly directed and lost efforts. For this reason I was unable to give your objection an easy answer. I could not give it to you who ask me, in the name of your generation, why I, or others like me, have dedicated ourselves to the Church—to this Church against which you have piled up so much anger, as I have. Maybe the difference between you and me is only quantitative. I have lived longer than you and I know that an ideal society does not exist; I know that the conflict between prophets and Pharisees, between slaves and free men, is eternal and is within all structures. Che Guevara spoke of dogmatism within the vast area of Marxism, and he was certainly not referring to a Tridentine dogmatism. I reached a clear conclusion: the demarcation of the Church's boundaries, the difficult problem of living with men and with the world, cannot be a problem of quantity, decided from the outside by men. It is a permanent creation of the Holy Spirit. He is present in prophecy and overturns fears, traditions, and interests.

When the Church leaves the field of prophecy, man shows himself to be poor, naked, limited, with all his fears, his greed, and his shortcomings.

This play of light and shadow has always helped me to discover the Church and to live joyfully within her, despite the protest I feel in my mind and which comes to my lips. When I am alone, when I think and pray, my protest makes me smile, because I discover that in the last analysis everything is grace. Fidelity to the Church is not easy because it is not based on visible arguments, but on faith. The Church is not being inconsistent when she proclaims "the new man"—the one for whom the students of Paris are hoping and whom Che Guevara saluted with his dying eyes on the Bolivian altiplano. But then she herself makes deals with the oppressors, with those who will always block the way to the people so that they cannot participate in decisions. Yet, behind the man of daring, the visionary Church, the prophets who hail the promised land from afar, is the Spirit of God, who guides the world from chaos to community.

The other person, the diplomat, the pacifier, is a man like me, like you, who after eating and drinking well, with a roof over his head and tranquillity in his heart, protests: "What's all the fuss about? Come on, children, go to bed and don't quarrel!" To be and to see in a faithful manner is not the result of flesh and blood. It is a gift of faith. And faith is the reason, a demonstrative force for things that are not visible. And this faith is maturity in prayer and contemplation.

You will tell me that between fidelity to the Church and fidelity to the revolution and the liberation of man you choose the second. To what avail is fidelity to the Church and to traditions, to old and dehumanized things, in comparison to fidelity to man and his concrete objectives? You do not want to miss your appointment with history. Neither do I, although like Peter running to Jesus' tomb, I do not have your legs and your breath. Maybe my receptiveness is more limited than I suspect. But do you remember when you arrived in Florence and the streets were filled with mud and the water reached the second floor of the houses? Cimabue's Christ had been destroyed as it looked at the mirror of water that came up to its waist, and the codices of the Laurentiana were bobbing about like canoes. The Palazzo Vecchio, that old giant, survived in that bog of death in November 1966. It seemed to you like a masterwork of beauty and hope rising up out of death. If through some magic power you could have returned the deadly waters to their river bed and made the Arno the romantic mirror of the city that is the pearl of the world, if you could have changed it from an aggressor into a friend, from an instrument of death into a model of beauty and harmony, from a vehicle of mire into a channel of fertile life, you would certainly have done so. This is what the

Church seems to me. It is not excess baggage, a juxtaposition, a useless survival, but the great channel through which the water of history flows. For this reason it is essential for me to see history in the Church, that is, in Christ. Or to see it outside of Christ.

To marry outside of Christ means mere copulation. To marry in Christ means forming a couple in dialogue, the image of the Unity which is the peace of the individual. To build without Christ is to make towers of Babel, New York, Paris, Buenos Aires, Milan, where man is the more despairing and alone in proportion to the complexity, refinement, and comfort which the city organization offers him. To build with Christ is to build the city of peace, the community.

Here I must confess something. I have some sympathy with those pastors who want immediately to get to the city of peace and think they can do so as if in a chess game. But we must not stand off and cry, *All of us should be doing this.* "He who is not with me is against me, and he who does not gather with me scatters" *(Luke 11:23).* This is the profound reason for my faith and for my stubborn, tenacious clinging to the Church—to this visible Church, which is lucid and confused, futuristic and antiquated, daring and diplomatic, fleshly and spiritual.

Michael, if you see that little by little the current is carrying me off like a dry leaf in the Church's undertow, in those backwaters that form behind her where one is so comfortably protected from the rapids, stop me. If you have no other means, tear up a cobblestone and throw it hard. Remember the inscriptions of Paris: "I love you. . . . I say it with a cobblestone!" If possible, don't kill me so I can continue struggling at your side for freedom and peace. But it is better to be stoned to death "seeing the heavens open up" than to be drowned in the swamp with our own image as our only promise. Don't hold back, don't listen to our counsels to prudence. "Professors, you make us grow old," wrote the young people of Paris. And I would write in your universities which used to be ours, "Young people, rejuvenate us!" Behind you—who don't want more comfort but to be more a man, not more production but more freedom, not more markets but more community, not more police but more persons—Christ smiles at me, a young Christ, and says, "Why did you have to look for me? Didn't you know that I had to be about my father's business?" But they did not understand.

Remember that the companions of prophecy were amazement, incomprehension, and persecution. But only prophecy can bring man out of the forest and free him from the desert.